THE HAMLYN ENCYCLOPEDIA OF

SOCCER

THE HAMLYN ENCYCLOPEDIA OF

SOCCER

IAN MORRISON

HAMLYN

Photographic acknowledgements

The publishers would like to thank the following organisations and individuals for their permission to reproduce the photographs in this book:
Allsport 1–3, 18–9t, 146–7, 151; Simon Bruty 23, 27, 78–9, 82–3; David Cannon 10t, 181, 34–5, 46, 47, 79, 110–1, 174; Tony Duffy 150; Michael King 139t; Don Morley 123; Mike Powell 170; Steve Powell 87b, 106b; Ravezzani 100; Dan Smith 142b; Colorsport 5, 6, 8, 10–11, 11t, 13, 14, 15, 20, 21, 22, 24, 26, 28–9, 30, 30–1, 33, 34, 36, 37, 38, 39, 42, 43, 44, 45br, 49, 50–1, 54–5b, 56, 57, 58–9, 60, 61, 62, 65, 68–9, 71, 72, 73, 76, 77, 80, 82t, 84, 85, 86, 87t, 89, 90–1t, 91b, 92, 94, 95, 97, 98, 99b, 101, 102, 103, 105, 106t, 107, 108–9, 112–3, 114, 115, 118, 119, 120–1, 126, 127, 128, 129, 130–1, 131b, 132–3, 138, 139c&b, 142t, 143, 153, 154, 155, 158b, 159, 161, 162, 163, 154–5, 166, 167, 171, 172–3, 175; Hulton Picture Company 44, 82b, 158t; Popperfoto 40, 116; Sporting Pictures 19b; Syndication International 152; Bob Thomas Sports Photography 54, 55, 70, 90b, 98–9, 131t, 146; Topham Picture Library 75, 81

Title spread:
Brian Stein scored two goals in Luton's 3–2 win over Arsenal in the 1988 Littlewoods Cup final, the first major trophy for the Kenilworth Road club

Published by
The Hamlyn Publishing Group Limited
a division of the Octopus Publishing Group
Michelin House
81 Fulham Road
London SW3 6RB
and distributed for them by
Octopus Distribution Services Limited
Rushden, Northamptonshire NN10 9RZ

First published in 1989

ISBN 0 600 56370 7

Produced by Mandarin Offset
Printed and bound in Hong Kong

Foreword

You don't need me to tell you what a great game soccer is. It isn't only the excitement generated on the park every Saturday that has turned soccer into our national sport, but also the great characters in the game and the wealth of detailed statistics and records that surround them and their clubs.

The Hamlyn Encyclopedia of Soccer brings together masses of results, statistics and fascinating facts that any football fan, whether terrace fanatic or armchair follower, will find a vital addition to their soccer library.

The author has crammed the book to its fullest in such a limited space and has covered countless aspects of the game in a simple-to-read format. He has not only provided results of major tournaments like the Football League, FA Cup, World Cup, European competitions etc. but the Football combination, central League and anglo-Scottish Cup are also made welcome in what is truly an encyclopedia of soccer.

For those of you who like the conventional soccer charts and tables spiced up with some interesting tit-bits or if you enjoy reading biographies or following the history of the game, then the blend of player biographies and club histories are a must for you.

This excellent book is not just restricted to the British Isles, but covers the sport worldwide. Sadly, English clubs cannot play in Europe at the moment, but that doesn't stop British interest in the European scene these days, particularly with so many British players, and indeed managers, on the Continent.

With the 1994 World Cup being played in the United States it is good to see the game across the Atlantic featured. Contrary to public belief the game is thriving in the States. It may not have the same impact at professional level as it does in Britain and Europe, but at school level it is one of the most popular sports. That can only be good for the future of soccer in the United States.

You'll find this book compulsive reading. As a companion for watching and enjoying the thrills of soccer, there can be no better than *The Hamlyn Encyclopedia of Soccer*.

Abandoned matches

Bad weather is the most common cause of abandonments, followed by crowd invasions or riots. But the international match between Chile and Uruguay on 25 June 1975 was abandoned with ten minutes remaining because there weren't enough players left on the field: the referee had sent off ten Chileans and nine Uruguayans following a mass fight on the pitch.

In general, matches are abandoned because of bad weather and replayed later. However, there have been abandoned matches where, because of the circumstances, the result has been allowed to stand.

The Bradford City versus Lincoln City match at Valley Parade on 11 May 1985 was abandoned after 40 minutes because of the disastrous fire. The scoreline was goalless at the time, and the result stood. It is the shortest match on record for which the result has been allowed to stand.

When Manchester United played Manchester City at Old Trafford on 27 April 1974 they needed a win, or at least a draw, to avoid possible relegation to the 2nd division; a defeat almost guaranteed the drop. Former Old Trafford favourite Denis Law scored the only goal of the game in the 82nd minute. United fans invaded the pitch before play resumed three minutes later. A second invasion, and a fire at the Stretford End, caused referee David Smith to abandon the game with four minutes remaining. The result was allowed to stand and United were relegated.

The score in the 4th division game between Barrow and Gillingham on 9 October 1961, 7-0 to Barrow, was allowed to stand despite its being abandoned after 75 minutes. The game was late in starting because of Gillingham's delayed arrival.

The Middlesbrough versus Oldham Athletic game on 3 April 1915 was abandoned after 55 minutes when Oldham full-back Billy Cook refused to leave the field after being sent off. The Football League ordered the result to stand.

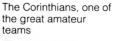
The Corinthians, one of the great amateur teams

Middlesbrough won 4-1.

The only case of a game being abandoned and finished on another day was in the 1898-99 season. On 26 November 1898 a Sheffield Wednesday-Aston Villa game was abandoned because of bad light after 79 ½ minutes, with Wednesday leading 3-1. The remaining 10 ½ minutes were played on 13 March the following year, when Wednesday added another goal.

Adidas Awards

See *Golden Boot Award*

Age

See *Oldest; Youngest*

Amateur Cup

See *FA Amateur Cup*

Amateur football

Since the 1974-75 season there has been no distinction between British professional and amateur footballers; this was brought about by the increase in 'shamateurism' — paying amateur players — and meant an end to the Amateur Cup and amateur international matches.

Up to the 1930s amateurs played a significant role in the professional game and many played League soccer. The *last amateur to captain the full England international side* was A.G. Bower (Corinthians) against Wales at Wrexham on 12 February 1927. The *last amateur to play for England at senior level* was Bernard Joy (Arsenal) against Belgium at Brussels on 9 May 1936.

The most appearances by an amateur in the Football League was 263 by J.C. Burns for Queen's Park Rangers and Brentford between 1927 and 1936. The most since 1945 was 89 by Mike Pinner for Aston Villa, Sheffield Wednesday, Queen's Park Rangers, Manchester United, Chelsea and Swansea Town between 1954 and 1963.

Three times, in 1928, 1929 and 1930, the amateur club Argonauts applied unsuccessfully to join the Football League. Optimistic, they had booked Wembley Stadium as their home ground if admitted.

Anglo-Italian Cup

When Swindon Town beat Arsenal to win the Football League Cup in 1968 they were not eligible to compete in the Fairs Cup as they were not a 1st Division side, so the two-legged Anglo-Italian League Cup was instituted. Out of it grew, in 1970, the Anglo-Italian Cup, which was for Italian and British Football League clubs with no other involvements in Europe, who

were nominated by their respective Leagues.

Six teams from each country competed, divided into three groups of four (two from each country per group). Teams played only teams from the opposing country within their group, on a two-legged system. After the group matches the overall top English team played the top Italian team in the final. Points were awarded for goals as well as for winning and drawing matches.

The first final, between Napoli and Swindon Town in 1970, was an ugly affair and was abandoned after 79 minutes because of a crowd disturbance.

The clubs which took part most often were AS Roma in the four years 1970 to 1973 and Blackpool, three times 1971-73.

Between 1970 and 1973 all finals were played on the home ground of the Italian club. The competition was discontinued in 1974 and when it was revived in 1976 was a two-team competition involving the FA Cup winners of England and Italy who played each other in a two-legged competition. It lasted only two seasons.

Finals			Attendance
1970	Napoli 0	Swindon T 3	40,000
1971	Bologna 1	Blackpool 2 aet	30,000
1972	AS Roma 3	Blackpool 1	40,000
1973	Fiorentina 1	Newcastle U 2	
1974	Not held		
1975	1st leg: Fiorentina 1	West Ham U 0	35,000
	2nd leg: West Ham U 1	Fiorentina 1	14,699
	(Fiorentina won 2-1 on aggregate)		
1976	1st leg: Southampton 1	Napoli 0	13,000
	2nd leg: Napoli 4	Southampton 0	60,000
	(Napoli won 4-1 on aggregate)		

Anglo-Italian League Cup Winners' Cup

This was inaugurated in 1969 to enable Football League Cup winners Swindon Town to compete in Europe, which as a non-1st division club they were ineligible to do. Because Italy did not have a League Cup competition their entrants were the National Cup Winners AS Roma. The competition lasted three years until the League Cup winners eventually gained automatic entry to the UEFA Cup.

Finals				Attendance
1969	1st leg: AS Roma	2	Swindon T 1	Not available
	2nd leg: Swindon T	4	AS Roma 0	
	(Swindon T won 5-2 on aggregate)			
1970	1st leg: Bologna	1	Manchester C 0	30,000
	2nd leg: Manchester C	2	Bologna 2	25,843
	(Bologna won 3-2 on aggregate)			
1971	1st leg: Torino	0	Tottenham H 1	38,000
	2nd leg: Tottenham H	2	Torino 0	33,000
	(Tottenham H won 3-0 on aggregate)			

Portsmouth's long-serving Jimmy Dickinson. After making 764 appearances for Pompey he later became club secretary and manager

Anglo-Scottish Cup

The successor of the Texaco Cup, the Anglo-Scottish Cup was open to English and Scottish teams which were not eligible for that season's European competitions. Sixteen English teams competed and were split into four groups with the four group winners progressing to the quarter-finals. The four Scottish quarter-finalists were by invitation. From that stage it was a knockout competition. All finals were two-legged matches.

The competition was discontinued in 1981 when the Scottish clubs withdrew because they felt the quality of English opposition was not strong enough, yet only one Scottish team, St Mirren, won the trophy during its six years. Blackburn Rovers, Blackpool, Bristol City, Fulham and Sheffield United all played in six competitions and Partick Thistle in four, the Scottish record.

Finals

			Attendance
1975-76	1st leg: Middlesbrough 1	Fulham 0	15,000
	2nd leg: Fulham 0	Middlesbrough 0	13,723
	(Middlesbrough won 1-0 on aggregate)		
1976-77	1st leg: Orient 1	Nottingham F 1	5,058
	2nd leg: Nottingham F 4	Orient 0	12,717
	(Nottingham F won 5-1 on aggregate)		
1977-78	1st leg: St Mirren 1	Bristol C 2	8,000
	2nd leg: Bristol C 1	St Mirren 1	16,110
	(Bristol C won 3-2 on aggregate)		
1978-79	1st leg: Oldham A 0	Burnley 4	10,456
	2nd leg: Burnley 0	Oldham A 1	10,865
	(Burnley won 4-1 on aggregate)		
1979-80	1st leg: Bristol C 0	St Mirren 2	3,731
	2nd leg: St Mirren 3	Bristol C 1	12,500
	(St Mirren won 5-1 on aggregate)		
1980-81	1st leg: Chesterfield 1	Notts C 0	10,190
	2nd leg: Notts C 1	Chesterfield 1	12,951
	(Chesterfield won 2-1 on aggregate)		

Appearances

Most by individual players

Football League

The most appearances in the Football League is 864 by Peter Shilton with Leicester City, Stoke City, Nottingham Forest, Southampton and Derby City between 4 May 1966, when he made his debut for Leicester City against Everton, and the end of the 1988-89 season.

Over 750 League appearances

824 – Terry Paine (Southampton and Hereford United) 1957-77
777 – Alan Oakes (Manchester City, Chester, Port Vale) 1959-84
770 – John Trollope (Swindon Town) 1960-80
764 – Jimmy Dickinson (Portsmouth) 1946-65
762 – Roy Sproson (Port Vale) 1950-72
758 – Ray Clemence (Scunthorpe United, Liverpool, Tottenham Hotspur) 1966-87

758 – Billy Bonds (Charlton Athletic, West Ham United) 1965-88
757 – Pat Jennings (Watford, Tottenham Hotspur, Arsenal) 1963-84
757 – Frank Worthington (Huddersfield Town, Leicester City, Bolton Wanderers, Birmingham City, Leeds United, Sunderland, Southampton, Brighton & Hove Albion, Tranmere Rovers, Preston North End, Stockport County) 1967-88

Scottish League

John Trollope's 770 games for Swindon Town is a record for one club.

The most appearances in the Scottish League is 626 by Bob Ferrier (Motherwell) 1918-37.

Consecutive

The most consecutive appearances in the Football League is 401 by Harold Bell, the Tranmere Rovers centre-half. He played in the opening game of the 1946-47 season against Rotherham United (31 August 1946) and did not miss a game until dropped for the match against Gateshead on 30 August 1955. During that period he also played in 58 FA Cup and other senior games, making a consecutive run of 459 games.

The most consecutive games in the 1st division is 365 by Phil Neal of Liverpool between 14 December 1975 (v Luton Town) and 24 September 1983 (v Manchester United).

Numbers of divisions

Ray Straw is believed to be the only player to have appeared in all six divisions of the Football League. He played for Derby County in divisions 1, 2 and 3(N) between 1951-57, and for Coventry City in divisions 3(S), 3 and 4 between 1957-61. He finished his career with Mansfield Town in the 4th division.

In 1947 outside-left Roy Clarke played in three divisions of the Football League in three consecutive games. A regular with Cardiff City in division 3(S), he transferred to Manchester City in the 2nd division in April that year. He played one game for City, who were then promoted. His next League game was in division 1.

Goalkeeper Chic Brodie repeated Clarke's feat in 1961. He played for Aldershot in division 4 until his transfer to 1st division Wolverhampton Wanderers in February. He played one game for Wolves before being transferred to Northampton Town. When he made his debut for them on 30 September, they were a 3rd division side.

Manchester City goalkeeper Eric Nixon became the first player to appear in all four divisions of the Football League in the same season when he played for Southampton and Manchester City in division 1, Bradford City in division 2, Carlisle United in division 3 and Wolverhampton Wanderers in division 4 during the 1986-87 season.

FA Cup
88 — Ian Callaghan (Liverpool, Swansea City, Crewe Alexandra)
86 — Stanley Matthews (Stoke City, Blackpool)
84 — Bobby Charlton (Manchester United, Preston North End)

Barry Stobart appeared for Wolverhampton Wanderers in the 1960 Cup final, yet he had only played four League games at the time.

International matches
British players with 100 + caps
119 — Pat Jennings (Northern Ireland) 1964-86
109 — Peter Shilton (England) 1970-89
108 — Bobby Moore (England) 1962-73
106 — Bobby Charlton (England) 1958-70
105 — Billy Wright (England) 1946-59
102 — Kenny Dalglish (Scotland) 1971-86
72 — Joey Jones (Wales) 1972-86
69 — Liam Brady (Ireland) 1974-89
Non-British
150 — Hector Chumpitaz (Peru) 1963-82
120 — Rivelino (Brazil) 1968-79
115 — Bjorn Nordqvist (Sweden) 1963-78
112 — Dino Zoff (Italy) 1968-83
111 — Pele (Brazil) 1957-71

World Cup
The most appearances in the final stages of the World Cup is 21 by Uwe Seeler of West Germany, who appeared in the 1958, 1962, 1966 and 1970 competitions, and Wladyslaw Zmuda of Poland, who also played in four tournaments, between 1974 and 1986.

The record for appearing in the most finals is five by Antonio Carbajal of Mexico in 1950, 1954, 1958, 1962 and 1966.

Apprentice

A player may register as an apprentice with a Football League club any time between his 15th and 17th birthday if he is not in full-time education. The period of apprenticeship must expire on the player's 18th birthday or any time after his 17th birthday if the club wishes to sign him as a contract player. A club is not allowed more than 15 apprentices on its books at a time.

Argentina

Football was introduced to Argentina in the 1860s by British workmen. British sailors also popularised the sport when they used to play friendly matches in Buenos Aires. The first Argentinian club, Buenos Aires FC, was founded by Britons in 1865. In the late 1880s many British-owned businesses and service industries in Argentina formed early football clubs, which were the basis of the Argentine League, founded in 1891. The league was a first-year flop but was re-formed in 1893 as the Association del Futbol Argentino, this time with more success. The first president was British-born Alexander Watson Hutton, underlining the big British influence.

Argentina joined FIFA in 1912, about the time that many Italians emigrated to Argentina, and it is to them that the real growth of soccer in Argentina is credited. In the 1920s Argentina emerged as a strong contender in world soccer. They reached the final of the 1928 Olympic soccer tournament, losing to Uruguay in a re-play. Two years later they lost to the same country in the first World Cup final.

After the Second World War, however, their neighbours, Brazil, became the dominant South American footballing country. In 1978 Argentina retrieved the honours by winning the World Cup final, led by the lethal goalscoring power of Mario Kempes. When they won the trophy a second time in 1986 they had another lethal goalscorer in their midst: Diego Maradona.

International competitions
World Cup winners
1978 (beat Netherlands 3-1), 1986 (beat West Germany 3-2)
South American Champions
1921, 1925, 1927, 1929, 1937, 1941, 1945-47, 1955, 1957, 1959

Arsenal

Arsenal was founded in 1886 as Dial Square by Scot David Danskin and fellow exiled northern munitions workers. Some of the first members of Dial Square were ex-Nottingham Forest players, and it was Forest which supplied the club's first strip. Their first ground was at Plumstead Common but by the turn of the century they had also played at the Sportsman's Ground, the Manor Ground, and the Invicta Ground. They had also changed their name to Royal Arsenal in 1886 and to Woolwich Arsenal in 1891. In 1913 they moved to their current home, Highbury, and the following year dropped 'Woolwich' from their title.

Since 1919 they have maintained a regular presence in the top flight, and their continuous run of 62 seasons is a record.

When Herbert Chapman was appointed man-

Above: Diego Maradona, who skippered Argentina to their second World Cup success in 1986

Right: Charlie Nicholas scores Arsenal's first goal against Liverpool in the 1987 Littlewoods Cup final as the Gunners won their first major honour since the 1979 FA Cup

ager he guided the club to a hat-trick of championship wins. They won the League in 1931 to become the first southern winners of the title. During the 1930s the Gunners won the League title five times and the FA Cup twice.

Arsenal won the championship twice and the FA Cup once between 1948 and 1953 but they then went into the doldrums until 1970 when, under manager Bertie Mee, they won the Fairs Cup. The following year, under the captaincy of Frank McLintock, Arsenal emulated their north London rivals Tottenham Hotspur to become only the second 20th-century team to complete the double.

In 1989 they thwarted Liverpool's chances of the double when the Gunners clinched the championship with virtually the last kick of the season.

Ground: Arsenal Stadium, Highbury, London
Nickname: Gunners
Record attendance: 73,295 — v Sunderland (Division 1), 9 March 1935
First Football League season: 1893-94, Division 2 (9th)
Seasons in Football League: 85 (72: Division 1, 13 Division 2)

Honours

Division 1 champions 1930-31, 1932-33, 1933-34, 1934-35, 1937-38, 1947-48, 1952-53, 1970-71, 1988-89
FA Cup winners 1930, 1936, 1950, 1971, 1979
Football League Cup winners 1987
European Fairs Cup winners 1970
Footballers of the Year Joe Mercer (FWA) 1950, Frank McLintock (FWA) 1971, Liam Brady (PFA) 1979
Manager of the Year Bertie Mee 1971
European Team of the Year 1971 (with Ajax)

Associate Members' Cup

See *Sherpa Van Trophy*

Aston Villa

One of the 12 founder members of the Football League, Aston Villa were runners-up to the invincible Preston North End team in the League's first season.

Formed in 1874 by members of the Aston Villa Wesleyan Chapel, their first ground was at Aston Park. They moved to nearby Perry Barr in 1876 and in 1897 settled at their present home, Villa Park, which is one of the finest stadiums in Britain.

Most of the club's triumphs came before the turn of the century when they were one of the leading sides of the day. Having won the League title a record six times by 1910, they narrowly missed the double for a second time in 1913 when they were Cup winners and runners-up in the League. They completed the double in 1897, the last club for 64 years to perform this rare achievement.

Beating Huddersfield Town 1-0 to win the FA Cup in 1920 was the club's last honour until 1957 when they beat the crack Manchester United team 2-1 in the Wembley showpiece. But after that Villa suffered the ignominy of a

Peter Withe turns away after scoring the winner for Aston Villa in the 1982 European Cup final against Bayern Munich

drop into the 3rd division in 1970. But they bounced back and with Ron Saunders at the helm the club won the League championship in 1981, their first triumph in the League for more than 70 years. However, before he could lead them into Europe Saunders quit, and that task fell to Tony Barton, but the team were good enough to carry off Europe's top honour when they beat Bayern Munich 1-0 in Rotterdam.

Since then, however, Villa have endured another drop from the top division, although they are now back among the first division elite.

Ground: Villa Park
Nickname: Villans
Record attendance: 76,588 — v Derby C (FA Cup 6th round), 2 March 1946
First Football League season: 1888-89 Football League (2nd)
Seasons in Football League: 90 (78 Division 1, 10 Division 2, 2 Division 3)

Honours

Division 1 champions 1893-94, 1895-96, 1896-97, 1898-99, 1899-1900, 1909-10, 1980-81
Division 2 champions 1937-38, 1959-60
Division 3 champions 1971-72
FA Cup winners 1887, 1895, 1897, 1905, 1913, 1920, 1957
Football League Cup winners 1961, 1975, 1977
European Cup winners 1982
European Super Cup winners 1982
Footballer of the Year Andy Gray (PFA) 1977
Manager of the Year Ron Saunders 1975, 1981

Attendances

Highest
World Cup
199,854 — Brazil v Uruguay, 16 July 1950, Maracana Stadium, Rio de Janeiro
World Cup (qualifier)
183,341 — Brazil v Paraguay, 31 Aug 1969, Marcana Stadium, Rio de Janeiro
European Championship
103,000 — USSR v Hungary, 11 May 1968, Moscow
Club match (world):
177,656 — Flamengo v Fluminese, Aug 1963, (Brazilian League), Maracana Stadium, Rio de Janeiro
Club match (Europe)
146,433 — Celtic v Aberdeen, 24 April 1937, (Scottish Cup final), Hampden Park, Glasgow
European Cup
136,505 — Celtic v Leeds U, 15 April 1970 (semi-final), Hampden Park, Glasgow
FA Cup final
126,047 — Bolton W v West Ham U, 28 April 1923, Wembley Stadium, London
FA Cup (other than final)
84,569 — Manchester C v Stoke C, 3 March 1934, (6th round), Maine Road, Manchester (record for a game in Britain outside London or Glasgow)
Football League Cup (other than final)
63,418 — Manchester U v Manchester C, 17 Dec 1969 (semi-final), Old Trafford, Manchester
Football League
Division 1: 83,260 — Manchester U v Arsenal, 17 Jan 1948, Maine Road, Manchester
Division 2: 68,029 — Aston Villa v Coventry C, 30 Oct 1937, Villa Park, Birmingham
Division 3: 49,309 — Sheffield W v Sheffield U, 26 Dec 1979, Hillsborough, Sheffield
Division 4: 37,774 — Crystal P v Millwall, 31 March 1961, Selhurst Park, London
Division 3(S): 51,621 — Cardiff C v Bristol C, 7 April 1947, Ninian Park, Cardiff
Division 3(N): 49,655 — Hull C v Rotherham U, 25 Dec 1948, Boothferry Park, Hull
Scottish League
Division 1/Premier Division: 118,567 — Rangers v Celtic, 2 Jan 1939, Ibrox Stadium, Glasgow
Division 2/Division 1: 27,205 — Queen's Park v Kilmarnock, 31 March 1961, Hampden Park, Glasgow
Scottish FA Cup
146,433 — Celtic v Aberdeen, 24 April 1937, Hampden Park, Glasgow
Scottish League Cup
107,647 — Celtic v Rangers, 23 Oct 1965, Hampden Park, Glasgow
International (Britain)
149,547 — Scotland v England, 17 April 1937, Hampden Park, Glasgow

Aggregate
The record aggregate attendance for any one match was 351,000 for the three matches between AC Milan and Santos in the 1963 World Cup Championship.

Average
Since 1945 Football League average attendances have slumped from 23,333 per club in 1948-49 to just 8,130 in 1985-86, the lowest in any post-Second World War season.

In that period the top individual averages have been:

57,552 — Manchester United 1967-68
56,283 — Newcastle United 1947-48
55,509 — Tottenham Hotspur 1950-51
54,982 — Arsenal 1947-48
54,890 — Manchester United 1947-48
54,750 — Manchester United 1975-76
54,111 — Tottenham Hotspur 1949-50

There have been 15 more instances of clubs averaging 50,000. Manchester United have achieved it six more times, Arsenal four, Tottenham Hotspur twice, Newcastle United twice and Everton once.

Lowest
Several matches have been played behind closed doors for different reasons, with no paying attendance. However, the following are low attendances under normal conditions:

Football League
450 — Rochdale v Cambridge U (Div 3), 5 Feb 1974
469 — Thames v Luton T (Div 3(S)), 6 Dec 1930
484 — Gateshead v Accrington S (Div 3(N)), 26 March 1952
1st Division
4,026 — Wimbledon v Norwich C, 18 Dec 1987
2nd Division
Stockport County v Leicester City, Old Trafford, 7 May 1921 is often recorded as having an official attendance of just 13, but it is believed that a couple of thousand were inside the ground at the time.

Scottish League
80 — Meadowbank v Stenhousemuir (Div 2), 22 Dec 1979
World Cup (qualifier)
500 — United States v Bermuda, Kansas City, Missouri, 3 Nov 1968
European Cup tie
483 — UEFA Cup tie Rapid Vienna v Juventus, 1971-72
Home international
2,315 — Wales v Northern Ireland, Wrexham, 27 May 1982.

Australia

Soccer in Australia has to compete with Australian Rules Football and the two Rugby codes, which are all more popular there. Additionally the country's isolation from the rest of the soccer world has meant it has been a constant battle by the Australian Soccer Federation to gain recognition for the sport in their vast country.

The Australian Football Association was founded in 1920, but it was not until the formation of a new organisation, the Australian Soccer Federation, in 1963 that Australian football started to grow internationally. The new federation was the idea of Dr Henry Seamonds, then president of the NSW Federation of Soccer Clubs. Australia rejoined FIFA in 1963 after being suspended in 1958 for illegally obtaining players from other countries.

Soccer was first played in Australia in 1870 when British coalminers introduced the game. Organised soccer began in Sydney in 1880 when an English schoolmaster, W.J. Fletcher, formed the first club, Wanderers. Their first match was against the King's School on 14 August at Parramatta Common. In 1883 Australia was granted affiliation to the Football Association, and two years later the first organised tournament, the Rainsford Trophy, was won by Granville FC of Sydney.

League soccer in Australia is organised regionally, with most players part-time professionals. Because their season does not coincide with the British season, Australian matches are used by football pools companies during the English summer.

International competitions

World Cup (best finish) 1974 Qualified for the first time, finished bottom of group (drew 0-0 with Chile)

The Aston Villa team proudly displaying the FA Cup and League Championship trophies which they won in 1896–97

Ball

The ball must be spherical and with the outer casing made of leather or other approved material, the circumference must be not less than 27 nor more than 28 inches (69-71 cm) and at the start of the game it should weigh between 14 and 16 ounces (396-453 grams). The measurements were adopted into the laws in 1883 and the current weights approved in 1937.

The ball must not be changed during a game unless authorised by the referee.

There have been many instances of a ball deflating during a game and being changed. But it has happened only twice in FA Cup finals, remarkably in consecutive years.

Just after the Second World War the quality of leather used for football manufacture was inferior and in the first post-war Cup final between Derby County and Charlton Athletic the ball burst towards the end of the 90 minutes play. Referee E.D. Smith of Sunderland had said on radio the night before the final that odds against such an occurrence were 'A million-to-one'. Even more remarkably, when the two teams met in a War-time League game at the Baseball Ground four days later the ball burst again. The following year the ball burst again in the Charl-ton-Burnley final . . . what odds against that happening again?

With the introduction of floodlighting in the 1950s, the old brown coloured leather ball became unsuitable and light-coloured balls, which are now in every day use, became popular. The great Herbert Chapman introduced a white ball at Arsenal in the 1930s when it was hailed as another piece of showmanship by the great man.

Beazer Homes League

See *Southern League*

Beckenbauer, Franz (1945-)

Franz Beckenbauer was the inspiration behind the rise of both his club side Bayern Munich and West German football in general in the 1960s. He was a great leader, a master tactician, and a fine passer of the ball.

He joined Bayern's youth team, Munchen 1806, at the age of 13 and was promoted into the first team squad before his 18th birthday. It was not long after making his senior debut that he caught the eye of national coach Helmut Schoen. After just 27 senior games for Bayern he made his international debut against Sweden on 26 September 1965. In 1966, when only 20, and the West German Footballer of the Year, he figured prominently in West Germany's World Cup plans, but in the final Schoen made the

'The Kaiser'... West Germany's Franz Beckenbauer. He was one of the game's great captains

George Best was a genius and his close ball-control was his trade mark

mistake of playing him in a defensive role marking Bobby Charlton. Tactically, this move probably cost the West Germans the world crown.

In 1974 Beckenbauer skippered the World Cup side as they beat the Netherlands 2-1 in the final. His League career with Bayern yielded four League titles, four West German Cup winners' medals, three successive European Champions Cup winners' medals, and a Cup-winners' cup medal. He had also led West Germany to the 1972 European Championship.

After more than 100 internationals he retired in 1977, but New York Cosmos asked him to fill the place left when Pele retired. He eventually returned to Germany and joined Hamburg, whom he helped to win the Bundesliga in 1982. 'The Kaiser', as he was known, finally quit and subsequently became the national coach in 1984. The West Germans presented him with the 'Cross of Merit' for services to football.

Born: 11 September 1945, Munich, West Germany
International caps: 103
Honours
World Cup 1974
European Championship 1972
European Cup 1974, 1975, 1976
European Cup-winners' Cup 1967
World Club Championship 1976
West German League 1969, 1972, 1973, 1974, 1982
West German Cup 1966, 1967, 1969, 1971
North American Soccer League 1977, 1978
Awards
European Footballer of the Year 1972, 1976

Benefits

See *Testimonials*

Best, George (1946-)

Belfast-born George Best was one of the most gifted players ever to appear in the Football

League. Spotted playing in Northern Ireland by Manchester United, he joined them as a 15-year-old but soon returned to his native country, homesick. Happily Matt Busby persuaded him to return, and the youngster's great talent was developed at Old Trafford under the manager's watchful eye.

Best made his League debut in 1963 and after just 15 full games made his international debut. He collected two championship medals and in 1968, after topping the 1st division's goalscoring list, scored a great goal in a 4-1 win over Benfica in the European Cup final at Wembley, as United became the first English winners of the trophy.

However, troubled times lay ahead for the star who became a victim of his own circumstance. Disagreements with the new management team at Old Trafford led to his eventual walk-out from United and he played his last game for the club on 1 January 1974 against Queen's Park Rangers.

Since then he has been a 'wanderer'. He had a loan spell at Stockport County in 1975, went to the United States, had a couple of seasons at Fulham, moved north of the border with Hibernian and Motherwell. He played his last Football League game, for Bournemouth, on 7 May 1983. Best also helped out several non-league clubs who, despite not getting the full benefit of Best's genius, enjoyed his crowd-pulling power at the turnstiles.

Born: 22 May 1946, Belfast, Northern Ireland
Football League debut: 14 September 1963, Manchester U v West Bromwich A
Football League appearances: 411 (361 Manchester U, 3 Stockport C, 42 Fulham, 5 Bournemouth)
Football League goals: 147 (137 Manchester U, 2 Stockport C, 8 Fulham)
International caps: 37
Honours
European Cup 1968
Football League 1965, 1967
Awards
European Footballer of the Year 1968
Footballer of the Year (FWA) 1968

Betting

The majority of betting on football matches is via the football pools and fixed odds betting.

Betting on the outcome of matches by players or club officials is prohibited by the Football Association, which banned it as long ago as 1892. In 1963 the soccer world was rocked when the *Sunday People* newspaper launched a soccer bribery probe. Subsequently ten players and former players, including well known internationals, were jailed and banned from football. Included in the scandal were England internationals Tony Kay and Peter Swan.

Blackburn Rovers

As Blackburn was formed by Old Boys of Blackburn Grammar School, Harrow and Malvern, it was hardly surprising they were the first northern team to challenge the supremacy of the southern 'Old Boy' teams.

Originally formed in 1874, the club was re-formed the following year as Blackburn Rovers. By the time the Football League was formed in 1888 Rovers had an excellent record in the game's senior competition, the FA Cup, winning it three times in succession (the only present-day League team to complete the hat-trick). Naturally they were founder members of the League.

Despite their excellent Cup record, which had increased to five wins by the turn of the century, they struggled to capture the League title. But in 1912 they finished top of the table for the first time and repeated the feat two years later.

Since then, apart from a brief spell in the 1960s, Rovers have not challenged for the title and in 1971 the club reached its lowest level when relegated to the 3rd division. Rovers were last in the 1st division in the mid 1960s but they have shown signs in the late 1980s that they are ready to move up from the 2nd division once more. In 1987 they won the Full Members Cup final at Wembley, beating Charlton Athletic 1-0. It was their first Wembley appearance since 1960 when Wolves beat them 3-0 in the FA Cup final.

Ground: Ewood Park
Nickname: Rovers
Record attendance: 61,738 — v Bolton W (FA Cup 6th round), 2 March 1929
First Football League season: Football League 1888-89 (4th)
Seasons in Football League: 90 (54 Division 1, 31 Division 2, 5 Division 3)
Honours
Division 1 champions 1911-12, 1913-14
Division 2 champions 1938-39
Division 3 champions 1974-75
FA Cup winners 1884, 1885, 1886, 1890, 1891, 1928
Full Members Cup winners 1987

Brazil

Brazil last won the World Cup in 1970 but whenever they play, the crowd still awaits the flashes of brilliance they have come to expect from the Latins over the years.

They first came to world dominance in 1958 when they won their first World Cup in Sweden. Playing for them that day, and the scorer of two goals, was a 17-year-old youngster who was to be acclaimed the greatest footballer of all time, Pele.

Brazil hold the enviable record of having qualified for all 13 World Cup competitions between 1930-86 and have won the trophy three times. As the first nation to win the original Jules Rimet trophy three times they kept it after beating Italy 4-1 in the 1970 final.

Brazilian soccer owes its existence to Charles Miller, a Brazilian-born English youngster who brought two footballs with him when he returned from schooling in Southampton in 1894. He immediately organised soccer matches between English residents in the Sao Paulo area of Brazil where he lived. Most early Brazilian teams, like the Sao Paulo Athletic club, were made up of British citizens, but in 1898 the first all-Brazilian team, Mackenzie College, Sao Paulo, was formed. A series of regional leagues sprang up at the turn of the century, and because of the country's size, it was not until transport was made easier that the National League was established in 1967. The national association, the Confederacao Brasileira de Desportos, was established in 1914 and three years later Brazil became affiliated to FIFA.

Many great teams were born and the oldest still in existence is CR Flamengo. Other great teams like Fluminese and Santos soon followed and they formed the schooling grounds for the unending wealth of talent that Brazilian football constantly produces. Leonidas, master at the bicycle kick, was one of the first Brazilians to have an impact on the world game. Since then the list is never-ending: Garrincha, Ademir, Augusto, the Santos brothers, Gylmar, Rivelino, Jairzinho, Zito, Didi, Pele, Vava, Tostao, Zagalo . . . and so on.

International competitions
World Cup winners 1958 (beat Sweden 5-2), 1962 (beat Czechoslovakia 3-1), 1970 (beat Italy 4-1)

South American Champions 1919, 1922, 1949

Broadcasting

The first *game broadcast on radio* was between Arsenal and Sheffield United at Highbury on 22 January 1927. The commentator was H.T. Wakelam, better known as a rugby commentator. That same year, on 23 April, Arsenal also figured in the *first FA Cup final* to be broadcast live when commentary of their 1-0 defeat by Cardiff City was broadcast throughout the country.

With radio coverage increasing after the Second World War, the Football League banned the broadcasting of any games from the start of the 1951-52 season to encourage personal attendances at games. It soon lifted this ban, but restricted it to second-half commentaries. No announcement was made as to which match was being broadcast, which is still the case today. Arsenal were also the 'pioneers' of television coverage and a practice match between the first team and their reserves on 16 September 1937 was the *first to be shown on television*. Parts of the match were shown in a programme entitled 'Soccer at Arsenal' and the commentators were John Snagge and George Allison.

The *first Cup final to be shown on television* was the 1937 final between Sunderland and Preston North End. The first *final to be shown in its entirety* was the Preston versus Huddersfield final on 30 April 1938. Since then the BBC has covered every final live with the exception of the Newcastle-Arsenal match in 1952 when the Football Association refused permission. The *first cup-tie, other than the final, to be televised* was the Charlton Athletic v Blackburn Rovers fifth-round tie on 8 February 1947.

Live football is now very much part of the British way of life, but the televising of live League games is not a new idea. The *first Football League game to be televised live* was on 9 September 1960 and featured the local 'derby' between Blackpool and Bolton Wanderers. Bolton won an uninspiring game and the idea of regular Friday night live soccer never caught on.

Recorded highlights on a Saturday night became acceptable and the BBC's *Match of the Day* programme became popular. *The first match covered on Match of the Day* was Liverpool v Arsenal on 22 August 1964. The cameras went to Anfield for the *first match to be shown in colour* when they showed the Liverpool-West Ham game on 15 November 1969.

The first match covered by Independent Television was the Bedford Town v Arsenal FA Cup tie on 12 January 1956.

The television war really got going in the 1988 close season when ITV and the BBC did battle off the screen to capture lucrative deals with the governing bodies and the League clubs. In the end ITV paid £44 million for the right to show live League soccer while the BBC paid £30 million to cover internationals and FA Cup matches.

The first of the current live Football League matches was at White Hart Lane on 2 October 1983 when Tottenham Hotspur beat Nottingham Forest 2-1. Fortunately it was a better game than its predecessor, the Blackpool-Bolton match in 1960.

Closed circuit television has been used many times to accommodate crowds who would otherwise be unable to watch the match live. *The first match to be relayed by closed circuit television to the ground of the away team* was between Cardiff City and Coventry City on 7 October 1965. A midweek game, the match was relayed to Coventry fans who were watching at their Highfield Road ground.

When Everton played Liverpool in the FA Cup fifth round on 11 March 1967 a crowd of 64,851 packed into Goodison Park. Another 40,149 watched the game on closed circuit television at Anfield. The combined total of 105,000 is a record attendance for any FA Cup tie other than a final tie.

Burnley

On 9 May 1987 Burnley faced the most crucial match of their long history. At home to Leyton Orient they had to win to avoid the ignominy of being the first club to lose its Football League status following the introduction of the automatic relegation rule. Nearly 16,000 fans packed into Turf Moor. Happily they saw their team win 2-1 and thus avoid the drop.

The club was formed in 1881 as Burnley Rovers by local YMCA members, but dropped the Rovers from their title the following year. They were good enough to be founder members of the Football League and had the distinction of being the first team to take a point off the all-conquering Preston North End team. They won the FA Cup in 1914 when they beat Liverpool in

The entrance to Brazil's Maracana Stadium which has housed crowds of nearly 200,000

the first final to be attended by a reigning monarch, George V.

In the 1960s Burnley was one of the country's leading sides and with such players as Jimmy McIlroy and Ray Pointer in the side they won the League title in 1960. But since then the drop from the top has been dramatic and in 1985 they went into the 4th division. Happily, things are looking up again for the central Lancashire side.

Ground: Turf Moor
Nickname: Clarets
Record attendance: 54,775 — v Huddersfield T (FA Cup 3rd round), 23 Feb 1924
First Football League season: 1888-89 Football League (9th)
Seasons in Football League: 90 (51 Division 1, 31 Division 2, 4 Division 3, 4 Division 4)

Honours
Division 1 champions 1920-21, 1959-60
Division 2 champions 1897-98, 1972-73
Division 3 champions 1981-82
FA Cup winners 1914
Anglo-Scottish Cup winners 1979
Footballer of the Year Jimmy Adamson (FWA) 1962

Above: Blackburn Rovers returned from the wilderness in 1987 to beat Charlton Athletic in the Full Members' Cup final at Wembley

Left: Action between South America's two greatest rivals, Argentina and Brazil

After more than 10 years of trying, and much heartache, Matt Busby eventually got his hands on the coveted European Champions' Cup trophy in 1968

Busby, Sir Matt (1910-)

Matt Busby built two great Manchester United teams, the second after his famous team of 'Busby Babes' was wiped out when the plane carrying them home from a European Cup tie in Belgrade crashed killing eight players.

As a player, Busby was an accomplished half-back with Liverpool, Manchester City and Scotland and won an FA Cup winners' medal in Manchester City's 1934 win over Portsmouth. In 1945 he accepted the job as Manchester United manager and adopted a youth policy which was to be the foundation of the great United teams of the future.

He guided the club to an FA Cup win over Blackpool in 1948 and in 1952 the first cham-pionship for 41 years arrived in the Old Trafford trophy room. He added two more titles in 1956 and 1957 but then came the Munich disaster. After a rebuilding programme he took the club to another FA Cup win, two more League titles in 1965 and 1967, and in 1968 the supreme honour, the European Cup.

He retired as manager in 1969 but made a temporary return in 1970-71 before eventually quitting finally. He was made a director of the club and today is still very much involved with club activities and those of the Football League.

Managerial honours
European Cup 1968
Football League 1951-52, 1955-56, 1956-57, 1964-65, 1966-67
FA Cup 1948, 1963

Caps

Players are awarded caps for playing in international matches. A cap is awarded for every friendly game, but for tournaments like the World Cup, European Championship, Rous Cup and formerly the Home International championship, only one cap is awarded per tournament, (including qualifying matches), with the names of all teams a player appears against in the tournament on the cap. Caps are awarded even if a player appears as a substitute. Under 21 and Youth internationals also receive caps.

For list of international appearances see *Appearances*

Captains

British records

National team

Between 9 October 1948 (versus Northern Ireland) and 28 May 1959 (versus USA) Billy Wright captained England 90 times. During that period he missed just three internationals, when he was replaced as captain by Alf Ramsey.

Bobby Moore, also England, equalled Wright's record on 14 November 1973 when he played the last of his 108 games for his country.

Cup finals

Leading a side up the steps at Wembley to collect the FA Cup is one of the game's most treasured moments for any player: to do so more than once must be beyond the wildest dreams of most players. The following have all done so.

Joe Smith (Bolton W 1923, 1926)
Joe Harvey (Newcastle U 1951, 1952)
Danny Blanchflower (Tottenham H 1961, 1962)
Billy Bonds (West Ham U 1975, 1980)
Steve Perryman (Tottenham H 1981, 1982)
Bryan Robson (Manchester U 1983, 1985)

Dave Beasant of Wimbledon is the only goalkeeper to have led a team up the famous steps.

Billy Wright is chaired off the field after completing his 100th match for England, against Scotland at Wembley in 1959. He was the first Briton to win 100 caps. The player on the right is Don Howe

In the three successive FA Cup finals 1982-85, the captains of the losing sides were each ruled out through suspension. In 1982 Queen's Park Rangers' skipper Glenn Roeder missed the replayed final through suspension; in 1983 Brighton's Steve Foster missed the first game with Manchester United although he played in the replay, and in 1984 Watford's Wilf Rostron missed the 2-0 defeat by Everton because of suspension. Keeping the run going, Sunderland's skipper Shaun Elliott missed the 1985 Milk Cup final because of a ban. Sunderland were also losing finalists.

Goalkeepers

Three goalkeepers have captained England in full internationals since 1945: Frank Swift, Ray Clemence and Peter Shilton.

● The opposing captains in the 1924 international between Wales and Scotland at Ninian Park were Fred Keanor (Wales) and Jimmy Blair (Scotland), who both played for Cardiff City at the time!

● Martin Buchan (Aberdeen 1970 and Manchester United 1977) is the only man to have skippered Scottish and English FA Cup winning teams.

Left: Bobby Moore, one of the finest skippers to lead England

Below: Peter Shilton made his Football League debut in May 1966 and is still going strong after more than 820 games

Central League

Founded in 1911-12 with 17 members, the Central League for many years consisted of reserve sides of northern Football League teams. Today, many midlands sides help make up the League. The first winners in 1912 were Lincoln City, which was the club's first team. All other subsequent winners have been reserve sides. The League was extended to 20 teams in 1913 and in 1919 was increased to 22. It remained unaltered until 1982 when the League was extended to 32 teams split into two divisions. It was further increased to its current total of 36 teams, with 18 in each division, and a four-up four-down promotion/relegation system.

To date Blackburn Rovers, Blackpool, Bolton Wanderers, Everton, Liverpool, Manchester City, Manchester United and Preston North End have had continuous membership.

Recent champions

1983-84	Division 1:	Liverpool
	Division 2:	Bradford City
1984-85	Division 1:	Liverpool
	Division 2:	Leicester City
1985-86	Division 1:	Derby County
	Division 2:	Oldham Athletic
1986-87	Division 1:	Manchester City
	Division 2:	Huddersfield Town
1987-88	Division 1:	Nottingham Forest
	Division 2:	Blackburn Rovers
1988-89	Division 1:	Nottingham Forest
	Division 2:	Hull City

Most wins
15 — Liverpool
7 — West Bromwich Albion
6 — Manchester United, Wolverhampton Wanderers
5 — Huddersfield Town (includes 1 2nd division title)

Channel Islands

The leading Channel Islands tournament is the Muratti Competition between teams from Jersey, Guernsey and Alderney. Introduced in 1905, the final is contested every May on the Channel Islands' Liberation Day.

The two larger islands take it in turns to play a preliminary match against Alderney, with the winners playing the other team. Jersey and Guernsey have each won 35 times outright and shared the honours in 1937. Alderney sprang a shock in 1920 by beating Guernsey 1-0 to lift the trophy.

The record attendance is 13,500 at 'The Track', Guernsey in 1951.

The leading club competition is the Upton Park Trophy (inaugurated 1907) played by the champion club of Guernsey (winners of the Priaulx League) and the winners of Jersey's premier league, the Marquis Memorial League.

Upton Park trophy
Most wins
15 — Northerners (Guernsey)
10 — First Tower (Jersey)
10 — Jersey Wanderers (Jersey)
10 — St Martins (Guernsey)
6 — St Paul's/Old St Paul's (Jersey)
5 — Rangers (Guernsey)
Recent winners
1980 St Paul's (Jersey)
1981 Vale Rec (Guernsey)
1982 St Paul's (Jersey)
1983 First Tower (Jersey)
1984 First Tower (Jersey)
1985 St Martin's (Guernsey)
1986 Wanderers (Jersey)
1987 St Paul's (Jersey)
1988 Vale Rec (Guernsey)

Chapman, Herbert (1873-1934)

Herbert Chapman is widely regarded as the man who guided Huddersfield Town to a hat-trick of League championships in the 1920s, and Arsenal to the same achievement in the next decade. But the truth of the matter is that he never actually saw out the completion of the hat-trick by his two charges. He left Huddersfield midway through their third championship year, and died during Arsenal's run up to the hat-trick.

A Yorkshireman, he was not an outstanding player; he was noted more for his bright yellow boots during his days as a reserve at Tottenham Hotspur. He then joined Southern League Northampton Town as player-manager. Within two years they were champions, but in 1912 he graduated to the League with Leeds City. In 1919 Leeds were thrown out of the League for making illegal payments to players and Chapman was suspended. Later pardoned, he took charge at Huddersfield in 1920 and turned them into Football League champions in 1924. The feat was repeated a year later but in 1925-26 as Town were heading for a hat-trick of wins he quit and joined Arsenal.

Herbert Chapman, one of the game's top managers

One of his first signings for the Gunners was Charles Buchan from Sunderland. Between them they developed the 'third back' game and so was born the stopper centre-half, now very much part of the modern game.

Chapman also bought David Jack and Alex James for then sizable fees. But it paid dividends because Arsenal were League champions in 1931 and again in 1933. Chapman died on 6 January 1934 with Arsenal three points clear at the top of the table. They went on to win the title and completed the hat-trick in 1935, only the second team after Huddersfield to achieve the feat.

Managerial honours
Football League 1923-24, 1924-25 (Huddersfield T), 1930-31, 1932-33 (Arsenal)
FA Cup 1922 (Huddersfield T), 1930 (Arsenal)

Charity Shield

This traditional curtain-raiser to the English season is now a contest between the Football League champions and FA Cup winners, and is played at Wembley Stadium each August.

The first Charity Shield, in 1908, was between the champions of the Football League and the Southern League. It succeeded the Sheriff of London's Charity Shield which had been held since 1898.

Most wins
11(4) — Liverpool
9(3) — Manchester U
8(1) — Everton
The most outright wins is seven by Arsenal, Everton and Liverpool (Figures in brackets are shared wins)

Most appearances
15 — Liverpool
12 — Manchester U
10 — Arsenal, Everton

Charlton, Bobby, (1937-)

Born in Ashington, Co. Durham, Bobby Charlton had soccer running through his blood. A nephew of the great Jackie Milburn (who died in 1988) Bobby and his brother Jack both went on to play League soccer, and both played for England, appearing together in the 1966 World Cup final win.

Bobby spent most of his career with Manchester United, joining them as a teenager and progressing through the famous youth team before making his League debut against Charlton Athletic in 1956, when he scored the first of his 247 goals for the club in nearly 750 appearances.

A member of United's pre-Munich championship-winning team, he was the backbone of the 'new' United after the disaster. An FA Cup win and two League titles after Munich, Bobby enjoyed his greatest moment in a United shirt when he skippered them to the 1968 European

Charity Shield

Year				Venue
1908	Manchester U	1	Queen's Park R 1	Stamford Bridge
	Manchester U	4	Queen's Park R 0	Stamford Bridge
1909	Newcastle U	2	Northampton T 0	Stamford Bridge
1910	Brighton & HA	1	Aston Villa 0	Stamford Bridge
1911	Manchester U	8	Swindon T 4	Stamford Bridge
1912	Blackburn R	2	Queen's Park R 1	White Hart Lane
1913	Professionals	7	Amateurs 2	The Den, Milwall
1920	West Bromwich A	2	Tottenham H 0	White Hart Lane
1921	Tottenham H	2	Burnley 0	White Hart Lane
1922	Huddersfield T	1	Liverpool 0	Old Trafford
1923	Professionals	2	Amateurs 0	Stamford Bridge
1924	Professionals	3	Amateurs 1	Highbury
1925	Amateurs	6	Professionals 1	White Hart Lane
1926	Amateurs	6	Professionals 3	Maine Road
1927	Cardiff C	2	Corinthians 1	Stamford Bridge
1928	Everton	2	Blackburn R 1	Old Trafford
1929	Professionals	3	Amateurs 0	The Den, Milwall
1930	Arsenal	2	Sheffield W 1	Stamford Bridge
1931	Arsenal	1	West Bromwich A 0	Villa Park
1932	Everton	5	Newcastle U 3	St James' Park
1933	Arsenal	3	Everton 0	Goodison Park
1934	Arsenal	4	Manchester C 0	Highbury
1935	Sheffield W	1	Arsenal 0	Highbury
1936	Sunderland	2	Arsenal 1	Roker Park
1937	Manchester C	2	Sunderland 0	Maine Road
1938	Arsenal	2	Preston NE 1	Highbury
1948	Arsenal	4	Manchester U 3	Highbury
1949	Portsmouth	1	Wolverhampton W 1*	Highbury
1950	England XI	4	Canadian XI 2	Stamford Bridge
1951	Tottenham H	2	Newcastle U 1	White Hart Lane
1952	Manchester U	4	Newcastle U 2	Old Trafford
1953	Arsenal	3	Blackpool 1	Highbury
1954	West Bromich A	4	Wolverhampton W 4*	Molineux
1955	Chelsea	3	Newcastle U 0	Stamford Bridge
1956	Manchester U	1	Manchester C 0	Maine Road
1957	Manchester U	4	Aston Villa 0	Old Trafford
1958	Bolton W	4	Wolverhampton W 1	Burnden Park
1959	Wolverhampton W	3	Nottingham F 1	Molineux
1960	Burnley	2	Wolverhampton W 2*	Turf Moor
1961	Tottenham H	3	FA XI 2	White Hart Lane
1962	Tottenham H	5	Ipswich T 1	Portman Road
1963	Everton	4	Manchester U 0	Goodison Park
1964	Liverpool	2	West Ham U 2*	Anfield
1965	Liverpool	2	Manchester U 2*	Old Trafford
1966	Liverpool	1	Everton 0	Goodison Park
1967	Manchester U	3	Tottenham H 3*	Old Trafford
1968	Manchester C	6	West Bromwich A 1	Maine Road
1969	Leeds U	2	Manchester C 1	Elland Road
1970	Everton	2	Chelsea 1	Stamford Bridge
1971	Leicester C	1	Liverpool 0	Filbert Street
1972	Manchester C	1	Aston Villa 0	Villa Park
1973	Burnley	1	Manchester C 0	Maine Road
1974	Liverpool	1	Leeds 1†	Wembley
1975	Derby C	2	West Ham U 0	Wembley
1976	Liverpool	1	Southampton 0	Wembley
1977	Liverpool	0	Manchester U 0*	Wembley
1978	Nottingham F	5	Ipswich T 0	Wembley
1979	Liverpool	3	Arsenal 1	Wembley
1980	Liverpool	1	West Ham U 0	Wembley
1981	Aston Villa	2	Tottenham H 2*	Wembley
1982	Liverpool	1	Tottenham H 0	Wembley
1983	Manchester U	2	Liverpool 0	Wembley
1984	Everton	1	Liverpool 0	Wembley
1985	Everton	2	Manchester U 0	Wembley
1986	Everton	1	Liverpool 1*	Wembley
1987	Everton	1	Coventry C 0	Wembley
1988	Liverpool	2	Wimbledon 1	Wembley

* Shared, both teams holding shield for six months
† Liverpool won 6-5 on penalties

Above: England's most prolific goalscorer, Bobby Charlton, who scored 49 times for his country during his long career

Cup win over Benfica.

After 20 years of Old Trafford he left in 1974 to take up the manager's job at Preston North End where he was not as successful as in his playing days. He has since returned to United as a director.

Born: 11 October, 1937, Ashington, Co. Durham
Football League debut: 6 Oct 1956 v Charlton A
Football League appearances: 644 (606 Manchester U, 38 Preston NE)
Football League goals: 207 (199 Manchester U, 8 Preston NE)
International caps: 106
Honours
World Cup 1966
European Cup 1968
FA Cup 1963
Football League 1956-57, 1964-65, 1966-67
Awards
Footballer of the Year (FWA) 1966
European Footballer of the Year 1966

Chelsea

For more than 75 years the Mears family was associated with Chelsea Football Club, and it is to one member, H.A. Mears, that the club owes its existence. In 1904 H.A. acquired the Stamford Bridge Athletic Ground and assembled a team to play at this new arena. They applied unsuccessfully to join the Southern League in 1905. Optimistically and enthusiastically they applied to join the Football League and to everyone's surprise were accepted into the 2nd division. Many critics were dubious that Chelsea could survive, but one member of the club boldly claimed: 'Chelsea will stagger humanity'. For 50 years it looked as though the critics would be proved right and the optimistic and nameless club member wrong.

In their first half century all Chelsea had to show was a defeat in the 1915 FA Cup final by Sheffield United, and three runners-up positions in the 2nd division. But then in their Golden Jubilee year they put an end to the music hall jokes and won the League title led by Roy Bentley and managed by the great Ted Drake.

The jinx had at last been beaten and over the next 20 years, with the help of such famous players as Jimmy Greaves, Bobby Tambling, Peter Osgood, Peter Bonetti, 'Chopper' Harris, and many more, the Chelsea trophy room was to house the FA Cup, Football League Cup and European Cup-winners' Cup.

In recent years the Mears family have severed connections with the club and the new chairman is Ken Bates. Sadly, boardroom problems and uncertainty about the future of the Stamford Bridge ground has not helped.

Ground: Stamford Bridge
Nickname: Blues or Pensioners
Record attendance: 82,905 — v Arsenal (Division 1), 12 Oct 1935
First Football League season: 1905-06 Division 2 (3rd)
Seasons in Football League: 73 (54 Division 1, 19 Division 2)

Honours
Division 1 champions 1954-55
Division 2 champions 1983-84, 1988-89
FA Cup winners 1970
Football League Cup winners 1965
European Cup-Winners' Cup winners 1971
Full Members Cup winners 1986

Right: The Charity Shield

Matthew Le Tissier (Southampton) one of the small band of Channel Islanders to enjoy a successful Football League career

Corner kick

A corner kick is awarded to the attacking team when the ball passes over the goal line, other than when a goal is scored, and the ball was last played by a member of the defending side. The kick is taken from the segment near the corner flags at the intersection of the side-line and goal line. Defending players must stand 10 yards (9.15 metres) from the ball at the kick.

The corner kick was adopted by the Football Association in 1872 and the 10-yard rule introduced in 1914. Before 1924 goals could not be scored direct from corner kicks but the rules were changed that year, since when there have been many such instances in senior football.

The *first player to score direct from a corner in the Football League* was Billy Smith for Huddersfield Town versus Arsenal on 11 October 1924. Seven weeks earlier a winger called Alston scored for St Bernard's in a Scottish 2nd division game against Albion Rovers. That was the first goal direct from a corner in Britain.

The *first player to score direct from a corner in a Home International* was Alex Cheyne of Aberdeen who scored for Scotland against England at Hampden Park on 13 April 1929.

The 1st division game between Newcastle United and Portsmouth at St James's Park on 5 December 1931 is unique: it is believed to be the only Football League game not to include a single corner kick.

Crossbar

This is the horizontal bar that joins the two uprights of the goal. The underside of the bar must be 8 feet (2.4 metres) from the ground.

Perhaps surprisingly, crossbars were specifically forbidden by the laws of the game in 1863. In 1866 the Laws stated: 'The goals shall be upright posts, eight yards apart, with a tape across them, eight feet from the ground'.

However, in 1875 the Football Association permitted the use of crossbars and subsequently amended the rules to read: '. . . with a tape or bar across them.' Crossbars became compulsory from 1883.

Cruyff, Johan (1947-)

The most exciting attacking player in the 1970s, his ability was rewarded by being honoured with the coveted European Footballer of the Year award three times in four years.

Identifiable in his No.14 shirt, Cruyff joined Dutch club Ajax when he was ten and after working his way through their extensive junior system made his League debut at 19. He was the Netherlands' top scorer in his first season with 33 goals, and played a part in Ajax's 5-1 demolition of Liverpool in the Champions' Cup.

After winning three successive European Championship winners' medals, six Dutch League titles and the Cup four times he followed his former boss Rinus Michels and signed for Barcelona for £922,000. Further League and Cup honours followed.

He then had a spell in the USA before retiring. But after a brief period out of the game he was tempted back by Spanish 2nd division side Levante in 1981. Surprisingly the following year he was playing for Ajax again and another League title came his way. In 1983 he played for Feyenoord, and they took the League from Ajax. He returned to Barcelona in 1988 as team manager.

On the international scene, he played for the Netherlands 48 times and was a member of their team beaten in the 1974 World Cup final by West Germany.

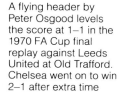

A flying header by Peter Osgood levels the score at 1–1 in the 1970 FA Cup final replay against Leeds United at Old Trafford. Chelsea went on to win 2–1 after extra time

Born: 25 April 1947, Amsterdam, Netherlands
International caps: 48
Honours
European Cup 1971, 1972, 1973, (all Ajax)
European Super Cup 1972, 1973 (both Ajax)
World Cup championship 1972 (Ajax)
Dutch League 1966, 1967, 1968, 1970, 1972, 1973, 1983
(all Ajax); 1984 (Feyenoord)
Spanish League 1974 (Barcelona)
Dutch Cup 1967, 1970, 1971, 1972, (all Ajax)
Spanish Cup 1978 (Barcelona)
Awards
European Footballer of the Year 1971, 1973, 1974

Dalglish, Kenny (1951-)

As a player Kenny Dalglish won most honours the game had to offer, both in Scotland and England. Since turning his attentions to managing Liverpool, the most successful club side in English history, he has continued to win trophies.

Born in Glasgow, he joined Celtic from local non-league side Cumbernauld United in 1967. He made his Celtic debut in 1969 and played more than 200 League games for the Scottish club, and scored over 100 goals. Uniquely, he repeated the feat when he moved south of the border in a £440,000 transfer deal that took him to Liverpool in 1977 as a replacement for the Kop's favourite son, Kevin Keegan. It was not long before 'King Kenny' became the new Anfield favourite. With both clubs Dalglish won 12 League Championship medals, and 10 domestic Cup winners' medals as a player.

He succeeded Joe Fagan as Liverpool manager in the summer of 1985 and immediately led them to the double, something which Paisley or Bill Shankly could not achieve at Anfield. Since then he has led the club to its record 17th League title.

Born: 4 March 1951, Glasgow, Scotland
Scottish League debut: 4 October 1969, Celtic v Raith R
Football League debut: 20 August 1977, Liverpool v Middlesbrough
Scottish League appearances: 204
Football League appearances: 354
Scottish League goals: 112
Football League goals: 118
International caps: 102
Honours (player)
European Cup 1978, 1981, 1984 (all Liverpool)
European Super Cup 1977 (Liverpool)
Scottish Premier/1st Division 1969-70, 1970-71, 1971-72, 1972-73, 1973-74, 1976-77
English 1st Division 1978-79, 1979-80, 1981-82, 1982-83, 1983-84, 1985-86
FA Cup 1986
Scottish FA Cup 1972, 1974, 1975, 1977
League Cup/Milk Cup 1981, 1982, 1983, 1984
Scottish League Cup 1974-75
Awards
Manager of the Year 1986, 1988
Player of the Year (FWA) 1979, 1983
Player of the Year (PFA) 1983

Debenhams Cup

Held just once, in 1977, this was a two-legged sponsored competition for the two 3rd/4th division clubs that went the furthest in the 1976-77 FA Cup. That honour went to Chester and Port Vale and it was Chester who won the one and only Debenhams Cup.

Debuts

The record for the *most goals on a debut in first-class football in Britain* is eight by Jim Dyet for King's Park against Forfar in the Scottish 2nd division on 2 January 1930.

The most goals by a player *making his debut in the Football League* is five by George Hilsdon for Chelsea against Glossop North End in the 2nd

Above: The finest footballer produced by the Netherlands, Johan Cruyff

Right: One of the Kop's favourites, Kenny Dalglish, scoring the only goal of the 1978 European Cup final against FC Bruges

division on 1 September 1906.

The *quickest goal by a Football League debutant* is six seconds by Barrie Jones of Notts County against Torquay United on 31 March 1962.

Playing his first game for his new club, Newcastle United, against Newport County on 5 October 1946, Len Shackleton scored six times in United's record 13-0 win.

Fulham's 'Tosh' Chamberlain *scored with his first kick in League football*, itself not a rarity. But against Lincoln City on 20 November 1954 his first kick was from inside his own half of the field . . . it sailed past the Lincoln 'keeper.

However, not everybody had such distinguished debuts.

Halifax Town's reserve goalkeeper Stan Milton was called up for first team duty for the game against Stockport County on 6 January 1934. Milton conceded 13 goals.

Former England full-back George Hardwick *scored an own goal within 60 seconds of his debut* for Middlesbrough against Bolton Wanderers on 18 December 1937.

Several players have *received their marching orders on their debut*. The first player known to have been sent off on his Football League debut was John Burns of Rochdale against Stockport County on 29 October 1921. Burns had to live with the unwanted record of being the *only* debutant to be sent off for 46 years until he was 'joined' by Gerald Casey of Tranmere Rovers, who was dismissed on his debut against Torquay United on 19 August 1967.

Apart from clubs playing their first Football

League game, *the most debutants in one Football League team* is 10 by Rochdale against Carlisle United on 27 August 1932.

In international football Scotland's Jim Craig *scored on his debut before he had even kicked the ball!* . . . he came on as substitute against Sweden at Hampden Park on 27 April 1977. His first touch of the ball was a scoring header.

The most goals scored by a player *making his debut for England* is five by Oliver Vaughton (Aston Villa) against Ireland at Belfast on 18 February 1882. England won 13-0 and in the same game Vaughton's Aston Villa team-mate Arthur Brown scored four goals on *his* debut. Charles Heggie (Rangers) equalled Vaughton's record on 20 March 1886 when he netted five times for Scotland on his debut against Ireland, also in Belfast.

Defeats

(For biggest individual defeats see *Wins*)

● Between 8 October 1983 and 23 April 1984 Cambridge United played 31 2nd division games without a win (21 lost, 10 drawn), the longest sequence in the Football League without a win.

● The worst start to a Football League season was by Manchester United in the 1st division in 1930-31 when they lost their first 12 matches.

● Rochdale hold the record for the most defeats in one season: 33 in the 3rd division (north) in 1931-32.

Most in single season
Football League

				Matches
33	Rochdale	1931-32	Division 3 (north)	40
33	Cambridge U	1984-85	Division 3	46
33	Newport C	1987-88	Division 4	46
32	Workington	1975-76	Division 4	46
31	St Mirren	1920-21	Scottish League*	42
31	Barrow	1925-26	Division 3 (north)	42
31	Tranmere R	1938-39	Division 2	42
31	Stoke C	1984-85	Division 1	42
31	Morton	1987-88	Scottish Premier	44
31	Crewe A	1956-57	Division 3 (north)	46
31	Crewe A	1957-58	Division 3 (north)	46
31	Newport C	1961-62	Division 3	46
31	Bradford PA	1968-69	Division 4	46
31	Barrow	1970-71	Division 4	46
31	Workington	1976-77	Division 4	46
31	Crewe A	1981-82	Division 4	46
29	Merthyr T	1924-25	Division 3 (south)	42
29	Walsall	1952-53	Division 3 (south)	46
29	Walsall	1953-54	Division 3 (south)	46

Scottish League (since 1975-76)

25	Queen of the South	1981-82	Division 1	39
29	Berwick R	1987-88	Division 2	39

Fewest in single season
Football League

0	Preston NE	1888-89	Football League	22
0	Liverpool	1893-94	Division 2	22
0	Celtic	1897-98	Scottish Division 1	18
0	Rangers	1898-99	Scottish Division 1	18
0	Kilmarnock	1898-99	Scottish Division 2	18

Minimum 38-game season

1	Rangers	1920-21	Scottish League*	42
1	Celtic	1916-17	Scottish Division 1	38
1	Rangers	1928-29	Scottish Division 1	38
2	Rangers	1919-20	Scottish Division 1	42
2	Celtic	1921-22	Scottish League*	42
2	Leeds U	1968-69	Division 1	42
2	Liverpool	1987-88	Division 1	40
2	St Mirren	1976-77	Scottish Division 1	39
2	Bristol C	1905-06	Division 2	38
2	Motherwell	1931-32	Scottish Division 1	38
2	Rangers	1932-33	Scottish Division 1	38
2	Rangers	1933-34	Scottish Division 1	38
2	Morton	1966-67	Scottish Division 2	38

3	Port Vale	1953-54	Division 3 (north)	46
3	Celtic	1919-20	Scottish League*	42†
3	Wolverhampton W	1923-24	Division 3 (north)	42
3	Rangers	1924-25	Scottish Division 1	42
3	Doncaster R	1946-47	Division 3 (north)	42
3	Leeds U	1963-64	Division 2	42
3	Nottingham F	1977-78	Division 1	42
3	Nottingham F	1978-79	Division 1	42†
3	Liverpool	1904-05	Division 2	38
3	Celtic	1913-14	Scottish Division 1	38
3	Celtic	1914-15	Scottish Division 1	38
3	Celtic	1915-16	Scottish Division 1	38
3	Rangers	1936-37	Scottish Division 1	38
4	Southampton	1921-22	Division 3 (south)	42
4	Plymouth A	1929-30	Division 3 (south)	42
4	Lincoln C	1975-76	Division 4	46
4	Sheffield U	1981-82	Division 4	46
5	Queen's Park R	1966-67	Division 3	46

*only one Scottish division at the time

Scottish League (since 1975-76)

3	Celtic	1987-88	Premier Division	44
2	St Mirren	1976-77	Division 1	39
2	Partick T	1975-76	Division 1	26
1	Raith R	1975-76	Division 2	26†

†didn't win League title

Most defeats for teams winning Football League titles

12	Everton	1931-32	Division 1
12	Notts C	1922-23	Division 2
12	Blackburn R	1938-39	
12	Millwall	1987-88	
12	Ipswich T	1956-57	Division 3 (south)
11	Nelson	1922-23	Division 3 (north)
11	Doncaster R	1934-35	
11	Barnsley	1954-55	
11	Southampton	1959-60	Division 3
11	Carlisle U	1964-65	
11	Oxford U	1967-68	
11	Millwall	1961-62	Division 4
11	Brentford	1962-63	
11	Doncaster R	1965-66	
11	Grimsby T	1971-72	
9	Celtic	1978-79	Scottish Premier
11	Morton	1986-87	Scottish Division 1
10	Falkirk	1974-75	Scottish Division 2

Henri Delaunay Cup

This is the trophy presented to the winners of the European Championship. It is named after Henri Delaunay, the former general secretary of UEFA and the French Football Federation who conceived the idea of the championship. Sadly he died before he could see its realisation.

Derby County

One of the 12 founder members of the Football League, Derby County was formed in 1884 as an offshoot of the Derbyshire County Cricket Club and played their matches at the nearby Racecourse Ground before moving to the Baseball Ground in 1895.

After fluctuating between the top two divisions County suffered a drop into the northern section of the 3rd division in 1955. Two years later they won the title. Before their drop they won their first major honour when they beat Charlton Athletic 4-1 after extra time to win the first post-Second World War FA Cup final.

The club enjoyed its greatest period in the early 1970s. Their revival started in 1967 when they appointed Brian Clough as manager. Along with right-hand man Peter Taylor, Clough led Derby to the 2nd division title in 1969. Three years later they were champions of the 1st division. Clough surprisingly quit in 1973 but

County went on to win a second title in 1975 under former player Dave MacKay.

Derby have had a second spell in the 3rd division in the 1980s but are now back amongst the top clubs in the 1st division.

Ground: Baseball Ground
Nickname: Rams
Record attendance: 41,826 — v Tottenham H (Division 1), 20 Sept 1969
First Football League season: 1888-89 Football League (10th)
Seasons in Football League: 90 (56 Division 1, 30 Division 2, 2 Division 3, 2 Division 3 (N))

Honours

Division 1 champions 1971-72, 1974-75
Division 2 champions 1911-12, 1914-15, 1968-69, 1986-87
Division 3 (north) champions 1956-57
FA Cup winners 1946
Texaco Cup winners 1972
Footballers of the Year Dave MacKay (FWA) 1969 (shared), Colin Todd (PFA) 1975

Derby matches

Derby matches are games between teams from the same town. They are named after the Shrove Tuesday games of 'football' played in Derby, Ashburton and other surrounding Derbyshire towns and villages for centuries before organised football started.

Derby County, along with manager Dave Mackay, after winning their second League title in three years in 1975

In 1953 he joined Real Madrid, who paid Millonarios £20,000 for him. Barcelona insisted they'd paid a fee to River Plate for him! The Spanish League ruled that Real should have him for the first season and Barcelona for the second, but he played so badly in his first season at Real that Barcelona said they could keep him!

What a mistake that proved to be: he played in seven European Cup finals for Madrid and scored in five consecutive finals between 1956 and 1960, including a hat-trick in 1960. In 510 games for Real he scored a staggering 428 goals. He retired in 1967 after a spell with Espanol of Barcelona, before going into club management

The Henri Delauny Cup, which is awarded to the winners of the European Championship

Di Stefano, Alfredo (1926-)

A rare triple international with Argentina, Colombia and Spain, Alfredo Di Stefano Lauthe was born in Buenos Aires and started his career at River Plate in 1944. His father before him played for River Plate.

He went on loan to Huracan for a year and scored 50 goals in 66 games; River Plate immediately recalled him. He won his first cap in 1947

with Boca Juniors and Valencia among others. He led Boca to two Argentinian titles and Valencia to the Spanish League title in 1971, their first title for 24 years.

Born: 4 July 1926, Buenos Aires, Argentina
International caps: 42 (7 Argentina, 4 Colombia, 31 Spain)
Honours
European Cup 1956-60
Spanish League 1954, 1955, 1957, 1958, 1961, 1962, 1963
Spanish Cup 1962
Argentine League 1945, 1947
Colombian League 1951, 1952
World Club Championship 1960
Awards
European Footballer of the Year 1957, 1959

Double

The double is winning both the cup and League Championship in the same season.

Double winners
Football League
Preston North End 1888-89   Tottenham Hotspur 1960-61
Aston Villa 1896-97   Arsenal 1970-71
                      Liverpool 1985-86

Thirteen teams have come close to completing the double:
FA Cup winners/runner-up in League
Manchester City 1904   Manchester United 1948
Aston Villa 1913

Everton–Liverpool matches are the most famous of all 'Derby' clashes, certainly in England

Football League cont.
West Bromwich Albion 1954
Wolverhampton Wanderers 1960
Leeds United 1972
Liverpool 1974

League Champions/FA Cup runners-up
Newcastle United 1905
Sunderland 1913
Manchester United 1957
Liverpool 1977
Everton 1985
Liverpool 1988

Scottish League
Celtic 1906-07, 1907-08, 1913-14, 1953-54, 1966-67, 1968-69, 1970-71, 1971-72, 1973-74, 1976-77, 1987-88
Rangers 1927-28, 1929-30, 1933-34, 1934-35, 1948-49, 1949-50, 1952-53, 1962-63, 1963-64, 1975-76, 1977-78
Aberdeen 1983-84

Draws

Most in single season
23	Norwich C	Division 1	1978-79	42
23	Exeter C	Division 4	1986-87	46
22	Tranmere R	Division 3	1970-71	46
22	Aldershot	Division 4	1971-72	46
22	Chester	Division 3	1977-78	46
22	Carlisle U	Division 3	1978-79	46
22	Halifax T	Division 4	1981-82	46
21	Plymouth A	Division 3*	1920-21	42
21	Halifax T	Division 3	1973-74	46
21	Halifax T	Division 4	1977-78	46
21	Leeds U	Division 2	1982-83	42
21	Oldham A	Division 2	1988-89	46
21	East Fife	Scottish Division 1	1986-87	44
20	Raith Rovers	Scottish Division 2	1986-87	39

*first season of 3rd division football, known as Division 3 and not Division 3 (south)

Preston North End in 1888–89, the first team to perform the 'Double'

Ian Botham, right, is one of several English test cricketers to have played in the Football League; he played for Scunthorpe United nine times

There have been 21 instances of teams going through an English or Scottish season without drawing a game. The first instance was in 1891-92 when both Aston Villa and Sunderland completed their 26-game programme without a draw. The last occasion was in 1907-08 when Ayr Parkhouse failed to draw in any of their 22 games in the Scottish 2nd division. The last instance of a team going through an English season without a draw was in the 2nd division in 1896-97 when Darwen played 30 2nd division games, winning 14 and losing 16.

Since the First World War, when the 1st division was increased to a 42-game season, the lowest number of drawn games in the Football League has been one by Barrow in division 3 (north) in 1932-33. In the same period six teams have gone through a Scottish League with only one draw to their credit. The last was Forfar Athletic in the 2nd division in 1969-70.

Highest scoring draws

6-6	Leicester City v Arsenal	21 April 1930	Division 1
6-6	Queen of the South v Falkirk	20 Sept 1947	Scot. Div. 1
6-6	Motherwell v Dumbarton	10 April 1954	Scot. Div. 2
6-6	Charlton v Middlesbrough	22 Oct 1966	Division 2

Dryborough Cup

This was a pre-season competition in Scotland similar to the English Watney Cup. The competition was open to the four highest scoring teams in each division the previous season and was a knockout tournament. It lapsed between 1975 and 1978 and has not been played since 1980.

Finals

		Attendance
1971	Aberdeen 2 Celtic 1	
1972	Hibernian 5 Celtic 3 at Hampden Park	49,462
1973	Hibernian 1 Celtic 0 at Hampden Park	49,204
1974	Celtic 2 Rangers 2 at Hampden Park	57,558

(Celtic won 4-2 on penalties)

Dual sportsmen

Over the years many men have enjoyed dual first-class cricket and soccer careers. In recent years the most famous has been England cricket captain Ian Botham who played League soccer with Scunthorpe United. He made his debut as

substitute against Bournemouth on 25 March 1980 and played nine League games for the Lincolnshire side.

Leicestershire and England cricketer Chris Balderstone enjoyed a 16-year career in the Football League with Huddersfield Town, Carlisle United and Doncaster Rovers, playing more than 500 League games. But on 15 September 1975 he uniquely played first-class cricket for Leicestershire against Derbyshire at Chesterfield before making a dash to Doncaster to play in Rover's 4th division match against Brentford.

One of the most versatile of ex-soccer players was Charles Burgess 'C.B.' Fry: he won an England soccer cap against Ireland in 1901 and played for Southampton in the 1902 FA Cup final; made his first-class cricketing debut for Surrey in 1891, going on to score nearly 40,000 first class runs, and appearing in 26 Test matches; played rugby for the Barbarians and broke the world long jump record at Iffley Road, Oxford, in 1893. He also stood as a Liberal party candidate in three elections, and was once offered the kingdom of Albania!

Since the Second World War only two men have played both soccer and cricket at full international level: Arthur Milton (Arsenal/Gloucestershire) and Willie Watson (Huddersfield Town and Sunderland/Yorkshire and Leicestershire). Contrary to the popular belief, neither Denis nor Leslie Compton were dual internationals at full level. Denis only played in war-time and a 'victory' soccer international, while brother Leslie never played cricket for England, although he did win two full soccer caps.

The only man to captain England at both soccer and cricket is Reginald E. Foster.

Makepeace had a remarkable record: he won an FA Cup winners' medal in 1906 and a League championship medal in 1915. In addition he won four England caps. He then went on to play cricket for England and in 1926-28 won the county cricket championship three times with Lancashire.

Arsenal have had an abundance of cricketers on their books over the years. In addition to Milton, Ducat and the Comptons there have been Joe Hulme of Middlesex, Ted Drake of Hampshire and Brian Close of Yorkshire.

In other sports, Irishman Kevin O'Flannagan, another ex-Arsenal player, played soccer and rugby for Ireland on consecutive Saturdays in 1946. His brother Michael was also a dual rugby-soccer international.

One senior Rugby League player has been capped at soccer: Dai Davies who played in goal for Bolton Wanderers in the 1904 FA Cup final was capped by Wales. He played Rugby League for Salford.

Full international soccer and cricket caps

	Football club(s)	Cricket club
John Arnold	Oxford C, Southampton, Fulham	Hampshire
Andy Ducat	Arsenal, Aston V, Fulham	Surrey
Reginald Foster	Oxford University	Worcestershire
Leslie Gay	Old Brightonians	Cambridge University
William Gunn	Notts County	Nottinghamshire
Harold Hardinge	Sheffield United	Kent
Hon. Alfred Lytteelton	Old Etonians	Middlesex
Harold Makepeace	Everton	Lancashire
Jack Sharp	Everton	Lancashire

Left: Asa Hartford (Manchester City, right) and Martin Peters (Norwich City) in action in 1978–79

Edwards, Duncan (1936-58)

One of the most stylish players to wear an England shirt, Duncan Edwards was only 18

Below: One of the finest wing-halves to pull on an England shirt, the great Duncan Edwards

when he made his international debut, but his stature belied his years.

Born in Dudley, Worcestershire, he played for the town's boys team at the age of 11 – the average age of the team was 15. Two hours after his 16th birthday Matt Busby personally went to the youngster's home to sign him for United. He was still only 16 when he made his senior debut. Edwards made his international debut in April 1955, the youngest person ever to pull on an England shirt.

A wing-half, he had a great natural talent and had great vision; he also had a fierce shot in either foot. In his five years at Old Trafford Edwards won two championship medals and appeared in the 1957 FA Cup final. Sadly the game lost a great talent when he died in the Munich air crash in 1958.

Born: 1 October 1936, Dudley, Worcestershire
Football League debut: 4 April 1953 v Cardiff City (Division 1)
Football League appearances: 151 (all Manchester U)
Football League goals: 20
International caps: 18
Honours
Football League 1955-56, 1956-57

England

For origins of soccer in England, see *Origins*. See also *Football Association* and *Football League*.

European Championship

The European Championship was the idea of Henri Delaunay, onetime secretary of the French Football Federation and general secretary of UEFA. It is a World Cup type competition held every four years for European countries.

The first matches got under way on 20 September 1958 and the first final was played in Paris on 10 July 1960. Sadly Delaunay died before the competition started. However, his name is immortalised in the championship trophy, the Henri Delaunay Trophy.

Initially known as the European Nations' Cup, it became simply the European Championship in 1966 when the qualifying group format of today was introduced. The final stages are held in a different country every four years.

European Cup

Known simply as the European Cup, its full title is the European Champion Clubs Cup. It was instituted in 1955 following a suggestion from the French daily sports newspaper *L'Equipe*.

European Championship

Finals

				Venue	Attendance
1960	USSR 2		Yugolavia 1 aet	Paris	17,966
1964	Spain 2		USSR 1	Madrid	120,000
1968	Italy 1		Yugoslavia 1	Rome	75,000
	Italy 2		Yugoslavia 0	Rome	60,000
1972	West Germany 3		USSR 0	Brussels	43,437
1976	Czechoslovakia 2		West Germany 2 aet	Belgrade	45,000
	(Czechoslovakia won 5-3 on penalties)				
1980	West Germany 2		Belgium 1	Rome	47,864
1984	France 2		Spain 0	Paris	80,000
1988	Netherlands 2		USSR 0	Munich	72,308

Leading goalscorers
Gerd Muller (West Germany) – 16
Johann Cruyff (Netherlands), Ferenc Bene (Hungary), Ole Madsen (Denmark), Zdenek Nehoda (Czechoslovakia), Tibor Nylasi (Hungary) – 12

Most goals in final stages (one tournament)
9 — Michel Platini (France) 1984

Biggest wins
12-1 — Spain v Malta (qualifying) 21 Dec 1983
9-0 — England v Luxembourg (qualifying) 15 Dec 1982

European Cup

Finals

			Venue	Attendance
1956	Real Madrid 4	Stade de Rheims 3	Paris	38,000
1957	Real Madrid 2	Fiorentina 0	Madrid	124,000
1958	Real Madrid 3	AC Milan 2 aet	Brussels	67,000
1959	Real Madrid 2	Stade de Rheims 0	Stuttgart	80,000
1960	Real Madrid 7	Eintracht Frankfurt 3	Glasgow	127,621
1961	Benfica 3	Barcelona 2	Berne	28,000
1962	Benfica 5	Real Madrid 3	Amsterdam	65,000
1963	AC Milan 2	Benfica 1	London	45,000
1964	Inter-Milan 3	Real Madrid 1	Vienna	74,000
1965	Inter-Milan 1	Benfica 0	Milan	80,000
1966	Real Madrid 2	Partizan Belgrade 1	Brussels	55,000
1967	Celtic 2	Inter-Milan 1	Lisbon	56,000
1968	Manchester U 4	Benfica 1 aet	London	100,000
1969	AC Milan 4	Ajax 1	Madrid	50,000
1970	Feyenoord 2	Celtic 1 aet	Milan	50,000
1971	Ajax 2	Panathinaikos 0	London	90,000
1972	Ajax 2	Inter-Milan 0	Rotterdam	67,000
1973	Ajax 1	Juventus 0	Belgrade	93,500
1974	Bayern Munich 1	Atletico Madrid 1	Brussels	65,000
	Bayern Munich 4	Atletico Madrid 0	Brussels	65,000
1975	Bayern Munich 2	Leeds United 0	Paris	48,000
1976	Bayern Munich 1	St Etienne 0	Glasgow	54,864
1977	Liverpool 3	Moenchengladbach 1	Rome	57,000
1978	Liverpool 1	FC Bruges 0	London	92,000
1979	Nottingham F 1	Malmo 0	Munich	57,500
1980	Nottingham F 1	SV Hamburg 0	Madrid	50,000
1981	Liverpool 1	Real Madrid 0	Paris	48,360
1982	Aston Villa 1	Bayern Munich 0	Rotterdam	46,000
1983	SV Hamburg 1	Juventus 0	Athens	80,000
1984	Liverpool 1	AS Roma 1 aet	Rome	69,693
	(Liverpool won 4-2 on penalties)			
1985	Juventus 1	Liverpool 0	Brussels	58,000
1986	Steaua Bucharest 0	Barcelona 0 aet	Seville	70,000
	(Steaua won 2-0 on penalties)			
1987	FC Porto 2	Bayern Munich 1	Vienna	59,000
1988	PSV Eindhoven 0	Benfica 0 aet	Stuttgart	70,000
	(Eindhoven won 6-5 on penalties)			
1989	AC Milan 4	Steau Bucharest 0	Barcelona	97,000

The champion club from each of the associations in UEFA is allowed to enter. The defending champions automatically enter, making it possible for one country to have two entrants.

All matches are played over two legs, with the exception of the final, which is held at a preselected venue before each year's competition by UEFA. In the two-legged matches, away goals count 'double' in the event of the scores being level at the end of the two legs.

Because of the tragedy at the Heysel Stadium, Brussels in 1985 English clubs have been barred from all European Club competitions until further notice. On re-instatement, the ban imposed on Liverpool FC will extend a further three years.

Clubs that have won in their own country
Real Madrid 1957, Inter-Milan 1965, Manchester U 1968, Ajax 1972, Liverpool 1978
Biggest win
single game
12-2 — Feyenoord v Reykjavic (1st round), 17 Sept 1969
aggregate
18-0 — (8-0:10-0) Benfica v Stade Dudelange (prelim round) Sept/Oct 1985
Most goals in career
49 — Alfredo di Stefano (Real Madrid) 1955-64
46 — Eusebio (Benfica) 1961-74
36 — Gerd Muller (Bayern Munich) 1969-77
Most goals one season
14 — Jose Altafini (AC Milan) 1962-63
12 — Ferenc Puskas (Real Madrid) 1959-60

Most wins
6 — Real Madrid
4 — Liverpool
3 — Ajax, Bayern Munich, AC Milan

Most finals appearances
9 — Real Madrid
6 — Benfica
5 — Bayern Munich, Liverpool

European Cup-winners' Cup

Started in 1960-61, this competition is open to the winners of major cup competitions in countries affiliated to UEFA. Matches are played over two legs, except the final on a neutral ground. The first final was played over two legs.

Real Madrid dominated the European Cup in its early years when Alfredo di Stefano was their most prolific goalscorer

European Cup-winners' Cup

Finals

			Venue	Attendance
1961	Rangers 0	Fiorentina 2	Glasgow	80,000
	Fiorentina 2	Rangers 1	Florence	50,000
1962	Atletico Madrid 1	Fiorentina 1	Glasgow	27,289
	Atletico Madrid 3	Fiorentina 0	Stuttgart	38,120
1963	Tottenham H 5	Atletico Madrid 1	Rotterdam	49,143
1964	Sporting Lisbon 3	MTK Budapest 3	Brussels	3,208
	Sporting Lisbon 1	MTK Budapest 0	Antwerp	19,924
1965	West Ham U 2	Munich 1860 0	London	97,974
1966	Borussia Dortmund 2	Liverpool 1 aet	Glasgow	41,657
1967	Bayern Munich 1	Rangers 0 aet	Nuremberg	69,480
1968	AC Milan 2	SV Hamburg 0	Rotterdam	53,276
1969	Slovan Bratislava 3	Barcelona 2	Basle	19,478
1970	Manchester C 2	Gornik Zabrze 1	Vienna	7,968
1971	Chelsea 1	Real Madrid 1 aet	Athens	42,000
	Chelsea 2	Real Madrid 1	Athens	24,000
1972	Rangers 3	Moscow Dynamo 2	Barcelona	24,701
1973	AC Milan 1	Leeds U 0	Salonika	45,000
1974	FC Magdeburg 2	AC Milan 0	Rotterdam	4,641
1975	Dynamo Kiev 3	Ferencvaros 0	Basle	10,897
1976	Anderlecht 4	West Ham U 2	Brussels	58,000
1977	SV Hamburg 2	Anderlecht 0	Amsterdam	65,000
1978	Anderlecht 4	Austria/WAC 0	Paris	48,679
1979	Barcelona 4	Fortuna Dusseldorf 3 aet	Basle	58,000
1980	Valencia 0	Arsenal 0 aet	Brussels	40,000
	(Valencia won 5-4 on penalties)			
1981	Dynamo Tbilisi 2	Carl Zeis Jena 1	Dusseldorf	9,000
1982	Barcelona 2	Standard Liege 1	Barcelona	100,000
1983	Aberdeen 2	Real Madrid 1 aet	Gothenburg	17,804
1984	Juventus 2	FC Porto 1	Basle	60,000
1985	Everton 3	Rapid Vienna 1	Rotterdam	35,000
1986	Dynamo Kiev 3	Atletico Madrid 0	Lyon	39,300
1987	Ajax 1	Lokomotiv Leipzig 0	Athens	35,000
1988	Mechelen 1	Ajax 0	Strasbourg	40,000
1989	Barcelona 2	Sampdoria 0	Berne	45,000

Most wins
3 — Barcelona

Most finals appearances
4 — Barcelona

Clubs that have won in their own country
Fiorentina 1961, West Ham U 1965, Bayern Munich 1967, Anderlecht 1976, Barcelona 1982

Biggest win
single game
16-1 — Sporting Lisbon v Apoel Nicosia (1st round) 13 Nov 1963
aggregate
21-0 — (8-0:12-0) Chelsea v Jeuness Hautcharage (1st round) Sept 1971

European Footballer of the Year

This award was inaugurated in 1956 by the French newspaper *France Football*, which invites nominees from selected football journalists across Europe. The winner receives *Le Ballon d'Or* (The Golden Ball) trophy.

Winner

1956	Stanley Matthews (Blackpool)
1957	Alfredo di Stefano (Real Madrid)
1958	Raymond Kopa (Real Madrid)
1959	Alfredo di Stefano (Real Madrid)
1960	Luis Suarez (Barcelona)
1961	Omar Sivori (Juventus)
1962	Josef Masopust (Dukla Prague)
1963	Lev Yashin (Dynamo Moscow)
1964	Denis Law (Manchester U)
1965	Eusebio (Benfica)
1966	Bobby Charlton (Manchester U)
1967	Florian Albert (Ferencvaros)
1968	George Best (Manchester U)
1969	Gianni Rivera (AC Milan)
1970	Gerd Muller (Bayern Munich)
1971	Johan Cruyff (Ajax)
1972	Franz Beckenbauer (Bayern Munich)
1973	Johan Cruyff (Barcelona)
1974	Johan Cruyff (Barcelona)
1975	Oleg Blokhin (Dynamo Kiev)
1976	Franz Beckenbauer (Bayern Munich)
1977	Allan Simonsen (B. Moenchegladbach)
1978	Kevin Keegan (SV Hamburg)
1979	Kevin Keegan (SV Hamburg)
1980	Karl-Heinz Rummenigge (Bayern Munich)
1981	Karl-Heinz Rummenigge (Bayern Munich)
1982	Paolo Rossi (Juventus)
1983	Michel Platini (Juventus)
1984	Michel Platini (Juventus)
1985	Michel Platini (Juventus)
1986	Igor Belanof (Dynamo Kiev)
1987	Ruud Gullit (AC Milan)
1988	Marco Van Basten (AC Milan)

Runner-up

1956	Alfredo di Stefano (Real Madrid)
1957	Billy Wright (Wolverhampton W)
1958	Billy Wright (Wolverhampton W)
1959	Raymond Kopa (Real Madrid)
1960	Ferenc Puskas (Real Madrid)
1961	Luis Suarez (Inter Milan)
1962	Eusebio (Benfica)
1963	Gianni Rivera (AC Milan)
1964	Luis Suarez (Inter Milan)

Ruud Gullit, who helped the Netherlands to win the 1988 European Championship

1965	Giacinto Facchetti (Inter Milan)
1966	Eusebio (Benfica)
1967	Bobby Charlton (Manchester U)
1968	Bobby Charlton (Manchester U)
1969	Gigi Riva (Cagliari)
1970	Bobby Moore (West Ham U)
1971	Sandro Mazzola (Inter Milan)
1972	Gerd Muller (Bayern Munich)
1973	Dino Zoff (Juventus)
1974	Franz Beckenbauer (Bayern Munich)
1975	Franz Beckenbauer (Bayern Munich)
1976	Rob Rensenbrink (Anderlecht)
1977	Kevin Keegan (Liverpool)
1978	Hans Krankl (Rapid Vienna)
1979	Karl-Heinz Rumminegge (Bayern Munich)
1980	Bernd Schuster (Barcelona)
1981	Paul Breitner (Bayern Munich)
1982	Alain Giresse (Bordeaux)
1983	Kenny Dalglish (Liverpool)
1984	Jean Tigana (Bordeaux)
1985	Preben Elkjaer (Verona)
1986	Gary Lineker (Barcelona)
1987	Paulo Futre (Atletico Madrid)
1988	Ruud Gullit (AC Milan)

Most wins

individuals

3 — Johan Cruyff, Michel Platini
2 — Alfredo di Stefano, Franz Beckenbauer, Kevin Keegan, Karl-Heinz Rummenigge

clubs

5 — Bayern Munich
4 — Juventus
3 — Real Madrid, Barcelona, Manchester United, AC Milan

● A dedicated fighter against apartheid, 1987 winner Gullit presented his trophy to the jailed black African leader Nelson Mandela.

European Super Cup

Following Ajax's second European Cup triumph in 1972, the Dutch newspaper *De Telegraaf* suggested a match between them and the winners of the Cup-winner's Cup, Glasgow Rangers, for a Super Cup.

The competition has had a chequered career since then. It was not officially recognised by UEFA until 1974, and there was no match in 1981 and 1985.

Normally played over two legs, the 1984 and 1986 matches were over a single game.

Results (aggregate scores)

1973	Ajax 6	Rangers 3
1974	Ajax 6	AC Milan 1
1975	Dynamo Kiev 3	Bayern Munich 0
1976	Anderlecht 5	Bayern Munich 3
1977	Liverpool 7	SV Hamburg 1
1978	Anderlecht 4	Liverpool 3
1979	Nottingham F 2	Barcelona 1
1980	Valencia 2	Nottingham F 2
	(Valencia won on away goals)	
1982	Aston Villa 3	Barcelona 1
1983	Aberdeen 2	SV Hamburg 0
1984	Juventus 2	Liverpool 0
	(one game; played in Turin)	
1986	Steaua Bucharest 1	Dynamo Kiev 0
	(one game; played in Monaco)	
1987	FC Porto 2	Ajax 0
1988	Mechelen 3	PSV Eindhoven 1

Eusebio, Ferreira da Silva (1942-)

The finest footballer ever produced by Africa, Eusebio started his career as a 15-year-old with local team Sporting Club of Lourenço Marques in Mozambique. In the summer of 1961 £7,500 was enough to take Eusebio to Benfica, who were then managed by the crack Hungarian trainer Bela Guttman. He impressed with a hat-trick on his debut and 25 games later was selected for the Portuguese national team: Mozambique never bothered to cap him!

Benfica retained the European Cup they had won in 1961 and their inspiration was new signing Eusebio. He helped Benfica to the final again in 1963 but AC Milan beat them 2-1 at

Terry McDermott scores Liverpool's opening goal in their first European Cup success in 1977

'The Black Pearl',
Eusebio

Right: Brothers Len
(top left) and Ivor
Allchurch (right) and
Mel (bottom left) and
John Charles
appeared together in
four internationals for
Wales in the mid-1950s

Wembley. He appeared in two more finals for his team but was on the losing side each time, including the 1968 defeat by Manchester United.

Eusebio will be remembered for his four magnificent goals for Portugal against the plucky North Koreans in the 1966 World Cup at Goodison Park when he hauled his team back from 3-0 down to win 5-3.

After winning ten Portuguese championships at Benfica he went across the Atlantic and won an NASL title with Toronto Metros. He returned to Portugal and played with the little known 1st division side Biera-Mar, but was forced to retire in 1977-78 with knee trouble. He had a spell training Biera-Mar before taking up a similar position with Benfica.

Born: 25 January 1942, Lourenço Marques, Mozambique
International caps: 77
Honours
European Cup 1962
Portuguese League 1963, 1964, 1965, 1967, 1968, 1969, 1971, 1972, 1973, 1975
Portuguese Cup 1962, 1964, 1969, 1970, 1972
NASL Championship 1976
Awards
European Footballer of the Year 1965
Adidas Golden Boot winner 1968, 1973

Everton

Founded in 1878 as a Sunday School team at St Domingo Church, their first grounds were at Stanley Road and Priory Road before they moved to Anfield Road, now Liverpool's home.

Founder members of the Football League in 1888, they moved to their present home four years later. Since joining the League Everton have spent a record number of 86 seasons in the 1st division, and have regularly been championship contenders, winning the title nine times, a figure bettered only by neighbours Liverpool, who for so long lived in the shadow of the Goodison Park club.

Everton has spent only four seasons out of the 1st division. In the 1927-28 season their centre-forward William Ralph 'Dixie' Dean scored 60 League goals, a record which still stands. Between 1931-33 Everton created a record by winning the 2nd division, 1st division and FA Cup in successive years.

Since 1945 Everton have twice won the FA Cup, in 1966 and 1984, and in 1984-85 emerged as Merseyside's leading club once more when they won the League title and beat Rapid Vienna to win the European Cup-winners' Cup. Two years later they regained the League title after letting it temporarily return to Anfield.

Ground: Goodison Park
Nickname: Toffees
Record attendance: 78,299 — v Liverpool (Division 1), 18 Sept 1948
First Football League season: 1888-89 Football League (8th)
Seasons in Football League: 90 (86 Division 1, 4 Division 2)

Honours
Division 1 champions 1890-91, 1914-15, 1927-28, 1931-32, 1938-39, 1962-63, 1969-70, 1984-85, 1986-87
Division 2 champions 1930-31
FA Cup winners 1906 1933, 1966, 1984
European Cup-Winners' Cup winners 1985
European Team of the Year 1985
Footballers of the Year
Neville Southall (FWA) 1985
Peter Reid (PFA) 1985
Gary Lineker (FWA/PFA) 1986

Fairs Cup

See *UEFA Cup*

Families

Many sons have followed their fathers and played for the same team but there has been

Marco van Basten (with the ball) was the 1988 European Footballer of the Year, and an inspiration behind the Netherlands' European Championship success

only one instance of a father and son playing in the same Football League team together. It happened on 5 May 1951 when Alec Herd and his son David both played for Stockport County in the 3rd division (north) game against Hartlepool United.

Many brothers have played together in the same side but the most playing together in one match is three. However, the Notts County side that played Nottingham Forest in the 1st round of the FA Cup on 16 November 1878 contained two sets of three brothers, the Curshams and

the Greenhalghs.

On 22 October 1988 against Sheffield Wednesday the three Wallace brothers, Danny, Ray and Rodney, all played for Southampton in a 1st division game. It was the first time since 1919-20 that three brothers had played together in the same 1st division side. On that occasion it was George, John and William Carr who played for Middlesbrough.

In 1925-26 Joseph, Thomas and Harold Keetley appeared in the same Doncaster Rovers side in the 3rd division (north). At the end of the season Joseph left the club but was replaced by another brother, Frank, who teamed up with Tom and Harold several times during the 1926-27 season.

The three Bambridge brothers, Arthur, Ernest and Edward, all played for England between 1876-87 but never more than two at any one time. In those days at the end of the last century, brothers playing in the same international team was not uncommon but when Jack and Bobby Charlton played together in the England team on 10 April 1965 against Scotland they were the first to represent their country in the same match since Frank and Fred Forman in 1899.

The Formans are unique as being the only brothers to play together in the same Football League team and the same England team. They both played for Nottingham Forest.

Former Chelsea wing-half John Hollins won one England cap in 1967 and his brother Dave was capped by Wales 11 times between 1962-66 as a goalkeeper. Dave was born in Bangor, John in Guildford, Surrey.

The Goodall brothers also played for different nations. John Goodall of Preston and Derby played for England 14 times between 1888-98, while his brother Archie (Derby and Glossop) played for Ireland 10 times 1899-1904.

On 20 April 1955 Wales played Northern Ireland at Belfast. Included in the Welsh team were two sets of brothers: John and Mel Charles and Ivor and Len Allchurch. The four men appeared together in three more internationals.

Fast scoring

Individual players

Fastest goals from kick-off
Football League
6 secs — Albert Mundy, Aldershot v Harlepools U, 25 Oct 1958, Division 4
6 secs — Barrie Jones, Notts C v Torquay U, 31 March 1962, Division 3
6 secs — Keith Smith, Crystal Palace v Derby C, 12 Dec 1964, Division 2
6 secs — Tommy Langley, Queen's Park R v Bolton W, 11 Oct 1980, Division 2

● Jim Fryatt of Bradford PA is often credited with having scored in 4 secs against Tranmere R on 25 April 1964, but as the ball was passed among three players before the goal was scored the claim must be disputed.

FA Cup
8 secs — Vic Lambden of Bristol R v Aldershot, 3rd round, 6 Jan 1951
FA Cup final
30 secs — Jack Devey, (own goal) West Brom v Aston Villa, 1985. (The goal is sometimes credited to Villa's Bob Chatt.)

Trevor Steven scores in the European Cup-Winners' Cup in May 1985. Everton beat Rapid Vienna 3–1

England international
27 secs-Bryan Robson v France, 16 June 1982, World Cup finals. It is also the fastest ever World Cup goal.

Fastest hat-trick
Football League
2½ mins — Ephraim 'Jock' Dodds, Blackpool v Tranmere R, 28 Feb 1942, War-time League
Jimmy Scarth, Gillingham v Leyton 0, 1 Nov 1952, Division 3 (S)

Since 1945
3 mins — Graham Leggat, Fulham v Ipswich T, 26 Dec 1963, Division 1
4 mins — Nigel Clough, Nottingham F v Queen's Park R, 13 Dec 1987, Division 1. *It is the fastest hat trick scored on a Sunday.*
Internationals
3½ mins — Willie Hall (Tottenham H) for England v Ireland, 16 Nov 1938

Other fast scoring
4 goals in 5 minutes
John McIntyre, Blackburn R v Everton, 16 Sept 1922, Division 1
4 goals in 5 minutes
William Richardson, West Bromwich A v West Ham U, (from kick-off) 7 Nov 1931, Division 1
8 goals in 21 minutes
Frank Keetley, Lincoln C v Halifax T, 16 Jan 1932, Division 3 (N)

Fastest own goal
8 secs-Pat Kruse, Torquay U v Cambridge U, 3 Jan 1977, Division 4

Teams
8 goals in 28 minutes
Sunderland v Newcastle U, 5 Dec 1908, Division 1 (Sunderland won 9-1. The spell as above came in the last 28 minutes of the game and their last five goals came in the 8 minute spell).
6 goals in 7 minutes
Preston NE v Hyde U, 15 Oct 1887, FA Cup 1st round (Preston won 26-0)
6 goals in 12 minutes
Notts C v Exeter C, 16 Oct 1948, Division 3 (S) (County won 9-0)
4 goals in 4 minutes
Halifax Town v Doncaster R, 21 Oct 1988, Division 4 (Halifax won 4-1)

Federation Internationale de Football Association (FIFA)

The controlling body of world soccer, FIFA has its headquarters in Zurich, Switzerland. Membership of FIFA is restricted to national associations and in 1988 there were 150 member countries.

Following the revival of the Olympic movement in 1896 officials from the French and Belgian football authorities pressed for an international soccer governing body and on 21 May 1904, following a meeting in Paris, FIFA was formed with seven founder members: France, Belgium, Netherlands, Denmark, Sweden, Switzerland and Spain.

England joined in 1906 and the other three British associations in 1910. However, all three resigned in 1920 because of the continued membership of Germany. They returned in 1924 before resigning once more four years later. It was not until 1954 that all four British associations were back in FIFA.

FIFA is responsible for organising the World Cup every four years and the current trophy is called the FIFA Trophy.

Presidents

1904-06	Robert Guerin (France)
1906-18	Daniel Burley Woodfall (England)
1921-54	Jules Rimet (France)
1954-55	Rodolphe Seeldrayers (Belgium)
1955-61	Arthur Drewry (England)
1961-74	Sir Stanley Rous (England)
1974-	Joao Havelange (Brazil)

Fines

The Football League and Football Association have fined clubs over the years for a variety of reasons. Fielding a weakened side before an important FA Cup tie has been one of the most common reasons and before the 1906 final both Everton and Newcastle United were fined £50 for fielding weakened sides in League games.

Leeds were fined £5,000 for fielding a weakened side towards the end of the 1969-70 season as the club challenged for the treble of League, FA Cup and European honours. In the end they won nothing.

Liverpool were fined £7,000 for fielding a team made up mostly of reserves in a League game with Manchester City on 26 April 1971. Twelve days later they played Arsenal in the FA Cup final with a full strength team and lost 2-1.

Tottenham Hotspur were fined £7,500 in 1984 for fielding eight reserves in a League game shortly before their UEFA Cup final with Anderlecht. Unlike Leeds and Liverpool, Spurs went on to win their final. Spurs were fined again in 1987 for fielding ten reserves before the FA Cup final against Coventry. They were initially fined a record £10,000, but this was reduced to £5,000 on appeal.

More recently, crowd behaviour has resulted in clubs being punished for the actions of some of their 'fans': Chelsea were fined a record £75,000 for failing to prevent crowd trouble at the play-off match against Middlesbrough on 28 May 1988.

Irregularities in clubs' books have led to some hefty fines over the years. In 1967 Peterborough United were fined £500 and had 19 points deducted from their total which assured them of relegation from the 3rd to the 4th division. The heaviest fine on a League club for financial irregularities was £15,000 on Fulham in 1978. Derby County were fined £10,000 in 1970 following irregularities in their books.

Derby County were also fined £10,000 in 1983 for illegally poaching Bradford City's manager Ray McFarland.

Sunderland were also fined the then large

amount of £5,000 in 1957 for making illegal payments to their players.

In 1974 Exeter City were fined £5,000 by the Football League for failing to fulfil a fixture against Scunthorpe United because nine of their players had flu.

Celtic were fined £17,000 in 1985 following crowd trouble at their European Cup-winners' Cup tie against Rapid Vienna on 7 November 1984.

Indiscipline among players has cost clubs dearly in recent seasons. In 1986-87 Wimbledon were fined £3,500 because of their poor disciplinary record and in Scotland Celtic and Rangers were each fined £5,000 by the Scottish FA following incidents in two separate matches. Rangers were also fined more than £5,000 by UEFA following an incident on the field during the UEFA Cup match with Borussia Moenchengladbach.

Wimbledon were fined for the second consecutive season in 1987-88 by the FA following their poor disciplinary record. This time the fine was £4,500 with another £5,000 suspended.

Finney, Tom (1922-)

Tom Finney spent his entire League career with his home-town club, Preston North End, resisting all temptations to move to more fashionable clubs both in Britain and Europe. Because of this loyalty he failed to win any major domestic honours.

He joined Preston just before the Second World War and won war-time honours in the shape of a cup winners' medal and 2nd division championship medal. He made his international debut in England's first post-war international against Northern Ireland. In 76 internationals, in which he played in four forward positions, he scored 30 goals, which was a record for a while.

In 1954 Finney appeared in the FA Cup final at Wembley but West Bromwich Albion won 3-2, depriving Finney of a chance of a major honour. However, he was Footballer of the Year that year and in 1957, the first man to win it twice. He retired in 1960 after more than 550 senior games, and was awarded the OBE for his services to the game. He was known as the 'Preston Plumber' because he continued running his plumbing business during his playing days.

In 1963 he came out of retirement to guest for Irish club Distillery in their European Cup tie against Benfica. It was Finney's only game in Europe at club level.

Born: 5 April 1922, Preston, Lancashire
Football League debut: 31 Aug 1946 v Leeds United
Football League appearances: 433 (all Preston NE)
Football League goals: 187
International caps: 76
Awards
Footballer of the Year (FWA) 1954, 1957

Floodlighting

On 14 October 1878 two representative Sheffield teams played each other under floodlights at Bramhall Lane. Two portable generators provided power for the four lights at each corner of the ground. The demonstration match drew a crowd of 20,000. Such was the interest that Birmingham staged a floodlit game a couple of weeks later and the following month London followed suit by staging a match at the Oval between the Wanderers and Clapham Rovers.

Floodlit football became popular in the 1920s but in 1930 the Football Association banned the use of lights for games that fell under their jurisdiction. This ban was lifted in December 1950.

Tom Finney of Preston, one of England's finest forwards

Wolves played several friendlies under floodlights in the 1950s. They are seen lining up before their game with Spartak Moscow at Molineux in 1954

The first competitive match under floodlights was at the Dell on 1 October 1951 when Southampton reserves played Tottenham Hotspur reserves in the Football Combination. That same month Arsenal played their annual challenge match against Glasgow Rangers under the Highbury lights, watched by a crowd of 62,000.

The first FA Cup tie to be played under floodlights was on 14 September 1955 when Kidderminster Harriers and Brierly Hill Alliance got their names into the record books.

The first floodlit game involving two Football League clubs was on 28 November 1955 when Carlisle United and Darlington met in an FA Cup first-round second replay at Newcastle's St James's Park.

The first Football League game to be played under lights was at Fratton Park on 22 February 1956

when Portsmouth played Newcastle United in a 1st division game which attracted a 30,000 crowd.

The first floodlit games in Scotland involving two senior clubs were the Scottish cup ties between Hibernian and Raith Rovers, and East Fife and Stenhousemuir, both played on 8 February 1956.

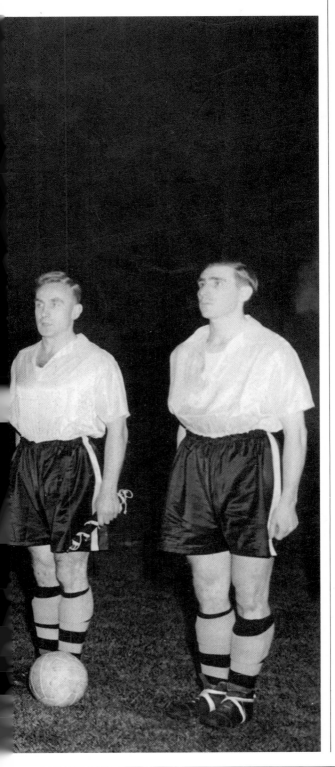

The first international in Britain to be played under lights was between England and Spain at Wembley on 30 November 1955 when the newly installed £22,000 lights were switched on for the last 15 minutes. The first international to be played entirely under floodlights was between England and Northern Ireland, also at Wembley, on 20 November 1983. Obviously the lights did not suit the Irish . . . England won 8-3.

● In 1932 a London XI of players from Spurs, Arsenal, Chelsea and West Ham defeated a Rest XI 3-0 under the White City floodlights. A white ball was used as an experiment . . . every time it went out of play it was washed and returned!

● Stranraer was the last British League club to install floodlighting.

Football Association

The ruling body of the game in England, the Football Association is the oldest such association in the world.

It was formed following a meeting at the Freemason's Tavern in Great Queen Street, London on 26 October 1863 with the prime function of unifying the various and conflicting rules of the game that existed.

The first headquarters of the Association were at Holborn Viaduct, London, and it has never left the capital. In 1972 it moved to its sixth and current address, 16 Lancaster Gate.

In February 1989 Graham Kelly, the former secretary of the Football League, succeeded Ted Croker as FA secretary.

FA Amateur Cup

Inaugurated in 1893, this was the most prestigious amateur competition until it was discontinued in 1974 after the Football Association no longer distinguished between professionals and amateurs.

The first final between Old Carthusians and Casuals was played at Richmond. From 1949, when Bromley beat Romford 1-0, all finals to 1974 were played at Wembley Stadium; replays in that period, however, were played on neutral Football League grounds.

Middlesbrough and Wimbledon are the only current Football League clubs to have won the Amateur Cup, and Wimbledon, Old Carthusians and Royal Engineers are the only dual FA Cup/Amateur Cup winners.

Most wins
10 — Bishop Auckland
5 — Clapton, Crook Town
4 — Dulwich Hamlet
3 — Bromley, Hendon, Leytonstone, Stockton
Biggest win (final)
Northern Nomads 7 Stockton 1 (1926)
Dulwich Hamlet 7 Marine (Liverpool) 1 (1932)

FA Challenge Cup

The oldest and most prestigious Cup competition in the world, the FA Cup was born following a meeting at the offices of *The Sportsman*, a London newspaper, in July 1871. Among the seven men present was Charles Alcock, the man whose brainchild the Cup had been in the first place.

At a subsequent meeting on 16 October that year the original proposal to run a cup competition was accepted and clubs taking part were invited to make a contribution towards the purchase of the original trophy, at a cost of £20.

Fifteen teams entered the first competition but only two were from north of Watford: Queen's Park, Glasgow, and Donington School in Derbyshire. Today more than 600 take part each year.

The Wanderers won the first trophy in front of a modest two thousand crowd at Kennington Oval.

The first trophy was stolen in 1895 after Aston Villa had won it. It was never recovered and Villa were fined £25 by the FA. It was not until 1958 that a man admitted to stealing the cup which he melted down to make counterfeit coins.

The FA acquired an exact replica as its replacement. The second trophy was withdrawn in 1910 when it was discovered a similarly designed trophy had been made for another competition, and as no copyright existed, the FA couldn't take any action. They took the step of presenting the trophy to Lord Kinnaird to mark his 21 years service as FA President.

The third, and current trophy was made by Messrs Fattorini & Sons of Bradford and the first winners in 1911 were . . . Bradford City.

Finals

Year			Venue	Attendance
1872	Wanderers 1	Royal Engineers 0	Kennington Oval	2,000
1873	Wanderers 2	Oxford University 0	Lillie Bridge	3,000
1874	Oxford University 2	Royal Engineers 0	Kennington Oval	2,000
1875	Royal Engineers 1	Old Etonians 1 aet	Kennington Oval	3,000
	Royal Engineers 2	Old Etonians 1	Kennington Oval	3,000
1876	Wanderers 1	Old Etonians 1	Kennington Oval	3,000
	Wanderers 3	Old Etonians 0	Kennington Oval	3,500
1877	Wanderers 2	Oxford University 0 aet	Kennington Oval	3,000
1878	Wanderers 3	Royal Engineers 1	Kennington Oval	4,500
1879	Old Etonians 1	Clapham R 0	Kennington Oval	5,000
1880	Clapham Rovers 1	Oxford University 0	Kennington Oval	6,000
1881	Old Carthusians 3	Old Etonians 0	Kennington Oval	4,500
1882	Old Etonians 1	Blackburn R 0	Kennington Oval	6,500
1883	Blackburn R 2	Old Etonians 1 aet	Kennington Oval	8,000
1884	Blackburn R 2	Queen's Park 1	Kennington Oval	4,000
1885	Blackburn R 2	Queen's Park 0	Kennington Oval	12,500
1886	Blackburn R 0	West Bromwich A 0	Kennington Oval	15,000
	Blackburn R 2	West Bromwich A 0	Baseball Ground Derby	12,000
1887	Aston V 2	West Bromwich A 0	Kennington Oval	15,500
1888	West Bromwich A 2	Preston NE 1	Kennington Oval	19,000
1889	Preston NE 3	Wolverhampton W 0	Kennington Oval	22,000
1890	Blackburn R 6	Sheffield W 1	Kennington Oval	20,000
1891	Blackburn R 3	Notts C 1	Kennington Oval	23,000
1892	West Bromwich A 3	Aston V 0	Kennington Oval	32,810
1893	Wolverhampton W 1	Everton 0	Fallowfield	45,000
1894	Notts C 4	Bolton W 1	Goodison Park	37,000
1895	Aston V 1	West Bromwich A 0	Crystal Palace	42,560
1896	Sheffield W 2	Wolverhampton W 1	Crystal Palace	48,836
1897	Aston V 3	Everton 2	Crystal Palace	65,891
1898	Nottingham F 3	Derby C 1	Crystal Palace	62,017
1899	Sheffield U 4	Derby C 1	Crystal Palace	73,833
1900	Bury 4	Southampton 0	Crystal Palace	68,945
1901	Tottenham H 2	Sheffield U 2	Crystal Palace	110,820
	Tottenham H 3	Sheffield U 1	Burnden Park	20,470
1902	Sheffield U 1	Southampton 1	Crystal Palace	76,914
	Sheffield U 2	Southampton 1	Crystal Palace	33,068
1903	Bury 6	Derby C 0	Crystal Palace	63,102
1904	Manchester C 1	Bolton W 0	Crystal Palace	61,374
1905	Aston V 2	Newcastle U 0	Crystal Palace	101,117
1906	Everton 1	Newcastle U 0	Crystal Palace	75,609
1907	Sheffield W 2	Everton 1	Crystal Palace	84,584
1908	Wolverhampton W 3	Newcastle U 1	Crystal Palace	74,967
1909	Manchester U 1	Bristol C 0	Crystal Palace	71,401
1910	Newcastle U 1	Barnsley 1	Crystal Palace	77,747
	Newcastle U 2	Barnsley 0	Goodison Park	69,000
1911	Bradford C 0	Newcastle U 0	Crystal Palace	69,098
	Bradford C 1	Newcastle U 0	Old Trafford	58,000

Year			Venue	Attendance
1912	Barnsley 0	West Bromwich A 0	Crystal Palace	54,556
	Barnsley 1	West Bromwich A 0 aet	Bramall Lane	38,555
1913	Aston V 1	Sunderland 0	Crystal Palace	120,081
1914	Burnley 1	Liverpool 0	Crystal Palace	72,778
1915	Sheffield U 3	Chelsea 0	Old Trafford	49,557
1920	Aston V 1	Huddersfield T 0 aet	Stamford Bridge	50,018
1921	Tottenham H 1	Wolverhampton W 0	Stamford Bridge	72,805
1922	Huddersfield T 1	Preston NE 0	Stamford Bridge	53,000
1923	Bolton W 2	West Ham U 0	Wembley	126,047
1924	Newcastle U 2	Aston V 0	Wembley	91,695
1925	Sheffield U 1	Cardiff C 0	Wembley	91,763
1926	Bolton W 1	Manchester C 0	Wembley	91,447
1927	Cardiff C 1	Arsenal 0	Wembley	91,206
1928	Blackburn R 3	Huddersfield T 1	Wembley	92,041
1929	Bolton W 2	Portsmouth 0	Wembley	92,576
1930	Arsenal 2	Huddersfield T 0	Wembley	92,488
1931	West Bromwich A 2	Birmingham C 1	Wembley	92,406
1932	Newcastle U 2	Arsenal 1	Wembley	92,298
1933	Everton 3	Manchester C 0	Wembley	92,950
1934	Manchester C 2	Portsmouth 1	Wembley	93,258
1935	Sheffield W 4	West Bromwich A 2	Wembley	93,204
1936	Arsenal 1	Sheffield U 0	Wembley	93,384
1937	Sunderland 3	Preston NE 1	Wembley	93,495
1938	Preston NE 1	Huddersfield T 0 aet	Wembley	93,479
1939	Portsmouth 4	Wolverhampton W 1	Wembley	99,370
1946	Derby C 4	Charlton A 1 aet	Wembley	98,215
1947	Charlton A 1	Burnley 0 aet	Wembley	99,000
1948	Manchester U 4	Blackpool 2	Wembley	99,000
1949	Wolverhampton W 3	Leicester C 1	Wembley	99,500
1950	Arsenal 2	Liverpool 0	Wembley	100,000
1951	Newcastle U 2	Blackpool 0	Wembley	100,000
1952	Newcastle U 1	Arsenal 0	Wembley	100,000
1953	Blackpool 4	Bolton W 3	Wembley	100,000
1954	West Bromwich A 3	Preston NE 2	Wembley	100,000
1955	Newcastle U 3	Manchester C 1	Wembley	100,000
1956	Manchester C 3	Birmingham C 1	Wembley	100,000
1957	Aston V 2	Manchester U 1	Wembley	100,000
1958	Bolton W 2	Manchester U 0	Wembley	100,000
1959	Nottingham F 2	Luton T 1	Wembley	100,000
1960	Wolverhampton W 3	Blackburn R 0	Wembley	100,000
1961	Tottenham H 2	Leicester C 0	Wembley	100,000
1962	Tottenham H 3	Burnley 1	Wembley	100,000
1963	Manchester U 3	Leicester C 1	Wembley	100,000
1964	West Ham U 3	Preston NE 2	Wembley	100,000
1965	Liverpool 2	Leeds U 1 aet	Wembley	100,000
1966	Everton 3	Sheffield W 2	Wembley	100,000
1967	Tottenham H 2	Chelsea 1	Wembley	100,000
1968	West Bromwich A 1	Everton 0 aet	Wembley	100,000
1969	Manchester C 1	Leicester C 0	Wembley	100,000
1970	Chelsea 2	Leeds U 2 aet	Wembley	100,000
	Chelsea 2	Leeds U 1 aet	Old Trafford	62,078
1971	Arsenal 2	Liverpool 1 aet	Wembley	100,000
1972	Leeds U 1	Arsenal 0	Wembley	100,000
1973	Sunderland 1	Leeds U 0	Wembley	100,000
1974	Liverpool 3	Newcastle U 0	Wembley	100,000
1975	West Ham U 2	Fulham 0	Wembley	100,000
1976	Southampton 1	Manchester U 0	Wembley	100,000
1977	Manchester U 2	Liverpool 1	Wembley	100,000
1978	Ipswich T 1	Arsenal 0	Wembley	100,000
1979	Arsenal 3	Manchester U 2	Wembley	100,000
1980	West Ham U 1	Arsenal 0	Wembley	100,000
1981	Tottenham H 1	Manchester C 1 aet	Wembley	100,000
	Tottenham H 3	Manchester C 2	Wembley	92,000
1982	Tottenham H 1	Queen's Park R 1 aet	Wembley	100,000
	Tottenham H 1	Queen's Park R 0	Wembley	90,000
1983	Manchester U 2	Brighton & HA 2	Wembley	100,000
	Manchester U 4	Brighton & HA 0 aet	Wembley	92,000
1984	Everton 2	Watford 0	Wembley	100,000
1985	Manchester U 1	Everton 0 aet	Wembley	100,000
1986	Liverpool 3	Everton 1	Wembley	98,000
1987	Coventry C 3	Tottenham H 2 aet	Wembley	98,000
1988	Wimbledon 1	Liverpool 0	Wembley	98,203
1989	Liverpool 3	Everton 2 aet	Wembley	82,800

Most wins
7 — Aston V, Tottenham H
6 — Blackburn R, Manchester U, Newcastle U
5 — Arsenal, Wanderers*, West Bromwich A
*unbeaten

Most finals appearances
11 — Arsenal, Newcastle U, Everton
10 — Manchester U, West Bromwich A
9 — Aston Villa

Most wins at Wembley
5 — Arsenal, Newcastle U, Tottenham H
4 — Bolton W, Liverpool
3 — Everton, Manchester C, Manchester U, West Bromwich A, West Ham U

Most appearances at Wembley
11 — Arsenal
9 — Manchester U
8 — Liverpool

Non-1st Division winners
1894 Notts C (2nd division)
1901 Tottenham H (Southern League)
1908 Wolverhampton W (2nd division)
1912 Barnsley (2nd division)
1931 West Bromwich A (2nd division)
1973 Sunderland (2nd division)
1976 Southampton (2nd division)
1980 West Ham U (2nd division)

3rd division sides to reach semi-final
1937 Millwall (lost 2-1 to Sunderland)

Dave Beasant of Wimbledon made history in 1988 as the first 'keeper to skipper a Wembley FA Cup winning team. He was also the first to save a penalty in the Wembley final

Left: Graeme Sharp scores Everton's first goal against Watford in 1984

Above: Andy Gray raises his arm in salute after scoring the second

1954 Port Vale (lost 2-1 to West Bromwich A)
1955 York C (lost 2-0 to Newcastle U after 0-0 draw)
1959 Norwich C (lost 1-0 to Luton T after 0-0 draw)
1976 Crystal P (lost 2-0 to Southampton)
1984 Plymouth A (lost 1-0 to Watford)

Penalty misses
Charlie Wallace, Aston Villa v Sunderland 1913 ('keeper Butler)
John Aldridge, Liverpool v Wimbledon 1988 ('keeper Dave Beasant)

Nottingham Forest hold the unique distinction of being drawn against clubs from England, Ireland, Scotland and Wales in the FA Cup.

Biggest Cup tie wins
26-0 — Preston North End v Hyde United, 15 Oct 1887
18-0 — Preston NE v Reading 1st round 1893-94
16-0 — Wanderers v Farningham 1st round 1874-75
15-0 — Royal Engineers v High Wycombe 1st round 1875-76
15-0 — Darwen v Romford 5th round 1880-81
15-0 — Notts C v Rotherham 1st round 1885-86
This century
Tottenham H 13   Crewe A 2   4th round replay 1959-60
Away win
Clapton 0   Nottingham F 14   1st round 1890-91

Ipswich Town are unique in having played *in every round of the FA Cup* including the rarely played pre-preliminary round. Current HFS Loans League side Southport have played in every round except the semi-final and final.

Most individual winners' medals
5 — James Forrest (Blackburn R 1884-86, 1890-91); Lord Kinnaird (Wanderers 1873, 1877-78; Old Etonians 1879, 1882); Charles Wollaston (Wanderers 1872-73, 1876-78)

Appearances in Wembley finals
5 — Joe Hulme (Arsenal 1927, 1930, 1932, 1936; Huddersfield T 1938), Johnny Giles (Manchester U 1963; Leeds U 1965, 1970, 1972-73), Pat Rice (Arsenal 1971-72, 1978-80), Frank Stapleton (Arsenal 1978-80; Manchester U 1983, 1985)

Left: Newcastle United skipper Joe Harvey with the FA Cup after their 1952 triumph

Right: Manchester United skipper Eddie Colman receives the FA Youth trophy in 1955

When West Brom won the FA Cup in 1888 they were the first club to win the trophy with an all-English XI. In contrast, when Liverpool won in 1986 they didn't have an Englishman in the team. Mark Lawrenson was born in Preston but was an Ireland international.

● In 1946 Charlton reached the Cup final yet lost in a third-round match because all matches before the semi-final were over two legs. Charlton lost their third-round second-leg match at Fulham 2-1, after winning 3-1 at home and qualifying 4-3 on aggregate.

FA Challenge Trophy

Inaugurated in 1970, this is for eligible non-league clubs and is the most prestigious competition for non-league teams. All finals (except replays) have been held at Wembley Stadium.

Scarborough are the only current Football League club to have won the Trophy while the 1973 final was between two current League clubs, Scarborough and Wigan Athletic. Wealdstone, Bishop's Stortford and Enfield have won the FA Challenge Trophy and FA Amateur Cup.

FA Challenge Vase

This competition is open to non-league teams not eligible for the FA Challenge Trophy. It was first held in 1974-75 as a replacement for the Amateur Cup. All finals have been at Wembley.

Winners

1975	Hoddesdon	1983	VS Rugby
1976	Billericay Town	1984	Stansted
1977	Billericay Town	1985	Halesowen Town
1978	Blue Star	1986	Halesowen Town
1979	Billericay Town	1987	St. Helens Town
1980	Stamford	1988	Colne Dynamoes
1981	Whickham	1989	Tamworth
1982	Forest Green Rovers		

FA Charity Shield

See *Charity Shield*

FA County Youth Cup

This competition for youth players eligible to play for county sides affiliated to the Football Association is a knockout competition decided by a single game final (two legs 1945-69). Inaugurated in 1944-45, the first winners were Staffordshire.

Most wins
5 — Liverpool (1949, 1954, 1977, 1978, 1980)
4 — Middlesex (1951, 1956, 1962, 1972)
3 — Durham (1947, 1963, 1975); Lancashire (1961, 1971, 1981); Hertfordshire (1970, 1973, 1979)

FA Challenge Trophy

Finals

			Attendance
1970	Macclesfield Town 2	Telford U 0	28,000
1971	Telford U 3	Hillingdon Borough 2	29,500
1972	Stafford Rangers 3	Barnet 0	24,000
1973	Scarborough 2	Wigan Athletic 1 aet	23,000
1974	Morecambe 2	Dartford 1	19,000
1975	Matlock Town 4	Scarborough 0	21,000
1976	Scarborough 3	Stafford Rangers 2 aet	21,000
1977	Scarborough 2	Dagenham 1	20,500
1978	Altrincham 3	Leatherhead 1	20,000
1979	Stafford Rangers 2	Kettering Town 0	32,000
1980	Dagenham 2	Mossley 1	26,000
1981	Bishop's Stortford 1	Sutton United 0	22,578
1982	Enfield 1	Altrincham 0 aet	20,000
1983	Telford United 2	Northwich Victoria 1	22,001
1984	Northwich Victoria 1	Bangor City 1 aet	14,200
	Northwich Victoria 2	Bangor City 1	5,805*
1985	Wealdstone 2	Boston United 1	20,775
1986	Altrincham 1	Runcorn 0	15,700
1987	Kidderminster Harriers 0	Burton Albion 0 aet	23,617
	Kidderminster Harriers 2	Burton Albion 1	15,500†
1988	Enfield 0	Telford United 0 aet	20,161
	Enfield 3	Telford United 2	6,916†
1989	Telford United 1	Macclesfield 0 aet	18,106

*Replay at Victoria Ground, Stoke City FC
†Replay at the Hawthorns, West Bromwich Albion FC

FA Sunday Cup

For many years the FA refused to recognise Sunday football but in 1964-65 it launched its Sunday Cup. Originally contested by county teams, it has been for club sides since 1966. The first final was a two-legged game, but since then all finals have been over a single game.

Winners

1965	London	1977	Langley Park
1966	Ubique United	1978	Arras
1967	Carlton United	1979	Lobster
1968	Drovers	1980	Twin Foxes
1969	Leigh Park	1981	Fantail
1970	Vention United	1982	Dingle Rail
1971	Beacontree Rovers	1983	Eagle
1972	Newtown Unity	1984	Lee Chapel North
1973	Carlton United	1985	Hobbies
1974	Newtown Unity	1986	Avenue
1975	Fareham Town	1987	Lodge Cottrell
1976	Brandon United	1988	Nextday
		1989	Alma Park

FA Youth Cup

This knockout competition for club sides made up of youth players is open to the youth sides of League and non-league clubs. All competitions have been dominated by Football League clubs to date. All finals with the exception of 1978, have been played over two legs.

Finals (aggregate scores)

Year			
1953	Manchester U 9	Wolverhampton W	3
1954	Manchester U 5	Wolverhampton W	4
1955	Manchester U 7	West Bromwich A	1
1956	Manchester U 4	Chesterfield	3
1957	Manchester U 8	West Ham U	2
1958	Wolverhampton W 7	Chelsea	6
1959	Blackburn R 2	West Ham U	1
1960	Chelsea 5	Preston NE	2
1961	Chelsea 5	Everton	3
1962	Newcastle U 2	Wolverhampton W	1
1963	West Ham U 6	Liverpool	5
1964	Manchester U 5	Swindon T	2
1965	Everton 3	Arsenal	2
1966	Arsenal 5	Sunderland	3
1967	Sunderland 2	Birmingham C	0
1968	Burnley 3	Coventry C	2
1969	Sunderland 6	West Bromwich A	3
1970	Tottenham H 4	Coventry C 3 (after 2 replays)	
1971	Arsenal 2	Cardiff C	0
1972	Aston Villa 5	Liverpool	2
1973	Ipswich T 4	Bristol C	1
1974	Tottenham H 2	Huddersfield T	1
1975	Ipswich T 5	West Ham U	1
1976	West Bromwich A 5	Wolverhampton W	0
1977	Crystal P 1	Everton	0
1978	Crystal P 1	Aston Villa	0
1979	Millwall 2	Manchester C	0
1980	Aston Villa 3	Manchester C	2
1981	West Ham U 2	Tottenham H	1
1982	Watford 7	Manchester U	6
1983	Norwich C 6	Everton 5 (after replay)	
1984	Everton 4	Stoke C	2
1985	Newcastle U 4	Watford	1
1986	Manchester C 3	Manchester U	1
1987	Coventry C 2	Charlton A	1
1988	Arsenal 6	Doncaster R	1
1989	Watford 2	Manchester C	1

Most wins

6 — Manchester U

2 — Arsenal, Aston V, Chelsea, Crystal P, Everton, Ipswich T, Newcastle U, Sunderland, Tottenham H, West Ham U, Watford

Attendance record

28,651 — 2nd leg 1954 final Wolverhampton Wanderers v Manchester United, Molineux.

Biggest win

23-0 — Manchester United v Nantwich 1953

Final

7-1 — Manchester United v Wolverhampton Wanderers, 4 May 1953.

Football Combination

First held in 1916, this competition was continued after the disbandment of First World War London League.

After the war it carried on as a league for the reserve teams of southern-based Football League clubs. All winners since 1920 have been reserve teams.

Recent winners

1980	Tottenham H
1981	Southampton
1982	Queen's Park R
1983	Queen's Park R
1984	Arsenal
1985	Chelsea
1986	West Ham U
1987	Tottenham H
1988	Tottenham H
1989	Tottenham H

Most wins

18 —	Tottenham H
17 —	Arsenal
11 —	Chelsea

Sammy McIlroy of Manchester United equalises in the 88th minute of the 1979 FA Cup final against Arsenal. Alan Sunderland, however, scored the winner for the Gunners.

Above: The 1938 Arsenal championship-winning team.

Right: The Huddersfield Town team which won the title in 1925.

Arsenal and Huddersfield were the first two teams to win a hat-trick of titles. Only Liverpool have since emulated them

Football League

The Football League was the brainchild of a Scotsman, William McGregor of the Aston Villa club, who saw a need for professional clubs to organise themselves into a professionally run League. The first formal meeting of the Football League was held at the Royal Hotel, Manchester, on 17 April 1888.

Twelve clubs formed the original Football League: Accrington, Aston Villa, Blackburn Rovers, Bolton Wanderers, Burnley, Derby County, Everton, Notts County, Preston North End, Stoke City, West Bromwich Albion and Wolverhampton Wanderers. The first fixtures were played on 8 September 1888.

A second division was introduced in 1892-93 with 12 clubs and a third division in 1920-21

with 22. When the League was increased the following season a third division (north) with 20 clubs was added, and the 3rd division became the 3rd division (south). These two divisions, by then with 24 clubs each, were replaced by the existing 3rd and 4th divisions in 1958-59.

Some sources quote the inaugural 3rd division season of 1920-21 as being 3rd division (south). It was not called this until the formation of the northern section the next year.

The total number of clubs in the League has increased from 12 to 92. In the late 1980s there are 20 in Division 1 and 24 each in Divisions 2, 3 and 4.

Champions
1888-89 Preston NE
1889-90 Preston NE
1890-91 Everton
1891-92 Sunderland

	Division 1	Division 2
1892-93	Sunderland	Small Heath
1893-94	Aston V	Liverpool
1894-95	Sunderland	Bury
1895-96	Aston V	Liverpool
1896-97	Aston V	Notts C
1897-98	Sheffield U	Burnley
1898-99	Aston V	Manchester C
1899-1900	Aston V	The Wednesday
1900-01	Liverpool	Grimsby T
1901-02	Sunderland	West Bromwich A
1902-03	The Wednesday	Manchester C
1903-04	The Wednesday	Preston NE
1904-05	Newcastle U	Liverpool
1905-06	Liverpool	Bristol C
1906-07	Newcastle U	Nottingham F
1907-08	Manchester U	Bradford C
1908-09	Newcastle U	Bolton W
1909-10	Aston V	Manchester C
1910-11	Manchester U	West Bromwich A
1911-12	Blackburn R	Derby C
1912-13	Sunderland	Preston NE
1913-14	Blackburn R	Notts C
1914-15	Everton	Derby C
1919-20	West Bromwich A	Tottenham H

	Division 1	Division 2	Division 3
1920-21	Burnley	Birmingham	Crystal P

	Division 1	Division 2	Division 3(S)	Division 3(N)
1921-22	Liverpool	Nottingham F	Southampton	Stockport C
1922-23	Liverpool	Notts C	Bristol C	Nelson
1923-24	Huddersfield T	Leeds U	Portsmouth	Wolverhampton W
1924-25	Huddersfield T	Leicester C	Swansea T	Darlington
1925-26	Huddersfield T	Sheffield W	Reading	Grimsby T
1926-27	Newcastle U	Middlesbrough	Bristol C	Stoke C
1927-28	Everton	Manchester C	Millwall	Bradford PA
1928-29	Sheffield W	Middlesbrough	Charlton A	Bradford C
1929-30	Sheffield W	Blackpool	Plymouth A	Port Vale
1930-31	Arsenal	Everton	Notts C	Chesterfield
1931-32	Everton	Wolverhampton W	Fulham	Lincoln C
1932-33	Arsenal	Stoke C	Brentford	Hull C
1933-34	Arsenal	Grimsby T	Norwich C	Barnsley
1934-35	Arsenal	Brentford	Charlton A	Doncaster R
1935-36	Sunderland	Manchester U	Coventry C	Chesterfield
1936-37	Manchester C	Leicester C	Luton T	Stockport C
1937-38	Arsenal	Aston V	Millwall	Tranmere R
1938-39	Everton	Blackburn R	Newport C	Barnsley

Continued on following page

	Division 1	*Division 2*	*Division 3(S)*	*Division 3(N)*
1946-47	Liverpool	Manchester C	Cardiff C	Doncaster R
1947-48	Arsenal	Birmingham C	Queen's Park R	Lincoln C
1948-49	Portsmouth	Fulham	Swansea T	Hull C
1949-50	Portsmouth	Tottenham H	Notts C	Doncaster R
1950-51	Tottenham H	Preston NE	Nottingham F	Rotherham U
1951-52	Manchester U	Sheffield W	Plymouth A	Lincoln C
1952-53	Arsenal	Sheffield U	Bristol R	Oldham A
1953-54	Wolverhampton W	Leicester C	Ipswich T	Port Vale
1954-55	Chelsea	Birmingham C	Bristol C	Barnsley
1955-56	Manchester U	Sheffield W	Leyton O	Grimsby T
1956-57	Manchester U	Leicester C	Ipswich T	Derby C
1957-58	Wolverhampton W	West Ham U	Brighton & HA	Scunthorpe U
	Division 1	*Division 2*	*Division 3*	*Division 4*
1958-59	Wolverhampton W	Sheffield W	Plymouth A	Port Vale
1959-60	Burnley	Aston V	Southampton	Walsall
1960-61	Tottenham H	Ipswich T	Bury	Peterborough U
1961-62	Ipswich T	Liverpool	Portsmouth	Millwall
1962-63	Everton	Stoke C	Northampton T	Brentford
1963-64	Liverpool	Leeds U	Coventry C	Gillingham
1964-65	Manchester U	Newcastle U	Carlisle U	Brighton & HA
1965-66	Liverpool	Manchester C	Hull C	Doncaster R
1966-67	Manchester U	Coventry C	Queen's Park R	Stockport C
1967-68	Manchester C	Ipswich T	Oxford U	Luton T
1968-69	Leeds U	Derby C	Watford	Doncaster R
1969-70	Everton	Huddersfield T	Orient	Chesterfield
1970-71	Arsenal	Leicester C	Preston NE	Notts C
1971-72	Derby C	Norwich C	Aston V	Grimsby T
1972-73	Liverpool	Burnley	Bolton W	Southport
1973-74	Leeds U	Middlesbrough	Oldham A	Peterborough U
1974-75	Derby C	Manchester U	Blackburn R	Mansfield T
1975-76	Liverpool	Sunderland	Hereford U	Lincoln C
1976-77	Liverpool	Wolverhampton W	Mansfield T	Cambridge U
1977-78	Nottingham F	Bolton W	Wrexham	Watford
1978-79	Liverpool	Crystal P	Shrewsbury T	Reading
1979-80	Liverpool	Leicester C	Grimsby T	Huddersfield T
1980-81	Aston V	West Ham U	Rotherham U	Southend U
1981-82	Liverpool	Luton T	Burnley	Sheffield U
1982-83	Liverpool	Queen's Park R	Portsmouth	Wimbledon
1983-84	Liverpool	Chelsea	Oxford U	York C
1984-85	Everton	Oxford U	Bradford C	Chesterfield
1985-86	Liverpool	Norwich C	Reading	Swindon T
1986-87	Everton	Derby C	Bournemouth	Northampton T
1987-88	Liverpool	Millwall	Sunderland	Wolverhampton W
1988-89	Arsenal	Chelsea	Wolverhampton W	Rotherham U

Most titles

Division 1
17 — Liverpool
9 — Everton, Arsenal
7 — Manchester U, Aston Villa
6 — Sunderland

Division 2
6 — Leicester C, Manchester C
5 — Sheffield W
4 — Derby C, Liverpool, Birmingham C
3 — Notts C, Preston NE, Middlesbrough

Division 3
2 — Portsmouth , Oxford U

Division 4
2-Chesterfield, Doncaster R, Peterborough U

Division 3(S)
3-Bristol C
2-Charlton A, Ipswich T, Millwall, Notts C, Plymouth A, Swansea T

Division 3(N)
3-Barnsley, Doncaster R, Lincoln C
2-Chesterfield, Grimsby T, Hull C, Port Vale, Stockport C

Teams overall
21-Liverpool (17 Div 1, 4 Div 2)
10-Everton (9 Div 1, 1 Div 2); Aston Villa (7 Div 1, 2 Div 2, 1 Div 3)
9-Manchester U (7 Div 1, 2 Div 2); Sheffield W (4 Div 1, 5 Div 2)
9-Arsenal (9 Div 1); Sunderland (6 Div 1, 1 Div 2, 1 Div 3); Manchester C (2 Div 1, 6 Div 2)
8-Wolverhampton W (3 Div 1; 2 Div 2; 1 Div 3; 1 Div 3N; 1 Div 4) Wolverhampton Wanderers is the only club to have won the titles of five different divisions.

Non-title winning teams

The following current League teams have not won a title: Aldershot, Chester, Colchester U, Crewe A, Exeter C, Halifax T, Hartlepool U, Rochdale, Scarborough, Torquay U, Wigan A.

Multiple division teams

Coventry City is the only team to have played in all six different divisions of the Football League.

Grimsby Town have played in all four divisions as well as the 3rd division (north) and the inaugural 3rd division, which was the forerunner of the 3rd division (south).

For details of most points, most wins, goals etc, see appropriate section

Football League Cup

Following a proposal at the Football League's AGM in 1960, it was agreed they would stage their own knockout competition for member clubs. The first matches were played on Monday 26 September 1960: Bristol Rovers beat Fulham 2-1 and West Ham United beat Charlton Athletic 3-1.

Left: A 2–0 win over QPR gave Everton their eighth League title in 1985

Above: Luton Town appeared in the League Cup final in both 1988 and 1989

Tony Book (Manchester City) shared the Footballer of the Year title with Dave Mackay (Derby County) in 1969

First- and second-round matches are played over two legs, as are the semi-final matches. All other matches are played over a single game. The final has been played at Wembley since 1967, before when all finals were over two legs. Since the move to Wembley, the competition has attracted all Football League clubs. Many top clubs shunned the competition in its early days and it was not until 1969-70 that all 92 clubs took part for the first time. Since 1971-72 entry has been compulsory.

With sponsorship from the Milk Marketing Board in 1982 the competition became known as the Milk Cup and in 1986 it became the Littlewoods Cup, sponsored by Littlewoods.

Finals

Year				Attendance
1961	Rotherham U 2	Aston Villa 0		12,226
	Aston Villa 3	Rotherham U 0 aet		31,202
1962	Rochdale 0	Norwich C 3		11,123
	Norwich C 1	Rochdale 0		19,708
1963	Birmingham C 3	Aston Villa 1		31,850
	Aston Villa 0	Birmingham C 0		37,920
1964	Stoke C 1	Leicester C 1		22,309
	Leicester C 3	Stoke C 2		25,372
1965	Chelsea 3	Leicester C 2		20,690
	Leicester C 0	Chelsea 0		26,958
1966	West Ham U 2	West Bromwich A 1		28,341
	West Bromwich A 4	West Ham U 1		31,952
1967	Queen's Park R 3	West Bromwich A 2		97,952
1968	Leeds U 1	Arsenal 0		97,887
1969	Swindon T 3	Arsenal 1		98,189
1970	Manchester C 2	West Bromwich A 1		97,963
1971	Tottenham H 2	Aston V 0		100,000
1972	Stoke C 2	Chelsea 1		100,000
1973	Tottenham H 1	Norwich C 0		100,000
1974	Wolverhampton W 2	Manchester C 1		100,000
1975	Aston V 1	Norwich C 0		100,000
1976	Manchester C 2	Newcastle U 1		100,000
1977	Aston Villa 0	Everton 0		100,000
	Aston Villa 1	Everton 1 aet		55,000
	Aston Villa 3	Everton 2 aet		54,749
1978	Nottingham F 0	Liverpool 0 aet		100,000
	Nottingham F 1	Liverpool 0		54,375
1979	Nottingham F 3	Southampton 2		100,000
1980	Wolverhampton W 1	Nottingham F 0		100,000
1981	Liverpool 1	West Ham U 1 aet		100,000
	Liverpool 2	West Ham U 1		36,693
1982	Liverpool 3	Tottenham H 1 aet		100,000
1983	Liverpool 2	Manchester U 1 aet		100,000
1984	Liverpool 0	Everton 0 aet		100,000
	Liverpool 1	Everton 0		52,089
1985	Norwich C 1	Sunderland 0		100,000
1986	Oxford U 3	Queen's Park R 0		90,396
1987	Arsenal 2	Liverpool 1		96,000
1988	Luton T 3	Arsenal 2		95,732
1989	Nottingham F 3	Luton T 1		76,130

Most wins
4 — Liverpool
3 — Aston Villa, Nottingham F

Most finals appearances
6 — Liverpool
5 — Aston Villa
4 — Norwich C, Arsenal, Nottingham F

Biggest wins
10-0 — West Ham U v Bury (2nd round, 2nd leg) 25 Oct 1983
10-0 — Liverpool v Fulham (2nd round, 1st leg) 23 Sept 1986

Division 2 winners
1962 Norwich City
1975 Aston Villa

Division 3 winners
1967 Queen's Park Rangers
1969 Swindon Town

Division 4 finalists
1962 Rochdale

Footballer of the Year

The British Football Writers' Association (FWA) Footballer of the Year Award was instituted in 1947-48. Soccer writers nominate their Player of the Year and the winner is announced shortly before the FA Cup final.

Since 1974 the Professional Footballers' Association have had their own awards and in addition to the main Player of the Year award, also have a prestigious Young Player of the Year Award, divisional awards, and a Merit Award for service to association football.

Winners
Football Writers' Association (FWA)
Footballer of the Year

1948 Stanley Matthews (Blackpool)
1949 Johnny Carey (Manchester United)
1950 Joe Mercer (Arsenal)
1951 Harry Johnston (Blackpool)
1952 Billy Wright (Wolverhampton W)
1953 Nat Lofthouse (Bolton W)
1954 Tom Finney (Preston NE)
1955 Don Revie (Manchester C)
1956 Bert Trautmann (Manchester C)
1957 Tom Finney (Preston NE)
1958 Danny Blanchflower (Tottenham H)
1959 Syd Owen (Luton T)
1960 Bill Slater (Wolverhampton W)
1961 Danny Blanchflower (Tottenham H)
1962 Jimmy Adamson (Burnley)
1963 Stanley Matthews (Stoke C)
1964 Bobby Moore (West Ham U)
1965 Bobby Collins (Leeds U)
1966 Bobby Charlton (Manchester U)
1967 Jackie Charlton (Leeds U)
1968 George Best (Manchester U)
1969 Tony Book (Manchester C)
     Dave Mackay (Derby C)
1970 Billy Bremner (Leeds U)
1971 Frank McLintock (Arsenal)
1972 Gordon Banks (Stoke C)
1973 Pat Jennings (Tottenham H)
1974 Ian Callaghan (Liverpool)
1975 Alan Mullery (Fulham)
1976 Kevin Keegan (Liverpool)
1977 Emlyn Hughes (Liverpool)
1978 Kenny Burns (Nottingham F)
1979 Kenny Dalglish (Liverpool)
1980 Terry Mc Dermott (Liverpool)

1981 Frans Thijssen (Ipswich T)
1982 Steve Perryman (Tottenham H)
1983 Kenny Dalglish (Liverpool)
1984 Ian Rush (Liverpool)
1985 Neville Southall (Everton)
1986 Gary Lineker (Everton)
1987 Clive Allen (Tottenham H)
1988 John Barnes (Liverpool)
1989 Steve Nicol (Liverpool)

● The 2nd division has provided three winners: Stanley Matthews (Stoke C) 1963; Dave Mackay (Derby C) 1969; Alan Mullery (Fulham) 1975

● Only three winners have not won international caps: Bert Trautmann 1956; Jimmy Adamson 1962; Tony Book 1969

FWA and PFA Player of the Year winners
Pat Jennings, Terry McDermott*, Kevin Keegan, Kenny Dalglish*, Ian Rush*, Gary Lineker*, Clive Allen*, John Barnes*
* in same season

● Ian Rush stands alone as the only man to win both senior awards as well as the PFA Young Player award.

Professional Footballers' Association (PFA) Awards

	Player of the Year	*Young Player of the Year*	*Merit Award*
1974	Norman Hunter (Leeds U)	Kevin Beattie (Ipswich T)	Bobby Charlton/Cliff Lloyd
1975	Colin Todd (Derby C)	Mervyn Day (West Ham U)	Denis Law
1976	Pat Jennings (Tottenham H)	Peter Barnes (Manchester C)	George Eastham
1977	Andy Gray (Aston Villa)	Andy Gray (Aston Villa)	Jack Taylor
1978	Peter Shilton (Nottingham F)	Tony Woodcock (Nottingham F)	Bill Shankly
1979	Liam Brady (Arsenal)	Cyrille Regis (West Bromwich A)	Tom Finney
1980	Terry McDermott (Liverpool)	Glen Hoddle (Tottenham H)	Sir Matt Busby
1981	John Wark (Ipswich T)	Gary Shaw (Aston Villa)	John Trollope
1982	Kevin Keegan (Southampton)	Steve Moran (Southampton)	Joe Mercer
1983	Kenny Dalglish (Liverpool)	Ian Rush (Liverpool)	Bob Paisley
1984	Ian Rush (Liverpool)	Paul Walsh (Luton T)	Bill Nicholson
1985	Peter Reid (Everton)	Mark Hughes (Manchester U)	Ron Greenwood
1986	Gary Lineker (Everton)	Tony Cottee (West Ham U)	England '66 World Cup squad
1987	Clive Allen (Tottenham H)	Tony Adams (Arsenal)	Sir Stanley Matthews
1988	John Barnes (Liverpool)	Paul Gascoigne (Newcastle U)	Billy Bonds
1989	Mark Hughes (Manchester U)	Paul Merson (Arsenal)	Nat Lofthouse

---

Football pools

The first football pools were started in 1922 by former Coldstream Guard John Jervis Bernard from his Birmingham office at 28 Martineau Street. At the first attempt the number of coupons returned was not enough to cover his outlay of postage. However, just as he was about to abandon the scheme the following year, his idea suddenly inexplicably took off and he continued to operate it as Jervis Pools until he sold out to Copes' in 1938.

John Moores founded the famous Littlewoods empire in 1923 and he produced a football coupon which he used to distribute outside Manchester United's Old Trafford ground, despite having his business in Liverpool. Only 35 people tried their luck at the Littlewoods' coupon. The income was £4 7s 6d (£4.38) and prize money paid out was £2 12s (£2.60).

Winnings

Before the Second World War the biggest prize was the £30,780 won by L Levy of London in April 1937.

Since then prize money has soared beyond the £1 million barrier.

First six figure win
£104,990, Mrs Knowlson, Manchester, 7 November 1950
First £500,000 win
£512,683, Cyril Grimes, Liss, Hampshire, 4 March 1972

First £1 million win
Margaret Francis and ten colleagues, Roundway Hospital, Devizes, Wiltshire, 30 April 1986
Biggest payout for a British football pools win
(to mid-1989)
£1,339,358.50p, Jim Anderson, Anderton, Northants, 11 July 1987

Ford Sporting League

Known as the Ford Motor Company Sporting League, this was a competition for the 92 Football League clubs sponsored by the Ford Motor Company. The idea was to promote attacking football, and at the same time cut down on poor discipline on the field. Points were awarded for goals scored, with extra points for scoring away from home. Five points were deducted for every player booked and ten for players sent off.

It only lasted one season, 1970-71, and was won by Oldham Athletic who took the £50,000 first prize which had to be spent on ground facilities. Crewe Alexandra were second, while Bolton Wanderers were in 92nd place with Millwall one place above them.

Freight Rover Trophy

See *Sherpa Van Trophy*

Full Members' Cup

See *Simod Cup*

Germany, West

See *West Germany*

Giant-killing

The FA Cup provides opportunity for little clubs from outside the League to meet auspicious opposition in the greatest cup competition in the world. Occasionally the giants are humbled, and over the years many non-league clubs have claimed the scalp of League opposition. The following non-league clubs stand alone as beating 1st division opposition since the First World War:

1920	Sheffield W 0	Darlington 2 (after 0-0 draw)
1924	Corinthians 1	Blackburn R 0
1948	Colchester U 1	Huddersfield T 0
1949	Yeovil T 2	Sunderland 1
1972	Hereford U 2	Newcastle U 1 (after 2-2 draw)
1975	Burnley 0	Wimbledon 1
1986	Birmingham C 1	Altrincham 2
1989	Sutton U 2	Coventry C 1

The last 2nd division club to lose to non-league opposition was Leicester City who lost 1-0 at Harlow Town in 1980. Leicester went on to win the 2nd division title that season.

There have been five instances of non-league sides beating League opposition by a score of 6-1:

1935	Carlisle U 1	Wigan A 6
1937	Walthamstow A 6	Northampton T 1
1956	Derby C 1	Boston U 6
1958	Hereford U 6	Queen's Park R 1
1971	Barnet 6	Newport C 1

The furthest a non-league team has progressed in the FA Cup is to the fifth round:

1948	Colchester United
1949	Yeovil Town
1978	Blyth Spartans
1985	Telford United

● One of the biggest shocks in the history of the FA Cup was on 14 January 1933 when Arsenal, the greatest team of the day, were humbled by Walsall of the 3rd division (north) by two goals to nil. The equivalent shock in Scotland took place on 26 January 1967 when the mighty Rangers lost 1-0 at Berwick Rangers, a middle-of-the table 2nd division side.

(All the above records are since 1925 when the FA Cup was re-organised, unless otherwise stated)

Glasgow Celtic

The club was founded in 1888 by Irish Roman Catholics in Glasgow's East End to finance soup kitchens for the needy of the area. Within a few years its popularity made it one of the wealthiest clubs in Britain, and with one of the finest stadiums.

Founder members of the Scottish League in 1890, they were runners-up in the Scottish Cup a year earlier at their first attempt. The rivalry with Rangers started almost immediately with the first of many Celtic-Rangers finals played in 1894.

Celtic play in green and white hooped jerseys without numbers on the backs, and have won the Scottish League 35 times and the Cup on 28 occasions. The key to their success over the years has been their managers. Initially there was Willie Maley who spent 50 years with the club from its inception. He was succeeded by Jimmy McStay, and between 1946-65 the man at the helm was Jimmy McGrory, the most prolific goalscorer in Scottish football. When Jock Stein was appointed in 1965 he was only the club's fourth manager. He led them to Celtic's finest hour in 1967 when they became the first British club to win the European Cup.

Ground: Celtic Park
Nickname: Bhoys
Record attendance: 92,000 — v Rangers (Division 1), 1 Jan 1938
First League season: 1890-91 Scottish League (3rd)

Honours
League champions 1st Division 1892-93, 1893-94, 1895-96, 1897-98, 1904-05, 1905-06, 1906-07, 1907-08, 1908-09, 1909-10, 1913-14, 1914-15, 1915-16, 1916-17, 1918-19, 1921-22, 1925-26, 1935-36, 1937-38, 1953-54, 1965-66, 1966-67, 1967-68, 1968-69, 1969-70, 1970-71, 1971-72, 1972-73, 1973-74
Premier Division 1976-77, 1978-79, 1980-81, 1981-82, 1985-86, 1987-88

Scottish FA Cup winners 1892, 1899, 1900, 1904, 1907, 1908, 1911, 1912, 1914, 1923, 1925, 1927, 1931, 1933, 1937, 1951, 1954, 1965, 1967, 1969, 1971, 1972, 1974, 1975, 1977, 1980, 1985, 1988, 1989

Scottish League Cup winners 1956-57, 1957-58, 1965-66, 1966-67, 1967-68, 1968-69, 1969-70, 1974-75, 1982-83

European Cup winners 1967

Scottish Footballers of the Year
Billy McNeill (FWA) 1965, Ronnie Simpson (FWA) 1967, Bobby Murdoch (FWA) 1969, George Connelly (FWA) 1973, Danny McGrain (FWA) 1977, Davie Provan (PFA) 1980, Charlie Nicholas (FWA/PFA) 1983, Brian McClair (FWA/PFA) 1987, Paul McStay (FWA/PFA) 1988

Glasgow Rangers

The fourth oldest club in Scotland, Rangers was founded in 1872 (not 1873 as often recorded) when three youngsters formed a team after watching football on Glasgow Green. One of the

England has always produced top-class goalkeepers and there were few better than Gordon Banks

three youngsters was Moses McNeill whose brothers William, Peter and Harry helped swell the numbers of the first team. Their first match was in May 1872 when they played under the name of Argyle. They changed their name to Rangers after Moses McNeill spotted the name in an English rugby annual.

Since then the club has gone on to become one of the biggest names in Europe. The first great era in Rangers' history followed the appointment of Willie Struth as manager in 1920. Between then and the outbreak of the Second World War Rangers won the Scottish League 14 times and the Cup six times, including four doubles.

In the 1960s Rangers had to live in the shadow of their great rivals Celtic, but in 1972 the 'Gers emulated their fellow Glaswegians by winning in Europe when they beat Moscow Dynamo to win the European Cup-Winners' Cup.

Ground: Ibrox Stadium
Nickname: 'Gers
Record attendance: 118,567 — v Celtic (Division 1), 2 Jan 1939
First League season: 1890-91 Scottish League (jt. 1st)

Honours
League champions 1st Division 1890-91 (shared), 1898-99, 1899-1900, 1900-01, 1901-02, 1910-11, 1911-12, 1912-13, 1917-18, 1919-20, 1920-21, 1922-23, 1923-24, 1924-25, 1926-27, 1927-28, 1928-29, 1929-30, 1930-31, 1932-33, 1933-34, 1934-35, 1936-37, 1938-39, 1946-47, 1948-49, 1949-50, 1952-53, 1955-56, 1956-57, 1958-59, 1960-61, 1962-63, 1963-64, 1974-75
Premier Division 1975-76, 1977-78, 1986-87, 1988-89
Scottish FA Cup winners 1894, 1897, 1898, 1903, 1928, 1930, 1932, 1934, 1935, 1936, 1948, 1949, 1950, 1953, 1960, 1962, 1963, 1964, 1966, 1973, 1976, 1978, 1979, 1981
Scottish League Cup winners 1946-47, 1948-49, 1960-61, 1961-62, 1963-64, 1964-65, 1970-71, 1975-76, 1977-78, 1978-79, 1981-82, 1983-84, 1984-85, 1986-87, 1987-88, 1988-89
European Cup-winners' Cup winners 1972
Scottish Footballers of the Year
John Greig (FWA) 1966, 1976, Dave Smith (FWA) 1972, Sandy Jardine (FWA) 1975, Derek Johnstone (FWA/PFA) 1978

GM Vauxhall Conference

Founded in 1979 by leading Southern League and Northern Premier League clubs, it was initially called the Alliance Premier League, changed its name to the Gola League in 1984-85 and to its present style in 1986-87. Its object was to become a feeder League to the Football League, which it achieved in 1986-87 when champions Scarborough gained automatic entry to the Football league at the expense of the League's 92nd placed club, Lincoln City.

The first Football Alliance dates to 1890 when one was formed by leading northern clubs who could not gain admittance into the Football League.

Champions
1979-80 Altrincham
1980-81 Altrincham
1981-82 Runcorn
1982-83 Enfield
1983-84 Maidstone United
1984-85 Wealdstone
1985-86 Enfield
1986-87 Scarborough
1987-88 Lincoln City
1988-89 Maidstone United

average was the 2nd division in 1895-96 when Liverpool won the title with an average of 3.3125 to Manchester City's 1.6579.

The *closest finish* to a season involving promotion or relegation was in the 2nd division in 1926-27. Portsmouth and Manchester City both finished on 54 points behind champions Middlesbrough. Portsmouth scored 87 goals and conceded 49 for an average of 1.7755, while City's goals for were 108 and 61 against for an average of 1.7705. Portsmouth were promoted by 5/1,000ths of a goal.

The *first club to be relegated on goal average* was Nottingham Forest from the 1st division in 1905-06. Their average of 0,734 was inferior to the 0.789 of Middlesbrough, who retained their 1st division status.

The first division title was decided on goal average four times:

	Winners	for	agst	avge	Runners-up	for	agst	avge
1923-24	Huddersfield T	60	33	1,818	Cardiff C	61	34	1,794
1949-50	Portsmouth	74	38	1,947	Wolverhampton	76	49	1,551
1952-53	Arsenal	97	64	1,516	Preston NE	85	60	1,417
1964-65	Manchester U	89	39	2,282	Leeds U	83	52	1,596

Goal difference

Goal difference superseded goal average in 1976-77 as a means of separating teams level on points in the Football League. Calculated by deducting the number of goals conceded from the goals scored, the system had been used on the continent for many years, and had been the method of deciding teams level in the World Cup. When goal difference is identical the team scoring the most goals is deemed to be the better of the two. If clubs are still level there is a play-off match on a neutral ground.

The only Football League titles to have been decided by goal difference have been:

	Division	Champions	pts	diff	Runner-up	pts	diff
1981-82	3	Burnley	80	+23	Carlisle U	80	+15
1983-84	2	Chelsea	88	+50	Sheffield W	88	+38
1988-89	1	Arsenal	76	+37	Liverpool	76	+37

(Arsenal won title because they scored more goals, 73 to 65)
Had the title been decided on goal average Liverpool would have won.

Goal average

Goal average was first introduced into the Football League in 1895-96 as a means of separating teams level on points. The average was arrived at by dividing the goals scored by the goals conceded. Goal average was replaced by goal difference in 1976-77.

The *first championship to be decided on goal*

The first club to be relegated in the Football League using goal difference was Carlisle United, who went down from the 2nd division in 1976-77. Their difference was -26. The two clubs with them on points were Orient and Cardiff City with differences of -18 and -9 respectively.

Goalkeepers

Goalkeepers were first mentioned in the Sheffield Rules around 1870, but only as the players of the defending side nearest to the goal at any one time. The first mention of a goalkeeper as a player permitted to use his hands was in the FA Rules of 1878.

The *first goalkeeper to captain an FA Cup winning team at Wembley* was Dave Beasant of Wimbledon in 1988.

Only two *goalkeepers have skippered World Cup winning teams* and both were Italian. The first was Giampiero Combi in 1934 and the second Dino Zoff in 1982. Both World Cup final captains were 'keepers in 1934: Italy's opponents Czechoslovakia were skippered by Frantisek Planicka.

The record for *keeping a clean sheet the longest in international football* belongs to Dino Zoff (Italy) who went from September 1972 to June 1974 without conceding a goal. His run of 1,142 minutes was eventually broken on 15 June 1974 when Emanuele Sanon of Haiti scored in the 46th minute of their World Cup match in Munich. The *world record* is 1,221 minutes by Manuel Lopez of Spanish 2nd Division team (Group IV) Cueta. He conceded his first goal of the season on 4 December 1988. The *British record* is held by Chris Woods (Glasgow Rangers) who kept a clean sheet for 1,196 minutes from 26 November 1986 to 31 January 1987. The run was eventually broken by Adrian Sprott's 70th minute goal for Hamilton in their shock 1-0 win over Rangers in the Scottish Cup. The *Football League record* is 1,103 minutes by Steve Death of Reading between 24 March and 18 August 1979. His run was ended in the opening match of the 1979-80 season when his own full-back Stewart Henderson scored a first-half own goal!

Goalkeepers have been known to score goals, but none has had a finer record than Arnold Birch of Chesterfield who scored five in the 3rd division N in 1923-24, all from penalties.

After 21 games of Manchester United's relegation season in 1973-74 goalkeeper Alex Stepney was the club's top scorer in the League after converting two penalties.

In a Scottish 1st division game in 1910 both goalkeepers, Jimmy Brownlie of Third Lanark and Clem Hampton of Motherwell, scored.

For most appearances, League and Internationals, by a goalkeeper see *Appearances*

Goal nets

Introduced by an unknown Birmingham man, they were later patented and manufactured by 32-year-old Liverpool City engineer John Alexander Brodie. They were first used in a major match in January 1891 when the North played the South at Nottingham. The Football League insisted that all clubs should have nets installed during the 1891-92 season and the first FA Cup final to use goal nets was the Aston Villa-West Brom final in 1892. Brodie was also involved with the construction of the first Mersey Tunnel shortly before his death in 1934.

Goalscoring

Individual records – single game

Internationals

World record
10 — Sofus Nielsen, Denmark v France, 1908 Olympics
10 — Gottfried Fuchs, Germany v Russia, 1912 Olympics

Right: In recent years Ian Rush has been one of the most prolific of British goalscorers. Sadly for Juventus he could not maintain his scoring rate in the Italian league

Opposite: Ray Clemence. After a successful career with Liverpool he enjoyed a spell with Tottenham Hotspur

World Cup (final stages)
4 — Leonidas, Brazil v Poland, 5 June 1938
4 — Ernst Willimowski, Poland v Brazil, 5 June 1938
4 — Gustav Wetterstrom, Sweden v Cuba, 12 June 1938
4 — Juan Schiaffino, Uruguay v Bolivia, 2 July 1950
4 — Ademir, Brazil v Sweden, 9 July 1950
4 — Sandor Kocsis, Hungary v West Germany, 20 June 1954
4 — Juste Fontaine, France v West Germany, 28 June 1958
4 — Eusebio, Portugal v North Korea, 23 July 1966
4 — Emilio Butragueno, Spain v Denmark, 18 June 1986

British Internationals
6 — Joe Bambrick, N. Ireland v Wales, 1 Feb 1930

England
5 — Oliver Vaughton, v Ireland 18 Feb 1882 (on debut)
5 — Steve Bloomer, v Wales 16 March 1896
5 — Gilbert Smith, v Ireland 18 Feb 1899
5 — Willie Hall, v Ireland 16 Nov 1938
5 — Malcolm Macdonald, v Cyprus 16 April 1975

Major European championships
6 — Lothar Emmerich, Borussia Dortmund v Floriana, Cup-winners' Cup, 13 Oct 1965

British record in Europe
5 — Ray Crawford, Ipswich T v Floriana (European Cup) 25 Sept 1962
5 — Peter Osgood, Chelsea v Jeunesse Hautcharage (Cup-winners' Cup) 29 Sept 1971

Any first-class game
16 — Stephan Stanis, Racing Club Lens v Abry Asturies (French Cup) 13 Dec 1942

FA Cup
Competition proper
9 — Ted MacDougall, Bournemouth v Margate (1st round), 20 Nov 1971

Above: The first post-war goalkeeper to captain England, the giant Frank Swift of Manchester City. In 1958, while working as a journalist, Swift lost his life in the Munich air crash

Right: Jimmy Greaves scores the first of his three goals in England's 9–3 rout of Scotland at Wembley in 1961

Preliminary competitions
10 — Chris Marron, South Shields v Radcliffe B, 20 Sept 1947

Football League Cup
5 — Derek Reeves, Southampton v Leeds U (4th round), 5 Dec 1960
5 — Alan Wilks, Queen's Park R v Oxford U (3rd round), 10 Oct 1967
5 — Bob Latchford, Everton v Wimbledon (2nd round), 28 Aug 1978
5 — Cyrille Regis, Coventry v Chester C (2nd round), 9 Oct 1985

Football League
10 — Joe Payne, Luton T v Bristol R (Division 3(S)) 13 April 1936

Division 1
7 — Jimmy Ross, Preston NE v Stoke, 6 Oct 1888
7 — Ted Drake, Arsenal v Aston Villa, 14 Dec 1935

Division 2
7 — Tommy Briggs, Blackburn R v Bristol R, 5 Feb 1955
7 — Neville Coleman, Stoke C v Lincoln C, 23 Feb 1957

Division 3
5 — Barrie Thomas, Scunthorpe U v Luton T, 24 April 1965
5 — Keith East, Swindon T v Mansfield T, 20 Nov 1965
5 — Steve Earle, Fulham v Halifax T, 16 Sept 1969
5 — Alf Wood, Shrewsbury T v Blackburn R, 2 Oct 1971
5 — Tony Caldwell, Bolton W v Walsall, 10 Sept 1983

5 — Andy Jones, Port Vale v Newport C, 4 May 1987

Division 4
6 — Herbert Lister, Oldham A v Southport, 26 Dec 1962

Division 3(N)
9 — 'Bunny' Bell, Tranmere R v Oldham A 26 Dec 1935

Scottish League
8 — Owen McNally, Arthurlie v Armadale, (Division 2), 1 Oct 1927
8 — Jimmy McGrory, Celtic v Dunfermline A, (Division 1), 14 Jan 1928
8 — Jim Dyet, King's Park v Forfar A, (Division 2), 2 Jan 1930
8 — John Calder, Morton v Raith R, (Division 2), 18 April 1936
8 — Norman Haywood, Raith R v Brechin C, (Division 2), 20 Aug 1937

Scottish Cup
13 — John Petrie, Arbroath v Bon Accord, 12 Sept 1885

Scottish League Cup
5 — Jim Fraser, Ayr U v Dumbarton, 13 Aug 1952
5 — Jim Forrest, Rangers v Stirling A, 17 Aug 1966

● Gerry Baker scored 10 goals for St Mirren against Glasgow University in a Scottish Cup tie on 30 January 1960.

● Billy Minter scored 7 goals for St Albans City in an FA Cup qualifying tie against Dulwich Hamlet on 22 Nov 1922 yet was on the losing side . . . Dulwich won 8-7! Denis Law was once on the losing side after scoring 6 goals in an FA Cup tie. He scored all six in Manchester City's abandoned 4th round tie with Luton Town on 28 Jan 1961. Luton won the replayed game 3-1.

Individual records — season

World record
127 — Pele (Santos, Brazil), 1959

World Cup
13 — Juste Fontaine (France), 1958

European Cup
14 — Jose Altafini (AC Milan), 1962-63

European Cup-winners' Cup
14 — Lothar Emmerich (Borussia Dortmund), 1965-66

Football League
Division 1
60 — Dixie Dean, Everton 1927-28
Division 2
59 — George Camsell, Middlesbrough, 1927-28
Division 3
39 — Derek Reeves, Southampton, 1959-60
Division 4
52 — Terry Bly, Peterborough U, 1960-61
Division 3(S)
55 — Joe Payne, Luton T, 1936-37
Division 3(N)
55 — Ted Harston, Mansfield T, 1936-37
The last time at least 35, 40, and 50 goals in a season
1983-84 36 — Trevor Senior, Reading (Division 4)
1970-71 42 — Ted MacDougall, Bournemouth (Division 4)
1960-61 52 — Terry Bly, Peterborough U (Division 4)

Scottish League
66 — Jim Smith, Ayr U (Division 2) 1927-28

1st Division
52 — William McFadyen, Motherwell, 1931-32

FA Cup
15 — Albert Brown (Tottenham H) 1900-01

Football League Cup
12 — Clive Allen (Tottenham H) 1986-87

Individual records – career

World record
1,329 — Arthur Friedenreich (Germanio, CA Ipiranga, Americano, CA Paulistano, Sao Paulo, Flamengo, Brazil) 1909-35

1,000+ first-class goals
Pele 1,280 1956-77, Franz Binder 1,006 1930-50

Internationals
97 — Pele (Brazil) 1957-70

Leading British international scorers
England
49 — Bobby Charlton
44 — Jimmy Greaves
30 — Tom Finney
30 — Nat Lofthouse
29 — Vivian Woodward
26 — Steve Bloomer
26 — Gary Lineker
Scotland
30 — Denis Law
30 — Kenny Dalglish

Northern Ireland
12 — Joe Bambrick, Billy Gillespie, Gerry Armstrong

Wales
23 — Ivor Allchurch, Trevor Ford

Ireland
19 — Don Givens

European Cup
49 — Alfredo de Stefano (Real Madrid) 1955-64
British player
30 — Peter Lorimer, (Leeds U) 1965-77

Football League
434 — Arthur Rowley (West Bromwich A, Fulham, Leicester C, Shrewsbury T) 1946-65
349 — Dixie Dean (Everton) 1925-37

Scottish League
410 — Jimmy McGory (Celtic, Clydebank) 1922-38

FA Cup
41 — Denis Law (Huddersfield T, Manchester C, Manchester U)

The first man to score 100 goals in both the Scottish League and Football League was Neil Martin who achieved the feat with Alloa, Queen of the South and Hibernian in Scotland and Sunderland, Coventry C, Nottingham F, Brighton HA and Crystal P in England. He reached the milestone of 100 goals in the English League against Sheffield Wednesday at Hillsborough on 21 September 1974.

● The last club to score 100 were Northampton T (103) in 1986-87

● The last team to score 100 goals in the 1st division were Tottenham H (111) in 1962-63

● Lincoln City, Sheffield Wednesday and Wolverhampton Wanderers have each scored 100 goals on a record five occasions

● In 1948-49 season Notts County was the only Football League team to score 100 goals (102) yet they finished 11th in the 3rd division (south)

● Bristol City scored 100 goals in the 3rd division (south) in 1962-63 and were 14th in the table.

● Between 1958-61 Wolverhampton Wanderers scored a century of goals four years in succession for a total of 422 goals

● Southampton (Divisions 2, 3, 3S) and Northampton T (Divisions 3, 4, 3S) have scored 100 goals a season in three different divisions

● The champions of all four divisions of the Football League each scored a century of goals in the following season: 1931-32, 1956-57 and 1960-61.

● In 1930-31 and again in 1931-32 a staggering 8 teams scored a century of League goals in each of those seasons

Team records
For individual match records see *Scores (Record)*

Football League season

Most

		Div	
134	Peterborough U	4	1960-61
128	Bradford C	3N	1928-29
128	Aston Villa	1	1930-31
127	Millwall	3S	1927-28
127	Arsenal	1	1930-31
123	Doncaster R	3N	1946-47
122	Middlesbrough	2	1926-27
121	Everton	1	1927-28
121	Lincoln C	3N	1951-52
111	Queen's Park R	3	1961-62

Fewest

		Div	
24	Watford	2	1971-72
24	Stoke C	1	1984-85
26	Woolwich A	1	1912-13
26	Leicester C	1	1977-78
27	Stockport C	3	1969-70
27	Huddersfield T	1	1971-72
27	Wolverhampton W	1	1983-84
29	Crewe A	4	1981-82
33	Crystal P	3S	1950-51
32	Crewe A	3N	1923-24

Scottish League season
Most
(Pre-1975)

		Div	
142	Raith R	2	1937-38
135	Morton	2	1963-64
132	Falkirk	2	1935-36
132	Hearts	1	1957-58
122	Ayr U	2	1936-37
122	Clyde	2	1956-57
120	Cowdenbeath	2	1938-39
120	Dunfermline A	2	1957-58

(Since re-organisation in 1975)

95	Ayr U	2	1987-88
92	Motherwell	1	1981-82
91	St Mirren	1	1976-77
91	Dundee	1	1977-78
91	Dunfermline A	2	1985-86
90	Dundee	1	1976-77
90	Celtic	P	1982-83
90	Dundee U	P	1982-83
90	Celtic	P	1986-87

Single day records
Most
1st division 66 — 26 December 1963

Blackpool 1		Chelsea 5	
Burnley 6		Manchester U 1	
Fulham 10		Ipswich T 1	
Leicester C 2		Everton 0	
Liverpool 6		Stoke C 1	
Nottingham F 3		Sheffield U 3	
Sheffield W 3		Bolton W 0	
W Bromwich A 4		Tottenham H 4	
Wolverhampton W 3		Aston Villa 3	
West Ham U 2		Blackburn R 8	

Golden Boot Award

This is an annual award made by the Adidas sport shoe manufacturers to the European footballer who scores the most goals in a domestic League season.

Winners

1968	Eusebio	Benfica 43
1969	Peter Jekov	CSKA Sofia 36
1970	Gerd Muller	Bayern Munich 38
1971	Josip Skoblar	Marseilles 44
1972	Gerd Muller	Bayern Munich 40
1973	Eusebio	Benfica 40
1974	Hector Yazalde	Sporting Lisbon 46
1975	Dudu Georgescu	Dinamo Bucharest 33
1976	Sotiris Kaiafas	Omonia Nicosia 39
1977	Dudu Georgescu	Dinamo Bucharest 47
1978	Hans Krankl	Rapid Vienna 41
1979	Kees Kist	AZ 67 Alkmaar 34
1980	Erwin Van Den Bergh	Lierse 39
1981	Georgi Slavkov	Trakia 31
1982	Wim Kieft	Ajax 32
1983	Fernando Gomes	FC Porto 36
1984	Ian Rush	Liverpool 32
1985	Fernando Gomes	FC Porto 39
1986	Marco Van Basten	Ajax 37
1987	Rodion Camataru	Dinamo Bucharest 44
1988	Tanju Colak	Galatasary 39

Grounds

Largest capacity
World
Marcana (Mario Filho) Stadium, Rio de Janeiro, Brazil (205,000)
Morumbi Stadium, Sao Paulo, Brazil (150,000)
Pyongyang Stadium, Pyongyang, North Korea (150,000)
Castelao Stadium, Fortaleza, Brazil (130,000)
Nou Camp Stadium, Barcelona, Spain (120,000)

Britain
Wembley Stadium, London (83,000 — to be reduced further in 1989)
Hampden Park, Glasgow (74,730)
Celtic Park (Glasgow Celtic), Glasgow (60,800)
Highbury Stadium (Arsenal), London (57,000)
Maine Road (Manchester City), Manchester (58,385)
Hillsborough (Sheffield Wednesday), Sheffield (54,101)
Goodison Park (Everton), Liverpool (52,691)
Old Trafford (Manchester United), Manchester (52,600)

Smallest capacity
Football League

Shay Ground (Halifax) (4,021)
Belle Vue Ground (Doncaster Rovers) (4,859)
Plainmoor Ground (Torquay United) (4,999)
Gresty Road (Crewe Alexandra) (5,000)

Scotland

Clifton Hall Stadium, Albion Rovers (878)
Recreation Park, Alloa Athletic (3,100)
Glebe Park, Brechin City (3,491)
(These capacities are subject to change)

Everton's Dixie Dean scored 60 1st division goals in 1927–28, still a Football League record more than 60 years later

Arthur Rowley scored a
Football League record
434 goals between
1946–65

● Queen's Park Rangers in 1981-82 was the first Football League club to adopt an artificial pitch. They were followed by Luton Town in 1985-86 and Preston North End and Oldham Athletic in 1986-87. Queen's Park Rangers reverted to a conventional grass pitch in 1988-89. The first Scottish club to install an artificial pitch was Stirling Albion in 1987.

● Aberdeen was the first British club to adopt an all-seater stadium when they opened their new ground for a friendly against Tottenham Hotspur on 5 August 1978. Coventry City was the first English League club to have an all-seater stadium.

● Chesterfield have the longest continuous tenure of any League club in Britain. They have played at their Saltergate ground since their formation in 1866. Dumbarton have played at their Boghead Park ground continuously since 1872.

● The two closest League grounds to each other in Britain are Dens Park and Tannadice Park in Dundee. They are only 200 yards apart.

Gullit, Ruud (1962-)

Born in Amsterdam of a Dutch mother and Surinamese father, Ruud Gullit emerged in the second half of the 1980s as the world's most outstanding player. He displayed his full skills during the summer of 1988 when he helped the Netherlands to their first major international honour, the European Championship in West Germany.

Gullit's first team was Merrboys FC, a team of under-8s. As a junior he went to DWS Amsterdam and then to Haarlem in 1979. He made his League debut against MVV in August 1979 as a 15-year-old and he celebrated his 19th birthday in September 1981 by making his international debut in a 2-1 defeat by Switzerland.

He moved to Feyenoord in 1982 and after helping them to the League and Cup double in 1984 moved to PSV Eindhoven in 1985. The Netherlands Footballer of the Year that season, he won two more League championship medals before his £5.5 million transfer to AC Milan in the summer of 1987, the same year that he became the second Dutchman after Johan Cruyff to win the European Footballer of the Year award.

A very skilful player, he has magnificent ball control, is very quick, and is easily identifiable by his dreadlock hairstyle.

Born: 1 September 1962, Amsterdam
International caps: 40
Honours
European Championship 1988
Dutch League 1984 (Feyenoord), 1986, 1987 (Eindhoven)
Dutch Cup 1984 (Feyenoord)
Awards
European Footballer of the Year 1987

Hampden Park

The biggest club ground in Britain, Hampden Park in Glasgow is owned by the Queen's Park club, the only amateur team in League soccer in Britain.

The current stadium is the third to carry the name Hampden Park. Queen's Park, who were one of the pioneers of Scottish football, acquired 12 acres of land for less than £10,000 in the 1870s, and developed the first ground. The second Hampden opened in 1894 and in October 1903 the current stadium staged its first match when Celtic visited Queen's Park.

Before the First World War six-figure crowds were commonplace and in 1931 the capacity was increased to accommodate the 131,273 that watched the Celtic versus Motherwell Cup final. After the completion of the North Stand in 1937 the capacity was increased and a staggering 149,547 watched the Scotland-England game that year. A week later 146,433 watched the Scottish Cup final between Celtic and Aberdeen.

The automatic choice of venue for all major matches in Scotland, Hampden has also played host to a world championship boxing contest between Jackie Paterson and Peter Kane (fly-weight) in 1943. Scotland has played rugby union at Hampden, and the Scottish women have played hockey at the famous stadium. Leading tennis player Suzanne Lenglen also once gave an exhibition at Hampden Park.

Hat-trick

The term derives from the cricket custom of presenting a bowler with a new hat when he took three wickets with consecutive balls. It is now widely used for any triple sporting achievement. In football it is the scoring of three goals in one match. Strictly speaking, it is not a hat-trick if the sequence is broken by a goal scored by another player.

Football League records
Most
37 — Dixie Dean (Tranmere R, Everton, Notts C) 1923-37
In one season
9 — George Camsell (Middlesbrough), Division 2, 1926-27

● Only one player has scored a *hat-trick* of *hat-tricks* (hat-tricks in three consecutive League games): Jack Balmer (Liverpool) v Portsmouth 9 Nov, v Derby C 16 Nov (4 goals), v Arsenal 23 Nov 1946.

● Tom Keetley of Notts Country scored hat-tricks in *three consecutive away games* in the 2nd division in 1931: v Plymouth A 10 Oct, v Manchester U 26 Oct, v Chesterfield 7 Nov.

● Cliff Holton of Watford once scored hat-tricks on consecutive days: on Friday 15 April 1960 against Chester and the following day in Watford's 5-0 win over Gateshead.

The scoring of hat-tricks by players from opposing sides in one Football League game is not rare, but the last time it happened in the 1st division was 18 January 1977 when Trevor Francis scored three for Birmingham City and Malcolm MacDonald did the same for Arsenal.

There have been three instances of three players of one side scoring a hat-trick in the same match:

Nottingham F (Enoch West, Billy Hooper, Arther Spounder) v Leicester, Fosse, Division 1,

21 April 1909

Wrexham (Ron Barnes, Roy Ambler, Wyn Davies) v Hartlepools U, Division 4, 3 March 1962

Manchester C (Tony Adcock, Paul Stewart, David White) v Huddersfield T, Division 2, 7 Nov 1987

In the 1968-69 FA Cup competition Billy Best and Gary Moore scored hat-tricks in Southend United's 9-0 win over King's Lynn in the first round. In the next round they both scored hat-tricks again (Best actually scored 5 and Moore 4) as Southend beat Brentwood Town 10-1.

The last player to score a hat-trick of penalties in a 1st division game was Ken Barnes for Manchester C v Everton on 7 December 1957.

Since the formation of the Football League in 1888 only two men have scored hat-tricks for England in full internationals on their home ground. Ted Drake of Arsenal did so against Hungary at Highbury on 3 December 1936 and Jack Rowley of Manchester United emulated the feat against Ireland at Maine Road on 16 November 1949. Manchester United were using Maine Road as their home ground at the time.

In 1926–27 Middlesbrough's George Camsell scored a record 59 League goals including a record 9 hat-tricks

Major finals

World Cup
Geoff Hurst, England v West Germany, 30 July 1966
European Championship
None
European Cup
Ferenc Puskas (4 goals), Real Madrid v Eintracht, 8 May 1960
Alfredo di Stefano, Real Madrid v Eintracht, 8 May 1960
Ferenc Puskas, Real Madrid v Benfica, 2 May 1962
(Puskas was on losing side)
Pierino Prati, AC Milan v Ajax, 28 May 1969
European Cup-winnners' Cup
None
UEFA/Fairs Cup
Vicente Guillot, Valencia v Barcelona, 8 Sept 1962
Luis Pujol, Barcelona v Real Zaragoza, 21 Sept 1966
Jupp Heynckes, Borussia M'bach v Twente Enschede, 21 May 1975

FA Cup
William Townley, Blackburn R v Sheffield W, 29 March 1890
Jimmy Logan, Notts C v Bolton W, 31 March 1894
Stanley Mortensen, Blackpool v Bolton W, 2 May 1953
Football League cup
None
Scottish FA Cup
John Smith, Queen's Park v Dumbarton, 5 Feb 1881
Jimmy Quinn, Celtic v Rangers, 16 April 1904
Dixie Deans, Celtic v Hibernian, 6 May 1972
Scottish League Cup
Davie Duncan, East Fife v Falkirk, 1 Nov 1948
Willie Bauld, Hearts v Motherwell, 23 Oct 1954
Billy McPhail, Celtic v Rangers, 19 Oct 1957
Jim Forrest (4 goals), Rangers v Morton, 26 Oct 1963
Bobby Lennox, Celtic v Hibernian, 5 April 1969
Dixie Deans, Celtic v Hibernian, 26 Oct 1974
Joe Harper, Hibernian v Celtic, 26 Oct 1974
(Harper was on the losing side)

Hampden Park, the biggest football ground in Britain

Ally McCoist, Rangers v Celtic, 25 March 1984

Dixie Deans is the only British player to have scored hat-tricks in the final of two different major competitions.

Against England in full internationals
Richard Hofmann, Germany, 10 May 1930
Nandor Hideguti, Hungary, 25 Nov 1953 (at Wembley)
Alexandr Petakovic, Yugoslavia, 11 May 1958
Juan Seminario, Peru, 17 May 1959
Marco Van Basten, Netherlands, 15 June 1988

Home internationals

See *International Championship*

The Netherlands' Ruud Gullit

Huddersfield Town

Huddersfield are immortalised in the record books as the first club to win the Football League title in three consecutive years. Only Arsenal and Liverpool have emulated their feat.

Although a Huddersfield football team had existed since the 1890s, the current club was not formed until 1908. After a season in the Midland league they were admitted into the 2nd division of the Football League in 1910, and so began a remarkable sequence of successes that took them to those three League titles.

They gained promotion to the 1st division in 1920 and then appointed the great Herbert Chapman as manager. It was under him that Town won their first title in 1924. They repeated the achievement a year later and completed the hat-trick in 1926. Chapman left the club to take charge at Arsenal before they completed one of soccer's greatest achievements.

A very young Denis
Law during his days at
Huddersfield in
1956–57

Huddersfield had preceded their great League run with an FA Cup win over Preston North End in 1922 when Billy Smith became the first man to win an FA Cup final with a penalty kick.

Since those heady days of the 1930s there has been little for the West Yorkshire fans to cheer. Manager Bill Shankly and his protegée Denis Law brought renewed hoped to the club in the 1950s, but since then, apart from a brief spell back in the 1st division, Huddersfield have languished amongst the lower divisions of the Football League.

Ground: Leeds Road
Nickname: Terriers
Record attendance: 67,037 — v Arsenal (FA Cup 6th round), 27 Feb 1932
First Football League season: 1910-11, Division 2 (13th)
Seasons in Football League: 68 (30 Division 1, 27 Division 2, 6 Division 3, 5 Division 4)

Honours
Division 1 champions 1923-24, 1924-25, 1925-26
Division 2 champions 1969-70
Division 4 champions 1979-80
FA Cup winners 1922

Inter-city Fairs Cup

See *UEFA Cup*

International Championship

Inaugurated in 1883-84, this was a four-nation tournament involving the four British home countries. The first match was at Belfast on 26 January 1884 when Scotland had a resounding 5-0 win against Northern Ireland.

The championship was discontinued after the 1983-84 season because it was felt the fixtures involving Northern Ireland and Wales were no longer attractive. Ironically, Northern Ireland won the last championship with Wales second. The last match in the championship was at Hampden Park on 26 May 1984 when Scotland and England drew 1-1 in front of 73,064 fans. The last goal in the championship was scored by England's Tony Woodcock.

The championship was won by the country with the most points each season (2 for a win, 1 for a draw), and if two teams were level at the top of the table they shared the championship.

Winners
Outright
England 34 – 1888, 1891-93, 1895, 1898-99, 1901, 1904-05, 1909, 1911, 1913, 1930, 1932, 1938, 1947-48, 1950, 1954-55, 1957, 1961, 1965-66, 1968-69, 1971, 1973, 1975, 1978-79, 1982-83
Scotland 24 – 1884-85, 1887, 1889, 1894, 1896-97, 1900, 1902, 1910, 1921-23, 1925-26, 1929, 1936, 1949, 1951, 1962-63, 1975, 1976-77
Wales 7 – 1907, 1920, 1924, 1928, 1933-34, 1937
Ireland/N. Ireland 3 – 1914, 1980, 1984
Shared
England/N. Ireland/Scotland/Wales 1956
England/Ireland/Scotland 1903, 1964*
England/Scotland/Wales 1939, 1960, 1970
England/Scotland 1886, 1890, 1906, 1908, 1912, 1927, 1931, 1935, 1953, 1972, 1974
England/Wales 1952
England/N. Ireland 1958-59
*Northern Ireland
The 1980-81 competition was not completed and no champions were declared.

England–Scotland matches were the highlight of the International Championship. In this game at Wembley in 1951 Scotland won 3–2 despite this goal from Tom Finney

Above: England's goalkeeper Gordon Banks in action against Northern Ireland

Below: Scotland's greatest day when the 'Wembley Wizards' beat England 5–1 at Wembley

Since the end of the Home Internationals, the England-Scotland fixture has continued.

Biggest win
13-0 — England v Ireland at Belfast, 18 February 1882.
Most appearances
48 — Billy Meredith (Wales) 1895-1920
Consecutive
33 — Danny Blanchflower (Northern Ireland) 1952-62

England–Scotland matches still take place each year despite the demise of the International Championship

Internationals

Earliest
Home
Scotland v England (0-0) at West of Scotland Cricket Ground, Hamilton Crescent, Partick, Glasgow, 30 November 1872, attendance 4,000.
Scotland: (all Queen's Park) R. Gardner, W. Ker, J. Taylor, J.J. Thomson, J. Smith, R. Smith, R. Leckie, A. Rhind, W.W. M'Kinnon, J.B. Weir, D.N. Wotherspoon.
England: W.J. Maynard (1st Surrey Rifles), E.H. Greenhalgh (Notts C), R. de C. Welch (Wanderers), F.B. Maddison (Oxford Univ), R. Barker (Herts. R), J. Brockbank (Cambridge U), J.C. Clegg (Sheffield W), A.K. Smith (Oxford Univ.), C.J. Ottaway (Oxford Univ.), C.J. Chenery (Crystal P), C.J. Morice (Barnes).

Between four home countries
England v Wales: 18 Jan 1879 at Kennington Oval. England won 2-1
England v Ireland: 18 Feb 1882 at Belfast. England won 13-0
Scotland v Wales: 25 March 1876 at Glasgow. Scotland won 4-0
Scotland v Ireland: 26 Jan 1884 at Belfast. Scotland won 5-0
Wales v Ireland: 25 Feb 1882 at Wrexham. Wales won 7-1

Non-British
France v Belgium (3-3) at Uccle, nr. Brussels, 1 May 1904.

British full internationals
England v Austria (6-1) at Vienna, 6 June 1908
Scotland v Norway (7-3) at Bergen, 26 May 1929
Wales v France (1-1) at Paris, 25 May 1933
N. Ireland v France (3-1) at Paris, 11 Nov 1952

Defeats
England's by Spain (4-3) in Madrid, 15 May 1929.
Scotland's by Austria (5-0), 16 May 1931

Home
England's by Ireland (2-0) at Goodison Park, Everton, 21 Sep 1949.

Teams supplying most international players
Individual matches — Britain

Corinthians 11 for England side; 12 March 1894 v Wales at Wrexham, and 18 March 1895 v Wales at Queen's Club, Kensington. (Strictly speaking, as Corinthians was a representative club itself, the players were all members of other clubs. Corinthians were asked by the FA to assemble the international teams for those two matches).

Individual matches — World

Anderlecht 11 for Belgium v the Netherlands, 30 September 1964.
Torino 10 for Italy v Hungary, 11 May 1947.

Johnny Carey skippered the Republic of Ireland to a memorable victory over England at Goodison Park in 1949

In total for England

Corinthians 83
Aston Villa 51
Everton 50
Tottenham H 42
West Bromwich A 41

● The following current Football league clubs have not had one of their players capped at full international level: Colchester U, Darlington, Halifax T, Rochdale, Scarborough, Scunthorpe U, Torquay U, Wigan A.

● The first player from the 4th division to play in a full international was Viv Rouse (Crystal P) for Wales against Northern Ireland on 22 April 1959.

● Since 1945 four 3rd division players have appeared for England; Tommy Lawton (Notts C), Reg Matthews (Coventry C), Johnny Byrne (Crystal P), Peter Taylor (Crystal P)

● English players with overseas clubs playing for England are now commonplace but the first man to play for England while playing League soccer outside England was Joe Baker (Hibernian) who played against Yugoslavia at Wembley on 11 May 1960.

● Many players have represented two nations at international level, but the list of those who have played for three countries is considerably smaller:

Ladislav Kubala – Hungary, Czechoslovakia, Spain
Alfredo di Sterfano – Argentina, Colombia, Spain
Joe Kennaway – Scotland, Canada, United States

● Terry Venables is the only player to represent England at schoolboy, youth, amateur, under-23, and full international level.

(For biggest wins, most appearances and top goalscorers in international matches, see appropriate sections)

Ipswich Town

Since replacing Gillingham in the Football League in 1938 Ipswich have won every championship on offer to them, including the coveted 1st division at the first attempt in 1961-62. They have also added victories in the FA Cup and UEFA Cup to confirm them as one of the top teams in British football, despite their recent demise and drop into the 2nd division.

The club was formed in 1883, although it is believed another club bearing the name of the town was formed c.1878. Ipswich Town were strictly amateur and won local Suffolk League and Cup titles. They turned professional in 1936 and joined the Southern League. They appointed Scott Duncan (previously manager of Manchester United) as their first secretary-manager and he took the club into the 3rd division (south) of the Football League. At the same time the club secured the financial help of the Cobbold family, local brewers. The family is still associated with the club, whose greatest asset is its warm and friendly atmosphere.

Most of their success came under two men who both went on to manage the English national side, Alf Ramsey and Bobby Robson. It was Ramsey who took the club to 2nd division and 1st division titles in successive seasons, and it was Robson who led the Suffolk club to their great FA Cup win over Arsenal.

Ground: Portman Road
Nickname: Blues or Town
Record attendance: 38,010 — v Leeds United (FA Cup 6th round), 8 March 1975
First Football League season: 1938-39 Division 3(S) (7th)
Seasons in Football League: 44 (21 Division 1, 12 Division 2, 11 Division 3(S))

Honours

Division 1 champions 1961-62
Division 2 champions 1960-61, 1967-68
Division 3 champions 1953-54, 1956-57
FA Cup winners 1978
UEFA Cup winners 1981
Texaco Cup winners 1973
European Team of the Year 1981
Footballers of the Year Frans Thijssen (FWA) 1981, John Wark (PFA) 1981

Ireland, Northern

Football was first played in Ireland in 1878 and from the formation of the Irish football Association two years later, until the establishment of the Republic in 1921, Irish soccer was played under just one banner, that of Ireland. Founded in 1880, the Irish Football Association first joined FIFA in 1911 but, like the English Association, quit in 1920 and again in 1924. However, they have been members continuously since 1946.

The first club devoted entirely to playing soccer was Cliftonville, founded in 1879. The Irish Cup was inaugurated in 1881 and won by Moyola Park. Linfield, who were founded in 1887, won the first Irish League title in 1891 and have since been the most successful club side in Ireland. Ireland's first international match was at Belfast on 18 February 1882 against England when they suffered an embarrassing 13-0 defeat. They had to wait five years and 16 matches before registering their first win, 4-1 against Wales at Belfast on 12 March 1887. Northern Ireland's first international against non-British opposition was at Belfast on 12 May 1951 when they drew 2-2 with France. Their first win against overseas opposition was at Belfast on 1 May 1957 when they beat Portugal 3-0.

The first match against the Republic of Ireland was a goalless draw on 20 September 1978 in Dublin.

Domestic competitions

League Champions	Cup winners
(recent)	(recent)
1980 Linfield	1980 Linfield
1981 Glentoran	1981 Ballymena U
1982 Linfield	1982 Linfield
1983 Linfield	1983 Glentoran
1984 Linfield	1984 Ballymena U
1985 Linfield	1985 Glentoran
1986 Linfield	1986 Glentoran
1987 Linfield	1987 Glentoran
1988 Glentoran	1988 Glentoran
1989 Linfield	1989 Ballymena U
Most wins	**Most wins**
40 — Linfield	33 — Linfield
19 — Glentoran	14 — Glentoran
14 — Belfast Celtic	12 — Distillery

International competitions

World Cup
1958 reached quarter-finals, lost to France 4-0
1982 won group, failed to get past second phase
1986 failed to qualify from first phase

European Championship
Have never reached quarter-final stage

Ireland, Republic

Following the foundation of the Irish Republic in 1921 a new association was formed to control the game there: the Cumann Peile Nah-Eireann (Football Association of Ireland).

Billy Bingham wearing a Northern Ireland shirt in 1954. Twenty-six years later he was appointed manager of the team

Above: John Wark, later to find fame at Liverpool, scored for Ipswich in the 1981 UEFA Cup final against AZ 67 Alkmaar

Right above: Italy's Paulo Rossi (right), the 1982 European Footballer of the Year

Right: It's all over! And the celebrations start after Italy's 1982 World Cup triumph over West Germany

Southern clubs had already defected from the Irish FA after the First World War and these clubs joined the newly formed FAI. The new association joined FIFA in 1923. The League of Ireland and Cup of Ireland were instituted in the 1921-22 season.

The 'new' country made its international debut at the 1924 Olympic Games in Paris. However, it was not until 1946 that any of the four home countries played the Republic of Ireland, when England won a friendly 1-0 in Dublin on 30 September 1946. On 21 September 1949 the Irish enjoyed their greatest hour when they beat England 2-0 at Goodison Park. It was England's first home defeat other than by any of the home countries.

The constant drain of their best players to England meant Ireland fared badly at international level, until Jackie Charlton was appointed as national team manager in February 1986. Charlton took the country to its first major finals, the 1988 European Championships, and but for the Netherlands scoring a winner 8 minutes from time, they would have reached the semi-final stage.

Domestic competitions
League champions
(recent)
1980 Limerick
1981 Athlone Town
1982 Dundalk
1983 Athlone Town
1984 Shamrock Rovers
1985 Shamrock Rovers
1986 Shamrock Rovers
1987 Shamrock Rovers
1988 Dundalk
1989 Derry C
Most wins
24 — Shamrock Rovers
7 — Shelbourne, Bohemians, Dundalk

Cup winners
(recent)
1980 Waterford
1981 Dundalk
1982 Limerick
1983 Sligo
1984 University College Dublin
1985 Shamrock Rovers
1986 Shamrock Rovers
1987 Shamrock Rovers
1988 Dundalk
1989 Derry C
Most wins
23 — Shamrock Rovers
8 — Dundalk
5 — Drumcondra

International competitions
World Cup
Have never qualified for the final stages

European Championship
Reached final stages 1988, failed to qualify for semi-final

Italy

A form of football-style kicking game is believed to have been played by the Romans thousands of years ago. The Italian soccer Federation's name, Federazione Italiana Giuoco Calcio translates literally as Italian Kickball Game Federation, reflecting its Roman links. But the British were responsible for taking the modern game of soccer to Italy, as to many other countries.

The FIGC was founded in 1898, eight years after the formation of the country's first organised club, Football Club Internationale of Turin (not to be confused with Inter Milan). The famous Juventus club was formed in 1897. Italy became one of the first nations to join the newly formed FIFA in 1905 and in 1910 Italy played their first international, beating France 6-2 in Milan. They did not compete in the first World Cup but were the host nation four years later and went on to beat Czechoslovakia 2-1 after extra time to win the trophy. They returned from France as World Champions four years later, and between their two triumphs also won the Olympic title.

They lost their world crown in Brazil in 1950 but 32 years later became the second club after Brazil to win the trophy three times when they beat West Germany 3-1 in an all-European final in Madrid. Italy has also won the European Championship: they are the only nation to win both the World Cup and European Championship on home soil.

International competitions

World Cup winners
1934 (beat Czechoslovakia 2-1 aet),
1938 (beat Hungary 4-2),
1982 (beat West Germany 3-1)

European Champions
1968 (beat Yugoslavia 2-0 after 1-1 draw)

Jennings, Pat (1945-)

Britain's most capped footballer, Pat Jennings played for Northern Ireland 119 times between April 1964, when he made his debut against Wales at Swansea, and June 1986, when he bowed out in the World Cup.

Born in Newry, Jennings started his Football League career with Watford who bought him from Newry Town for £6,000. He moved to Tottenham for £30,000 in 1964 and after taking over from Bill Brown was the regular first choice 'keeper for more than ten years. He played nearly 500 League games for Spurs, and won FA Cup, League Cup and UEFA Cup winners' medals. After a £40,000 move to north-London rivals Arsenal in 1977 Pat opened another successful chapter in his long career and went on to appear in three consecutive FA Cup finals with the Gunners.

At international level his skill and inspiration played a big part in Northern Ireland reaching the final stages of the World Cup in 1982 and 1986 and it was quite appropriate that he should end his international career in the finest tournament in the world, and against one of the world's greatest teams, Brazil.

Born: 12 June 1945, Newry, Northern Ireland
Football League debut: 23 May 1963 v Queen's Park R (let in 5 goals!)
Football League appearances: 757 (48 Watford, 472 Tottenham H, 237 Arsenal)
International caps: 119
Honours
FA Cup 1967 (Tottenham H), 1979 (Arsenal)
Football League Cup 1971, 1973 (both Tottenham H)
UEFA Cup 1972 (Tottenham H)
Awards
Footballer of the Year (FWA) 1973, (PFA) 1976

Keegan, Kevin (1951-)

When Bill Shankly plucked Kevin Keegan from the obscurity of the lower divisions in 1971 there were few who doubted the wisdom of the Liverpool manager's move. Any who did were soon proved wrong as Keegan went on to become a loyal servant to both Liverpool and England, serving both as a great player and captain. After three seasons playing with Scunthorpe, Keegan was bought for £35,000 by Liverpool on 1 May 1971 and was thrown into the Liverpool first team, quickly adapting to the change from 4th to 1st division football.

During his six years at Anfield he won three League championship medals, two UEFA Cup winners' medals, and European and FA Cup winners' medals. His performance in the 1974 FA Cup final against Newcastle, when he scored two goals, was one of his best for the club.

In 1977 he quit Anfield and moved to SV Hamburg but after three seasons made a surprise move back to England, joining Southampton. He finished his career at Newcastle United, having helped them back into the 1st division.

Born: 14 February 1951, Armthorpe, Doncaster, Yorkshire
Football League appearances: 590 (124 Scunthorpe U, 230 Liverpool, 68 Southampton, 78 Newcastle U)
Football League goals: 203 (18 Scunthorpe U, 68 Liverpool, 37 Southampton, 48 Newcastle U)
International caps: 63
Honours:
Division 1 Championship 1972-73, 1975-76, 1976-77
German League 1978-79
FA Cup 1974
European Cup 1977
UEFA Cup 1973, 1976
Awards:
Footballer of the Year (FWA) 1976
Player of the Year (PFA) 1982
European Footballer of the Year 1978, 1979

Law, Denis (1940-)

When Denis Law walked into the offices of Huddersfield Town in 1956 he looked very little like a footballer, bespectacled and frail looking as he was. The Huddersfield manager, Bill Shankly, was prepared to look at him play and liked what he saw. From that beginning was developed one of the most lethal of inside forwards ever to play for Scotland.

In 1958 Law became Scotland's youngest ever international at 18 and 236 days. He joined Manchester City for a then British record £55,000 in 1960 and when he joined Italian club Torino 15 months later, it was the first £100,000 deal involving a British club. Twelve months later Manchester United paid £115,000 for him, the first six-figure fee for a player paid by a British club.

At Old Trafford he teamed up with Bobby Charlton and George Best, making United one of the most lethal attacks in the country. He won an FA Cup winners' medal in 1963 and two championship medals in 1965 and 1967. Sadly, a knee injury ruled him out of the club's greatest success, the 1968 European Cup final win over Benfica.

Law returned to Maine Road in 1973 and in April 1974 he scored his last Football League goal at Old Trafford when his 82nd minute back-heeler sent United into the 2nd division.

Born: 24 May 1940, Aberdeen, Scotland
Football League debut: 24 Dec 1956 v Notts C
Football League appearances: 458 (81 Huddersfield T, 68 Manchester C, 309 Manchester U)
Football League goals: 217 (16 Huddersfield, 30 Manchester C, 171 Manchester U)
International caps: 55
Honours
Division 1 Championship 1964-65, 1966-67
FA Cup 1963
Awards
European Footballer of the Year 1964
Merit Award (PFA) 1975

Laws

The first uniform rules for football were drawn up at Cambridge University, probably in 1848. Other widely used rules at that time were the Sheffield Rules, drawn up in 1856. The first Football Association rules were published in 1863, the year the FA was formed.

The current game is played to the laws drawn up by the Football Association, with slight amendments made by the International Board of FIFA.

There are 17 laws of the game in the following categories:

Law I:	The field of play
Law II:	The ball
Law III:	Number of players
Law IV:	Players' equipment
Law V:	Referees
Law VI:	Linesmen
Law VII:	Duration of the game
Law VIII:	The start of play
Law IX:	Ball in and out of play
Law X:	Method of scoring
Law XI:	Off-side
Law XII:	Fouls and misconduct
Law XIII:	Free-kick
Law XIV:	Penalty-kick
Law XV:	Throw-in
Law XVI:	Goal-kick
Law XVII:	Corner-kick

A full copy of the Laws of the Game can be obtained from The Football Association, 16 Lancaster Gate, London W2 3LW.

Jackie Charlton opened the scoring for Leeds in the 1970 FA Cup but Chelsea eventually won the trophy after a replay and Leeds had to wait two more years for their first FA Cup success

Leeds United

The first Leeds soccer club was formed as Hunslet AFC in 1880 following the disbanding of a local rugby team. Out of them was born Leeds City, who successfully applied to join the 2nd division of the Football League in 1905. However, after allegations of illegal payments to players during the First World War, and their subsequent failure to produce their books, the club was expelled from the Football League in October 1919.

A new team was born in 1920, and that year Leeds United joined the Football League, winning promotion to the 1st division in 1924. The club was regularly involved in an up-and-down career between the top two divisions, but their fortunes took a turn for the better after the Second World War when Major Frank Buckley was appointed manager. His duty was to keep the club out of the third division. He did that and furthermore guided them back to the 1st division. He was also the man who discovered the 'Gentle Giant', John Charles. But sadly the club returned to the 2nd division.

Don Revie, who joined the club as a player in 1961, was appointed manager in 1962 and set

about a massive rebuilding programme. He brought Charles back from Italy and recruited the Scot Bobby Collins. He led Leeds into the 1st division as champions in 1964, and with men like Gary Sprake, Norman Hunter, Billy Bremner, Jackie Charlton, Alan Clarke, Paul Reaney and Johnny Giles, Revie produced one of the hardest British teams to beat. Had Liverpool not been in the ascendant at the same time, Leeds' record of two League championships, one FA Cup and two Fairs Cup wins would have been considerably greater.

Ground: Elland Road
Nickname: United
Record attendance: 57,892 — v Sunderland (FA Cup 5th round replay), 15 March 1967
First Football League season: Leeds City: 1905-06 Division 2 (6th) Leeds United: 1920-21 Division 2 (14th)
Seasons in Football League: (Leeds U): 62 (36 Division 1, 26 Division 2)

Honours
Division 1 champions 1968-69, 1973-74
Division 2 champions 1923-24, 1963-64
FA Cup winners 1972
Football League Cup winners 1968
European Fairs Cup winners 1968, 1971
Footballers of the Year Bobby Collins (FWA) 1965, Jackie Charlton (FWA) 1967, Billy Bremner (FWA) 1970, Norman Hunter (PFA) 1974
Manager of the Year Don Revie 1969-70, 1972

Left: Republic of Ireland goalkeeper Pat Bonner thwarts yet another Gary Lineker goal attempt

Below left: Kevin Keegan in action for his last League club, Newcastle United

Below: One of the game's most popular goalkeepers, Pat Jennings

Libertadores Cup

See *South American Championship*

Lightest player

The lightest player to have played in the Football League is believed to be W Hepworth, who played outside-right for Barnsley in the 1890s. He weighed in at a mere 7 stone 5 lb (47 kg).

Limited companies

The first Football League club to become a limited company was Birmingham City (as Small Heath Ltd) in 1888. The last of the current Football League clubs to become a limited company was Nottingham Forest in 1983. Tottenham Hotspur in 1986 was the first to go public and have their shares quoted on the stock exchange.

Lineker, Gary (1960-)

Since making his debut for England against Scotland in May 1984 Gary Lineker has become one of the most prolific scorers to play for his country. In his first 36 games he scored 26 goals, including four hat-tricks, to make him the seventh top scorer for his country.

Born in Leicester, Gary started his career with his home-town team and turned professional in December 1978 after coming through the junior ranks.

Leicester's top scorer every season from 1982-85, he joined Everton in 1985 and in his first

Everton goalkeeper Ted Sagar spent more than 24 years with the Merseyside club between 1929–53

season netted 30 goals as Everton finished runners-up to Liverpool in both the League and FA Cup.

The lure of the peseta took Gary to Barcelona in 1986 when he teamed up with Terry Venables who paid £2,750,000 for the striker shortly after England's World Cup exploits. Lineker soon became a favourite with the Catalan fans and in 1988 he won a Spanish Cup winners' medal.

Born: 30 November 1960, Leicester
Football League debut: 1 January 1979 v Oldham Athletic
Football League appearances: 235 (194 Leicester C, 41 Everton)
Football League goals: 125 (95 Leicester C, 30 Everton)
International caps: 38
Honours
Division 2 Championship 1979-80 (Leicester C)
Spanish Cup 1988 (Barcelona)
Awards
Footballer of the Year (FWA/PFA) 1986

Linesmen

At one time football matches were controlled by umpires, one on either side of the pitch, outside the field of play. A referee was called on if there was a dispute between the two umpires. In 1891 the referee was moved onto the playing area and the umpires abandoned in favour of linesmen.

Linesmen each control one half of the pitch and are responsible for assisting the referee in making his decisions and indicating when the ball is in or out of play.

In senior matches linesmen should be qualified referees able to take over from the referee if necessary.

Littlewoods Cup

See *Football League Cup*

Liverpool

The record of Liverpool FC tells its own story: they have been simply the most successful Football League club of all time.

Liverpool FC was founded on 15 March 1892 after Everton quit their Anfield Road ground and moved to Goodison Park. Anfield owner John Houlding had a ground but no team so he started one using the name of Liverpool. Under the chairmanship of John McKenna (later to be president of the Football League for 26 years) they successfully applied to join the 2nd division of the Football League in 1893. The Reds won the title at the first attempt and in 1901 won the first of their record 17 1st division titles.

The current era started in December 1959 when they appointed Bill Shankly as team manager. The canny Scot took the club to the 1st division, and since then their record has been unsurpassed in British football. Shankly was a shrewd man and it was his ebullience which was the foundation for the atmosphere that spreads through the club today. He had the ability to bring the best out of the players.

Following Shankly into the management chair was his former assistant Bob Paisley, and since then the club has continued to promote from within, continuing its success story. The rest of the Liverpool story is told in the honours list below. They have won every domestic honour as well as the coveted European Champions' Cup a British record four times.

The 1988-89 season was the most traumatic in this great club's long history. Ninety-five fans lost their lives in the Hillsborough tragedy. The club picked itself up and beat Everton to win the FA Cup and were only a minute away from completing the double for the second time when they were deprived of the title by a last minute goal from Arsenal's Michael Thomas.

Ground: Anfield Road
Nickname: Reds
Record attendance: 61,905 — v Wolverhampton W (FA Cup 4th round), 2 Feb 1952
First Football League season: 1893-94 Division 2 (1st)
Seasons in Football League: 85 (74 Division 1, 11 Division 2)

Honours
Division 1 champions 1900-01, 1905-06, 1921-22, 1922-23, 1946-47, 1963-64, 1965-66, 1972-73, 1975-76, 1976-77, 1978-79, 1979-80, 1981-82, 1982-83, 1983-84, 1985-86, 1987-88
Division 2 champions 1893-94, 1895-96, 1904-05, 1961-62
FA Cup winners 1965, 1974, 1986
Football League Cup winners 1981, 1982, 1983, 1984
Football League Super Cup winners 1985-86
European Cup winners 1977, 1978, 1981, 1984
UEFA Cup winners 1973, 1976
European Super Cup winners 1977
European Team of the Year 1976, 1978, 1982-84
Footballers of the Year Ian Callaghan (FWA) 1974, Kevin Keegan (FWA) 1976, Emlyn Hughes (FWA) 1977, Kenny Dalglish (FWA) 1979, 1983, (PFA) 1983, Terry McDermott (FWA) 1980, (PFA) 1980, Ian Rush (FWA) 1984, (PFA) 1984, John Barnes (FWA) 1988, PFA 1988, Steve Nicol (FWA) 1989
Managers of the Year Bill Shankly 1973, Bob Paisley 1976-77, 1979-80, 1982-83, Joe Fagan 1984, Kenny Dalglish 1986, 1988

Long service

The *longest serving manager in British football* was Willie Struth who was in charge of Rangers from August 1920 to April 1953. During his 33 year reign as manager Struth guided the club to ten championships, ten Scottish Cup wins and three League Cup successes.

The *longest in the Football League* was Matt Busby who managed Manchester United from October 1945 to June 1969, and again from

December 1970 to June 1971, a total of 24 years 3 months.

The *longest career with a single Football League club* by any player is 24 years 1 month by Ted Sagar, who joined Everton in March 1929 and retired in May 1953. In between making his debut at home to Derby County on 18 January 1930 and playing his last game at Plymouth on 15 November 1952 he played 463 games in a Football League career that spanned 22 years 10 months. Stanley Matthews' career spanned 32 years 10 months, but with two clubs, Stoke City (twice) and Blackpool. He made his League debut on 19 March 1932 and played his final game on 6 February 1965.

Willie Maley spent more than 51 years with Celtic as a player, secretary and manager between December 1887 and February 1939.

Left: England's current goalscorer Gary Lineker

Above: Ted Sagar, former Everton goalkeeper

Longest matches

The *longest first-class game* was the division 3 (north) Cup game between Stockport County and Doncaster Rovers on 30 March 1946. It was the second leg of a division 3 (north) Cup tie and in an effort to find a winner with the aggregate scores level at 4-4, play continued for a further 10 minutes each way, after which it was decided that play would go on until another goal was scored.

However, after 205 minutes' play (3 hours 25 minutes) play was abandoned because of bad light without any addition to the scoreline. Some of the 13,000 crowd went home and returned to see the closing stages of the match!

The *longest Football League match* lasted 135 minutes (two hours 15 minutes). It took place at Roker Park on 1 September 1894 and was between Sunderland and Derby. The referee did not arrive for the start and one of the linesmen officiated. At half-time Sunderland led 3-0. The referee then arrived and insisted on restarting the match. In the next 90 minutes Sunderland scored eight more goals. The result was recorded as 8-0, the first 45 minutes not counting.

The *longest FA Cup tie* was the fourth qualifying round tie between Alvechurch and Oxford City in 1971-72. The total playing time was 11 hours and the game was not resolved until the sixth meeting. Alvechurch eventually won 1-0 after 2-2, 1-1, 1-1 and two goalless draws. After all their hard work Alvechurch lost 4-1 at Aldershot in the next round.

The *longest FA Cup tie* in the competition proper, including replays, lasted 9 hours 22 minutes. It was the third-round tie between Stoke City and Bury in January 1955. In the fifth meeting between the two sides Stoke eventually won 3-2 at Old Trafford to qualify for the fourth round where they lost 3-1 to Swansea Town!

The *longest FA Cup final* was the 1970 final between Chelsea and Leeds United. It went to extra time in the first game at Wembley, and again in the replay at Old Trafford. The playing time was four hours.

McGrory, Jimmy (1904-)

Jimmy McGrory is the most prolific goalscorer in Scottish football. Between January 1923 and October 1937 he scored 410 League goals for Celtic and Clydebank, including a British record 397 for one club (Celtic). In all matches including cup ties, McGrory scored 550 first-class goals.

He joined Celtic from Glasgow junior side St Roch's in 1922, and apart from a season on loan to Clydebank in 1923-24 spent all his career at Celtic Park. Initially an outside-left, he was soon moved to centre-forward, a position he held for 15 seasons.

McGrory won two championship medals and appeared in four Cup finals with Celtic, on the winning side every time. He led the Scottish goalscoring list three times with tallies of 49-47-50. On 14 January 1928 he scored eight against Dunfermline, and against Motherwell on 14 March 1936 he scored four goals in five minutes.

Despite his goalscoring records, McGrory was picked for Scotland only seven times. He left Parkhead in 1938 to become manager at Kilmarnock. He returned to Celtic as manager in 1945 and held the position until 1965 when replaced by Jock Stein.

Born: 1904 Glasgow
Scottish League debut: 20 January 1923 Celtic v Third Lanark
Scottish League appearances: 408 (378 Celtic, 30 Clydebank)
Scottish League goals: 410 (397 Celtic, 13 Clydebank)
International caps: 7
Honours
Scottish League 1925-26, 1935-36 (all Celtic)
Scottish Cup 1925, 1931, 1933, 1937 (all Celtic)

Major Indoor Soccer League (MISL)

The MISL was formed in 1978 in North America to capitalise on outdoor soccer's projected popularity by incorporating elements of soccer, basketball and ice hockey to make it an attractive indoor sport.

The League was founded with six teams: Houston Summit, New York Arrows, Cincinatti Kids, Philadelphia Fever, Pittsburgh Spirit and Cleveland Force. Only Cleveland were still in the League in 1988. The end of season play-off final is the best-of-seven game series.

Sadly, the outdoor game collapsed in 1985 following the failure of the North American Soccer League (NASL). The MISL continues despite its troubled times.

After a troubled summer the League reduced from 11 to seven teams for the 1988-89 season.

Winners

1978-79 New York Arrows
1979-80 New York Arrows
1980-81 New York Arrows
1981-82 New York Arrows
1982-83 San Diego Sockers
1983-84 Baltimore Blast
1984-85 San Diego Sockers
1985-86 San Diego Sockers
1986-87 Dallas Sidekicks
1987-88 San Diego Sockers

(See also *North American Soccer League*)

Managers

Fewest in Football League
5 — West Ham United
Longest serving (at 22 May 1989)
Football League
John Lyall West Ham United 1974-.
Scotland
Jim McLean Dundee United 1971-.
Players and managers of FA Cup winners

Managers of two FA Cup winners
Charles Foweraker (3), Bolton W 1923, 1926, 1929
Bill Nicholson (3), Tottenham H 1961, 1962, 1967
Billy Walker, Sheffield W 1935, Nottingham F 1959
Stan Cullis, Wolverhampton W 1949, 1960
Matt Busby, Manchester U 1948, 1963
Stan Seymour, Newcastle U 1951, 1952
Bill Shankly, Liverpool 1965, 1974
John Lyall, West Ham U 1975, 1980
Keith Burkinshaw, Tottenham H 1981, 1982
Ron Atkinson, Manchester U 1983, 1985
Kenny Dalglish, Liverpool 1986, 1989

The most prolific goalscorer in British League soccer, Jimmy McGrory. He scored 410 goals for Celtic and Clydebank between 1923–37

Players and managers of FA Cup winners

	Player	Manager
Peter McWilliam	Newcastle U 1910	Tottenham H 1921
Billy Walker	Aston Villa 1920	Sheffield W 1935, Nottingham F 1959
Jimmy Seed	Tottenham H 1921	Charlton A 1947
Matt Busby	Manchester C 1934	Manchester U 1948, 1963
Joe Smith	Bolton W 1923, 1926	Blackpool 1953
Bill Shankly	Preston NE 1938	Liverpool 1965, 1974
Joe Mercer	Arsenal 1950	Manchester C 1969
Don Revie	Manchester C 1956	Leeds U 1972
Bob Stokoe	Newcastle U 1955	Sunderland 1973
Kenny Dalglish	Liverpool 1986	Liverpool 1986, 1989
Bobby Gould	West Ham U 1975 (sub)	Wimbledon 1988

Players and managers of Football League champions

	Player	Manager
Ted Drake	Arsenal 1933-34, 1934-35, 1937-38	Chelsea 1954-55
Bill Nicholson	Tottenham H 1950-51	Tottenham H 1960-61
Alf Ramsey	Tottenham H 1950-51	Ipswich T 1961-62
Joe Mercer	Everton 1938-39, Arsenal 1947-48, 1952-53	Manchester C 1967-68
Dave MacKay	Tottenham H 1960-61	Derby C 1974-75
Bob Paisley	Liverpool 1946-47	Liverpool 1975-76, 1976-77, 1978-79, 1979-80, 1981-82, 1982-83
Kenny Dalglish	Liverpool 1978-79, 1979-80, 1981-82, 1982-83, 1983-84, 1985-86 (player/manager)	Liverpool 1985-86 (player/manager), 1987-88
Howard Kendall	Everton 1969-70	Everton 1984-85, 1986-87
George Graham	Arsenal 1970-71	Arsenal 1988-89

● Only two managers have guided two different clubs to the Football League Championship: Herbert Chapman did so with Huddersfield Town and Arsenal, and Brian Clough repeated the feat with Derby County and Nottingham Forest.

The man who turned Liverpool into the great team they are today, Bill Shankly

England's managers
Walter Winterbottom (previously chief coach) 1946-July 1962
Alf Ramsey July 1962-May 1974
Joe Mercer (caretaker) May-July 1974
Don Revie July 1974-July 1977
Ron Greenwood Aug 1977-Aug 1982
Bobby Robson Aug 1982-

● Bill Lambton was manager of Scunthorpe United for just three days between 21-24 April 1959. This is the shortest reign of any manager in the Football League. The club played one game while he was in charge: they lost 3-0 to Liverpool at Anfield in a 2nd division game.

Most successful, Football League
Bob Paisley, Liverpool
6 Football League, 3 Milk Cups, 3 European Cups, 1 UEFA Cup.

● Since the Second World War hundreds of Football League managers have lost their jobs. The distinction of being the first to lose his position after the war belongs to Ernest Blackburn of Hull City who lost his job Jan 1946.

For longest serving managers see *Long service*

Left: Manager Joe Fagan with his Liverpool team and the Canon Trophy in 1984

Below: One of the game's great characters and top managers, Brian Clough

Manchester City

In recent years Manchester City have had to live in the shadow of United, but for many years the situation was reversed.

Founded in 1880, two years after United, as West Gorton FC, they changed to Gorton in 1884 when the club was considerably re-organised. They became known as Ardwick FC in 1887 before plumping for their current name in 1894. After playing in the Alliance they became founder members of the 2nd division in 1892. With the great Billy Meredith in their ranks City gained promotion to the 1st division in 1899 and have spent most of their Football League career in the top flight ever since. Although they beat Bolton to win the FA Cup in 1904 it was another 30 years before the glory returned to City, who had by then moved to their spacious Maine Road ground from their old Hyde Road Stadium.

They won the FA Cup in 1934 with Frank Swift in goal, and three years later won their

first League championship. When they won their second championship over 30 years later they were managed by two of the game's great characters, Malcolm Allison and Joe Mercer. They took City to League, FA Cup, League Cup and European honours as they enjoyed a spell as the top Manchester club once more.

Their Maine Road ground has attracted the biggest crowd for a soccer game in England outside Wembley Stadium.

Ground: Maine Road
Nickname: Blues or Citizens
Record attendance: 84,569 – v Stoke C (FA Cup 6th round), 3 March 1934
First Football League season: 1892-93 (as Ardwick FC) Division 2 (5th)
Seasons in Football League: 86 (65 Division 1, 21 Division 2)

Diego Maradona, one of South America's most talented footballers

Honours
Division 1 champions 1936-37, 1967-68
Division 2 champions 1898-99, 1902-03, 1909-10, 1927-28, 1946-47, 1965-66
FA Cup winners 1904, 1934, 1956, 1969
Football League Cup winners 1970, 1976
European Cup-winners' Cup winners 1970
Footballers of the Year
Don Revie (FWA) 1955
Bert Trautmann (FWA) 1956
Tony Book (FWA, shared) 1969

Manchester United

Manchester United was founded in 1878 by workmen from the Lancashire and Yorkshire Railway. They took their name, Newton Heath, from a local railway shed. They joined the Football Alliance in 1889 and in 1892 were accepted into the newly enlarged 1st division of the Football league.

Within two years they were bottom of the table and facing bankruptcy, but a fund-raising exercise saved the club. Another financial crisis hit the club and it was only thanks to benefactor John Davies that the club was saved. In 1902 he changed the name to Manchester United and moved the club to Old Trafford, where they played their first game in 1910. They had won their first League title in 1908 and in their first full season at Old Trafford lifted the title a second time. In between they had won the FA Cup.

During the inter-war period United spent nine seasons in the 2nd division, and in 1934 narrowly missed the drop to the 3rd. But after the war, following the appointment of Matt Busby as manager, United became one of the country's top sides and under him won five League titles and the FA Cup twice.

His youthful and successful team, known as the Busby Babes, was devastated in one of football's most notorious tragedies, the Munich air crash, in 1958. Matt Busby rebuilt the team and in 1968 they reached the pinnacle of the club's history by beating Benfica to win the European Cup, the trophy Busby had been chasing for more than ten years.

Since Busby retired United has had a succession of managers but none have been able to restore the League championship to the Old Trafford trophy room.

Ground: Old Trafford
Nickname: Red Devils
Record attendance: 76,962 – Wolverhampton W v Grimsby T (FA Cup semi-final) 25 March 1939
Club record: 70,504 – v Aston Villa (Division 1), 27 Dec 1920
First Football League season: 1892-93 Division 1 (16th)
Seasons in Football League: 86 (64 Division 1, 22 Division 2)

Honours
Division 1 champions 1907-08, 1910-11, 1951-52, 1955-56, 1956-57, 1964-65, 1966-67
Division 2 champions 1935-36, 1974-75
FA Cup winners 1909, 1948, 1963, 1977, 1983, 1985
European Cup winners 1968
Footballers of the Year Johnny Carey (FWA) 1949, Bobby Charlton (FWA) 1966, George Best (FWA) 1968, Mark Hughes (PFA) 1989
European Footballers of the Year
Denis Law 1964, Bobby Charlton 1966, George Best 1968
Manager of the Year Matt Busby 1968

Maradona, Diego (1960-)

South American countries have produced a host of talented footballers over the years. Occasionally a brilliant star emerges: first there was Pele, and now there is Diego Maradona.

Born in Argentina, he started his career with a local Buenos Aires youth team Los Cebollitos (Little Onions). A talent scout recommended him to the little known Argentinian 1st division team Argentinos Juniors, who signed the entire 'Little Onions' team.

Maradona became Argentina's youngest international in 1977 at 16 and 4 months when he played against Hungary. Two years later he skippered Argentina to win the 1979 World Youth Cup in Japan. He was then transferred to Boca Juniors for £1 million. In June 1982 he moved to Barcelona for a world record fee of about £5 million, and in 1984 Napoli broke the world record when they paid approximately £6.9 million for his services.

Maradona skippered Argentina to a great World Cup success in Mexico in 1986 despite a controversial goal against England.

Born: 30 October 1960, Lanus, Argentina
International caps: 64
Honours
Italian League 1987
Italian Cup 1987
Spanish Cup 1983
Awards
South American Footballer of the Year 1979, 1980
World Player of the Year 1986

Matthews, Sir Stanley (1915-)

Known as the 'Wizard of the Dribble' because of his close ball control, Stanley Matthews was the biggest crowd-puller in the 1950s.

Born in Hanley, Stoke-on-Trent, the son of a boxing barber, Matthews joined his home-town team Stoke City and in 1932 played for the Potters in the 2nd division at the age of 17. Two years later he made his international debut for England against Wales. He won a total of 54 caps, not including war-time and victory appearances for England.

In May 1947 he joined Blackpool for £11,500, despite a local public outcry.

He played for Blackpool in the 1948 FA Cup

Stanley Matthews during his first spell at his home-town team, Stoke City

final and was on the losing side against Manchester United. It was the same story against Newcastle in 1951 and in 1953 it looked like being a third losers' medal with 20 minutes to go when Blackpool trailed Bolton 3-1. But Matthews turned on a brilliant display and tore apart the Bolton defence. Blackpool won 4-3 and the match, one of the greatest seen at Wembley, is hailed as the 'Matthews Cup final'.

Matthews returned to Stoke in 1961 and the fans flooded back through the gates of the Victoria Ground. He helped Stoke into the 1st division and when he played his 701st and last Football League game on 6 February 1965 he was 50 years and 5 days old. Matthews now lives in Canada.

Born: 1 February 1915, Hanley, Stoke-on-Trent
Football League debut: 19 March 1932 Stoke C v Bury
Football League appearances: 701 (322 Stoke C, 379 Blackpool)
Football League goals: 71 (54 Stoke C, 17 Blackpool)
International caps: 54
Honours
FA Cup 1953
Awards
Footballer of the Year (FWA) 1948, 1963
European Footballer of the Year 1956

Right: Two of the game's great characters of the 1970s, Dave Watson (left) and Joe Jordan, during an all-Manchester battle

Below: One of the most talented players to wear a Manchester United shirt, George Best (red shirt, centre)

Medals

Individual British records

Most FA Cup winners'
5 — Charles Wollaston (Wanderers) 1872-73, 1876-78
5 — Lord Kinnaird (Wanderers) 1873, 1877-78, (Old Etonians) 1879, 1882
5 — James Forrest (Blackburn R) 1884-86, 1890-91

Most Scottish Cup
8 — Charles Campbell (Queen's Park) 1874-76, 1880-82, 1884-86

Most Football League championship (1st Division)

8 — Phil Neal (Liverpool)	1975-76, 1976-77, 1978-79, 1979-80, 1981-82, 1982-83, 1983-84, 1985-86
7 — Phil Thompson (Liverpool)	1972-73, 1975-76, 1976-77, 1978-79, 1979-80, 1981-82, 1982-83
7 — Alan Hansen (Liverpool)	1978-79, 1979-80, 1981-82, 1982-83, 1983-84, 1985-86, 1987-88
6 — Ray Kennedy (Liverpool/Arsenal)	1970-71, 1975-76, 1976-77, 1978-79, 1979-80, 1981-82
6 — Kenny Dalglish (Liverpool)	1978-79, 1979-80, 1981-82, 1982-83, 1983-84, 1985-86

Most in career

25 — Kenny Dalglish (Celtic and Liverpool) between 1970-85

● Many Scotsmen have won Scottish and English FA Cup winners' medals but only one *Englishman* has achieved the feat:
John Welford, Aston Villa 1895, Celtic 1899

● The only man to win Cup-winners' medals in England, Scotland and Ireland is Jimmy Delaney. His tally was as follows:

1937 Scottish FA Cup – Celtic
1948 English FA Cup – Manchester United
1954 Irish FA Cup – Derry City

Delaney also collected a runners-up medal with Cork Athletic in the FA of Ireland Cup in 1956.

Milk Cup

See *Football League Cup*

Moore, Bobby (1941-)

In 1964 Bobby Moore led West Ham up the Wembley steps after the Londoners beat Preston to win the FA Cup. A year later on the same pitch he led his club to victory over Munich 1860 in the European-Cup winners' Cup. And in 1966 he completed a unique treble by skippering England to their World Cup win.

Moore captained his country 92 times during his 11-year international career between 1962-73 when he made a record 108 appearances.

Brought up in the West End of London, he turned pro. with West Ham in 1958 and made the first of over 500 league appearances for the

Hammers later that same year.

After just 12 international appearances in May 1963, Alf Ramsey appointed Moore as England's youngest ever captain. He was seen as the man to lead England to the World Cup. How right Sir Alf was!

After 16 years at Upton Park Bobby Moore joined Fulham in 1974 and under him the 2nd division club reached the 1977 FA Cup final. But it was defeat for Moore this time as they lost to . . . West Ham. He eventually retired in 1977 and became a director and later manager of Southend United.

England and West Ham captain Bobby Moore

Born: 12 April 1941, Barking Essex
Football League debut: 8 September 1958 v Manchester United
Football League appearances: 668 (544 West Ham U, 124 Fulham)
Football League goals: 25 (24 West Ham U, 1 Fulham)
International caps: 108

Honours
World Cup 1966
European Cup-winners' Cup 1965
FA Cup 1964
Awards
Footballer of the Year (FWA) 1964

BB

Name changes

Football League clubs

Current name	Previous name(s)
Arsenal	Dial Square, Royal Arsenal, Woolwich Arsenal, The Arsenal
Barnsley	Barnsley St Peter's
Birmingham City	Small Heath Alliance, Small Heath, Birmingham
Blackpool	South Shore
Bolton Wanderers	Christ Church
AFC Bournemouth	Boscombe St John's, Boscombe, Bournemouth & Boscombe Athletic
Brighton & Hove Albion	Brighton United, Brighton & Hove Rangers
Bristol City	Bristol South End
Bristol Rovers	Black Arabs, Eastville Rovers, Bristol Eastville Rovers
Burnley	Burnley Rovers
Cambridge United	Abbey United
Cardiff City	Riverside, Riverside Albion
Chester City	Chester
Coventry City	Singers
Everton	St Domingo
Fulham	Fulham St Andrew's
Gillingham	New Brompton
Grimsby Town	Grimsby Pelham
Hartlepool United	West Hartlepool, Hartlepools United, Hartlepool
Leicester City	Leicester Fosse
Leeds United	Hunslet, Leeds City
Leyton Orient	Glyn Cricket & Football Club, Eagle, Orient, Clapton Orient, Leyton Orient, Orient
Manchester City	West Gorton, Gorton, Ardwick
Manchester United	Newton Heath LYR
Milwall	Millwall Rovers, Millwall Athletic
Newcastle United	Newcastle West End, Newcastle East End
Oldham Athletic	Pine Villa
Oxford United	Headington United
Plymouth Argyle	Argyle Athletic Club
Portsmouth	Portsmouth Town
Port Vale	Burslem Port Vale
Queen's Park Rangers	St Jude's Institute, St Jude's
Rochdale	Rochdale Town
Rotherham United	Thornhill United, Rotherham County
Scunthorpe United	Scunthorpe & Lindsey United
Sheffield Wednesday	The Wednesday
Southampton	Southampton St Mary's
Southend United	Southend Athletic
Stockport County	Heaton Norris Rovers, Heaton Norris
Stoke City	Stoke
Sunderland	Sunderland & District Teachers'
Swansea City	Swansea Town
Torquay United	Torquay Town
Tottenham Hotspur	Hotspur
Walsall	Walsall Town; Walsall Town Swifts
Watford	Hertfordshire Rangers, Watford Rovers
West Bromwich Albion	West Bromwich Strollers
West Ham United	Thames Ironworks
Wimbledon	Wimbledon Old Centrals
Wolverhampton Wanderers	St Lukes

The last club to change its name was Leyton Orient who reverted to one of its former names in 1987 after 21 years as Orient.

Scottish League clubs

Current name	Previous name
Ayr United	Ayr
Dundee United	Dundee Hibernians
East Stirling	East Stirlingshire-Clydebank
Hibernian	The Hibernians
Meadowbank Thistle	Ferranti Thistle

Nets

See *Goal Nets*

Newcastle United

One of the great institutions of British football, Newcastle United were founded in 1882 as Newcastle West End and played on the Leazes at a ground called St James's Park. In 1883 they merged with bitter rivals East End who played on a tiny ground at Heaton, but had a better playing squad. Ten years later the club changed its name to Newcastle United FC on being elected to the Football League.

Newcastle won promotion to the 1st division in 1898 and that is where they stayed until 1934, by which time they had won the League four times and the FA Cup on three occasions.

During the inter-war era Newcastle had the great Scottish forward Hughie Gallacher in their ranks and in five seasons he scored a remarkable total of 133 League goals. After winning the cup in 1932 Newcastle had little success again until after the Second World War when they won the FA Cup three times in five years between 1951 and 1955, skippered first by Joe Harvey and then by Jimmy Scoular.

The Geordie fans have always been loyal to their team and during the 1970s when they had little to cheer they still filed through the gates at St James' Park in their thousands.

Ground: St James' Park
Nickname: Magpies
Record attendance: 68, 386 – v Chelsea (Division 1), 3 Sept 1930
First Football League season: 1893-94 Division 2 (4th)
Seasons in Football League: 85 (63 Division 1, 22 Division 2)

Honours

Division 1 champions 1904-05, 1906-1907, 1908-09, 1926-27
Division 2 champions 1964-65
FA Cup winners 1910, 1924, 1932, 1951, 1952, 1955
European Fairs Cup winners 1969
Texaco Cup winners 1974, 1975
Anglo-Italian Cup winners 1973

North American Soccer League (NASL)

The North American Soccer League (NASL) was formed in 1968 following the merger of the United States Soccer Association and National

● When they joined the Scottish League in 1974 Ferranti Thistle were asked to change their name because it had commercial connections. They chose the name Meadowbank Thistle because they play at the Meadowbank Stadium.

Professional Soccer League.   The format of the League varied over the years depending on how many teams took part. Divisional champions met in play-offs each season for the title, with the exception of 1969 when only five teams competed in the League.

In the 1970s clubs recruited big name stars like Pele, Franz Beckenbauer, Johan Cruyff and George Best, and crowds often exceeded 70,000. However, interest declined when the big names drifted back to Europe and South America and in 1985 the NASL folded.
(see also *Major Indoor Soccer League*)

Northern Premier League

Formed in 1968-69 by an amalgamation of teams from the Cheshire League, Midland League and Northern League, it is now one of the three feeder Leagues into the GM Vauxhall Conference. The champions automatically get promoted to the Conference, subject to ground suitability.

Following sponsorship from Multipart in 1984 the League became known as the Multipart League for two seasons. Without a sponsor it reverted to being called the Northern Premier League in 1986-87 but, in November 1987, changed its name again to the HFS Loans League following a three-year sponsorship deal with Home Financial Services.

Since 1987-88 there have been two divisions, the Premier and the 1st division.

Nottingham Forest

Forest is one of the oldest clubs in the country, having been formed in 1865. Between then and 1898 they played at no fewer than seven different homes including the Forest Racecourse and Trent Bridge Cricket ground. When they were

NASL

Champions		Most Valuable Player
1967	USSA: Los Angeles Wolves	
	NPSL: Oakland Clippers	Ruben Navarro (Philadelphia Spartans)
1968	Atlanta Chiefs	John Kowalik (Chicago Mustangs)
1969	Kansas City Spurs	Cirilio Fernandez (Kansas Coty Spurs)
1970	Rochester Lancers	Carlos Metidieri (Rochester Lancers)
1971	Dallas Tornado	Carlos Metidieri (Rochester Lancers)
1972	New York Cosmos	Randy Horton (New York Cosmos)
1973	Philadelphia Atoms	Warren Archibald (Miami Toros)
1974	Los Angeles Aztecs	Peter Silvester (Baltimore Comets)
1975	Tampa Bay Rowdies	Steven David (Miami Toros)
1976	Toronto Metro-Croatia	Pele (New York Cosmos)
1977	New York Cosmos	Franz Beckenbauer (New York Cosmos)
1978	New York Cosmos	Mike Flanagan (New England Tea Men)
1979	Vancouver Whitecaps	Johan Cruyff (Los Angeles Aztecs)
1980	New York Cosmos	Roger Davies (Seattle Sounders)
1981	Chicago Sting	Georgio Chinaglia (New York Cosmos)
1982	New York Cosmos	Peter Ward (Seattle Sounders)
1983	Tulsa Roughnecks	Roberto Cabavia (New York Cosmos)
1984	Chicago Sting	Steve Zungul (Golden Bay Earthquakes)

Northern Premier League

Champions (Premier Division only)

1968-69	Macclesfield Town	1979-80	Mossley
1969-70	Macclesfield Town	1980-81	Runcorn
1970-71	Wigan Athletic	1981-82	Bangor City
1971-72	Stafford Rangers	1982-83	Gateshead
1972-73	Boston United	1983-84	Barrow
1973-74	Boston United	1984-85	Stafford Rangers
1974-75	Wigan Athletic	1985-86	Gateshead
1975-76	Runcorn	1986-87	Macclesfield Town
1976-77	Boston United	1987-88	Chorley
1977-78	Boston United	1988-89	Barrow
1978-79	Mossley		

elected into the 1st division in 1892 they played at the Town Ground. Six years later they moved to the City Ground which has been their home ever since.

Before the Second World War Forest spent their time between the top two divisions and in

Jackie Millburn heads Newcastle into the lead after less than a minute of the 1955 FA Cup final against Manchester City

Right: Nigel Clough, son of Nottingham Forest manager, Brian

Below: Congratulations to Trevor Francis after scoring Forest's winning goal in the 1979 European Cup final against Malmo

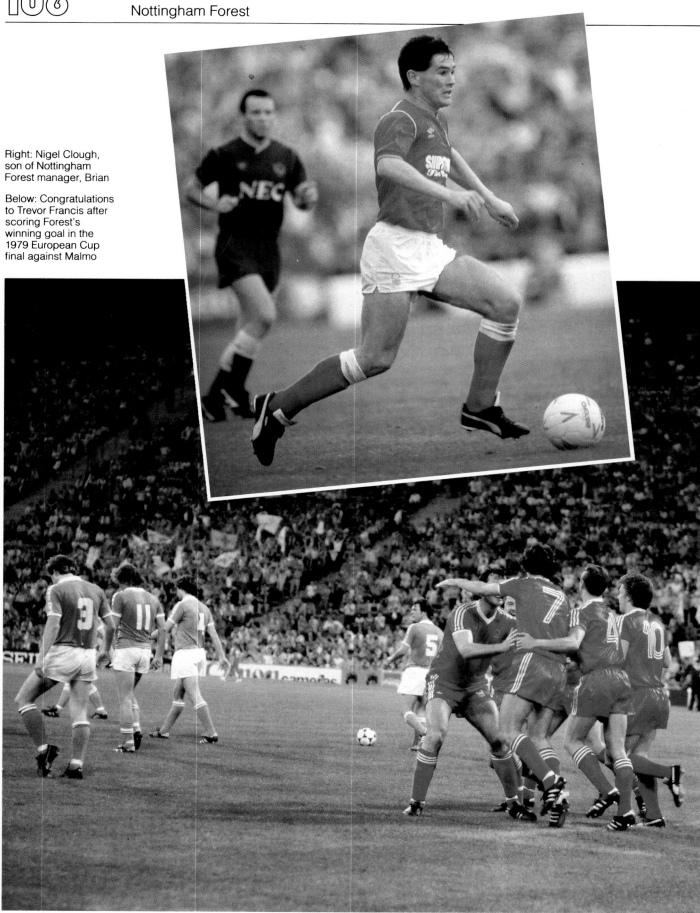

Soccer American style ... the player in white is Johan Cruyff

1949 they were relegated to the 3rd division (south). It was not until the arrival of Brian Clough at the City Ground in 1975 that the fortunes of Nottingham Forest took a turn for the better. He took them out of the 2nd division and to the 1st division title in successive seasons. Since then they have become one of the hardest clubs to beat as Clough has constantly moulded one successful team after another.

Before Clough's arrival, all the club had to show for its 110 years existence was two FA Cup wins and three minor League titles. Since the arrival of one of the game's shrewdest managers, Forest have won the 1st Division, Football League Cup twice, and the European Champions' Cup twice. Not to mention the likes of the Anglo-Scottish Cup and European Super Cup.

The shrewd buying of class players like Kenny Burns, John O'Hare, Peter Shilton, Trevor Francis, John McGovern, John Robertson, Gary Birtles and so on helped Forest win most of the game's top honours since the late 1970s.

Ground: City Ground
Nickname: Reds or Forest
Record attendance: 49,945 — v Manchester U (Division 1), 28 Oct 1967
First Football League season: 1892-93 Division 1 (10th)
Seasons in Football League: 86 (48 Division 1, 36 Division 2, 2 Division 3(s))

Honours

Division 1 champions 1977-78
Division 2 champions 1906-07, 1921-22
Division 3(S) champions 1950-51
FA Cup winners 1898, 1959
Football League Cup winners 1978, 1979, 1989
Anglo-Scottish Cup winners 1977
Simod Cup Winners 1989
European Cup winners 1979, 1980
European Super Cup winners 1979
European Team of the Year 1979
Footballers of the Year
Kenny Burns (FWA) 1978
Peter Shilton (PFA) 1978
Manager of the Year
Brian Clough 1978

Numbers

Players first wore numbers on their backs in two league games on 25 August 1928. Arsenal players wore them in the 1st division game against Sheffield Wednesday, and at Stamford Bridge, Chelsea players wore them against Swansea Town in a 2nd division fixture.

The first time numbers were worn in an FA Cup final was in 1933. The players were numbered from 1-22 starting with the Everton 'keeper Ted Sagar who wore No.1 through to the City goalkeeper Langford who wore No.22.

The numbering of players did not become compulsory until after the Football League's AGM in 1939.

Oddities

Aldershot's most capped player is Peter Scott of Northern Ireland. Scott is also York's most capped player. Coincidentally, Aldershot and York are the first and last teams in the Football league alphabetically . . .

Liverpool's Peter Beardsley once conceded a hat-trick in a Football League game . . . Playing for Newcastle United against West Ham on 21 April 1986, regular 'keeper Martin Thomas went off injured after letting in four first-half goals. Chris Hepworth then went in but dislocated a collar bone after conceding one goal. Beardsley then took over and let in three goals as the Hammers ran out the 8-1 winners.

Former Wimbledon assistant Manager Alan Gillett took charge of Japanese side Fujita in 1988 to become the first Englishman to coach in Japan.

Billy Holmes of Southport scored a hat-trick against Carlisle United on 30 October 1954 . . . he got married on the morning of the match.

August Starek holds the unique distinction of winning League championship medals with three different clubs in successive years. He won his first in 1967 with Rapid Vienna in the Austrian League and the second with FC Nuremburg in the German Bundesliga a year later. He completed the hat-trick with Bayern Munich in 1969.

A total of 121 different clubs have appeared in the Football League since 1888. Grimsby Town and Lincoln City have met a record 116 of them.

In 1965-66 Liverpool used only 14 players in winning the 1st division title. Aston Villa emulated their record in 1980-81. At the other end of the scale Darwen went through 45 players during their 2nd division campaign in 1898-99.

The most amazing recovery in a Football League was by Charlton Athletic against Huddersfield Town at the Valley on 21 December 1957. Trailing 5-1 with 28 minutes to go many of the 12,500 spectators made their way home having seen enough. But what a thrilling end they missed. Charlton scored five quick goals before Huddersfield equalised five minutes from time. But in the last minute Charlton scored the 13th and final goal of a remarkable match to win 7-6.

On 16 September 1967 Arsenal forward George Graham got married; his best man was Spurs forward Terry Venables. Later that same day the two men opposed each other in the north London derby, which Arsenal won 4-0. They renewed their rivalry when they became managers of the same two teams in the 1980s.

Gordon Nisbet made his Football League debut for West Brom as a goalkeeper. His next appearance was at full back, which is where he played the remainder of his career. In 1965-66

Luton Town 'promoted' their goalkeeper Tony Rad to striker. He scored 12 League goals that season, including a hat-trick in the 5-1 win over Notts County on 20 November 1965.

In 1888 West Brom and Renton, the English and Scottish Cup holders, met in a challenge match billed as the championship of the world. It was played at Hampden Park on 19 May, and Renton won 4-0.

Offside

The offside rule, which states that there must be *two defenders between a player kicking the ball in the opponent's half and the goal-line*, has been the biggest single influence in styling the modern game.

A form of offside rule has existed since the mid-1800s when Harrow school made it unlawful to receive a ball from a forward pass. This restriction made soccer a dribbling game.

The Cambridge Rules of 1848 allowed forward passes but *more* than three players had to be between the receiving player and the goal-line.

It was not until 1873 that the laws of the game referred to a player being offside at *the moment of kicking*, and in 1880 the part of the law relating to a player not being offside *if the ball was last played by an opponent* was incorporated.

Goal kicks had always been exempted from the offside rule and in 1881-82 corner kicks were also exempted. Offside was restricted to the *opponent's half of the field* in 1907, and throw-ins were exempted from the offside rule in 1921.

In 1925 following a proposal from the Scottish FA, the number of defenders needed between the receiving player and goal-line was reduced to two.

Oldest players

The *oldest player to appear in the Football League* is Neil McBain who was 52 years 4 months when

Neil McBain (defending) is the oldest Football League player at 52 years 4 months

Action from the 1988
Olympic final between
the Soviet Union and
Brazil. The Soviets won
2–1 after extra time

he played for New Brighton against Hartlepools United in the 3rd division (north) on 15 March 1947. McBain, an ex-Manchester United defender, was manager of New Brighton at the time, and helped out their injury crisis by playing in goal.

As McBain was born in Scotland, it means the *oldest Englishman to play in the Football League* was Bob Suter who was 50 years 9 months when he played for Halifax Town against Darlington on 24 April 1929.

The *oldest player to represent his country in a full international* is Billy Meredith who played for Wales against England at Highbury at the age of 45 years 8 months. Coincidentally the date of the match was the same as McBain's record

breaking appearance, 15 March, but 27 years earlier in 1920.

The *only player to appear in the 1st division over the age of 50* is Stanley Matthews who played his 701st and final Football League game on 6 February 1965 for Stoke City against Fulham. He was 50 years and 5 days at the time.

The *oldest player to appear in an FA Cup final* is Walter Hampson who was 41 years 257 days when he played for Newcastle United against Aston Villa on 26 April 1924.

The *oldest player to make his Football League debut* was Andy Cunningham who was 38 years 2 days old when he made his debut for Newcastle United in the 1st division game against Leicester City on 2 February 1929.

Origins

The exact origins of football are uncertain. Ancient Greeks and Romans certainly played some form of game with a ball, but what form it took is uncertain. A game which involved kicking and carrying a ball was played by the Chinese, Turks and Egyptians in ancient times. The Romans most probably brought football to Britain and there is evidence of it being played on a large scale in William the Conqueror's time.

By the beginning of the 19th century football began to take shape in a form that would be recognisable today. It was played largely in the public schools and universities, all of which had their own rules. In 1848 a meeting of public schools at Cambridge to bring some uniformity to the rules drew up the 'Cambridge Rules'.

Clubs sprang up in the provinces and one of the hotbeds of football by the mid-1800s was the Sheffield area. The Sheffield club was formed in 1855: they are the oldest football club still in existence.

Despite the Cambridge Rules, to which many clubs and schools played, there were still other forms of the game and in 1863 the Football Association was formed with the intention of standardising the game. Their part in the growth and development of British soccer, and their influence on the game worldwide, is apparent when one looks at the number of countries in

The *oldest player to make his international debut* was Leslie Compton who was 38 years 2 months when he played for England against Wales at Roker Park, Sunderland, on 15 November 1950.

Olympic Games

Soccer was first played in the Olympic Games in 1900 but the competition was not regarded as official. That was also the case in 1904, but since 1908 soccer has been officially recognised at the Games.

Because of the strength of the Eastern-bloc nations, FIFA ruled that from 1984 any player who appeared in the previous World Cup could not play in the Olympic competition.

Olympic Games

Unofficial finals

1900	Upton Park FC (GB) 4	UFSA (France) 0	
1904	Galt FC, Ontario (Canada) 7	Christian Brothers College (USA) 1	
1906	Denmark 5	Smyrna (Greece) 1	

Official finals

1908	Great Britain 2	Denmark 0
1912	Great Britain 4	Denmark 2
1920	Belgium 2	Czechoslovakia 0*
1924	Uruguay 3	Switzerland 0
1928	Uruguay 2	Argentina 1 (after 1-1 draw)
1936	Italy 2	Austria 1 (aet)
1948	Sweden 3	Yugoslavia 1
1952	Hungary 2	Yugoslavia 0
1956	USSR 1	Yugoslavia 0
1960	Yugoslavia 3	Denmark 1
1964	Hungary 2	Czechoslovakia 1
1968	Hungary 4	Bulgaria 1
1972	Poland 2	Hungary 1
1976	East Germany 3	Poland 1
1980	Czechoslovakia 1	East Germany 0
1984	France 2	Brazil 0
1988	USSR 2	Brazil 1 (aet)

* Czechoslovakia walked off the field in protest against the referee. Spain were awarded the silver medal.

● Record score: 17-1 Denmark v France 'A' 1908.
● Italy and Uruguay have both won the World Cup and Olympic title.
● Since the Football Association stopped recognising amateurs in 1972, a Great Britain team has not entered the Olympic Games.

German–born Bert Trautmann was a prisoner-of-war in England and stayed to pursue a career with Manchester City. He was the hero of the 1956 FA Cup final and played the last stages with a broken neck

which soccer is now played, all of which started playing the game to the rules of the Football Association.

Overseas players

In recent years there has been a big influx of overseas players into the Football League. The first to play in the League is believed to have been Max Seeburg, a German who played for Chelsea, Tottenham Hotspur, Burnley, Grimsby Town and Reading between 1907-14.

Own goals

In major finals

European Cup

Antonio Ramellets (Barcelona) v Benfica 1961

European Cup-winners' Cup

Dansky (MTK Budapest) v Sporting Lisbon 1964
Ron Yeats (Liverpool) v Borussia Dortmund 1966
Lanzi (AC Milan) v FC Magdeburg 1974

Fairs Cup/UEFA Cup

Brian Farmer (Birmingham C) v AS Roma, 2nd leg 1961
Van Daele (Feyenoord) v Tottenham H, 1st leg 1974

FA Cup

Lord Kinnaird (Oxford U) v Wanderers 1877
Bert Turner (Charlton A) v Derby C 1947
Mick McGrath (Blackburn R) v Wolverhampton W 1960
Tommy Hutchison (Manchester C) v Tottenham H 1981
Gary Mabbutt (Tottenham H) v Coventry C 1987
Turner, Hutchison and Mabbutt all scored for both sides in an FA Cup final.

Football League Cup

Roger Kenyon (Everton) v Aston Villa 1977
Gordon Chisholm (Sunderland) v Norwich C 1985

The *first own goal in the Football League* was scored on the opening day (8 September 1888) by George Cox of Aston Villa against Wolverhampton Wanderers.

The *quickest own goal* was scored by Pat Kruse of Torquay United just 8 seconds after the start of their 4th division game with Cambridge United on 3 January 1977.

Two men have *scored two goals for each side in a Football League game*. The first was Sam Wynne who scored two for his own team, Oldham Athletic, and two for Manchester United, in the 2nd division game on 6 October 1923. The feat was equalled by Aston Villa's Chris Nicholl on 20 March 1976 when he scored two for each side in the 1st division game against Leicester City.

Paisley, Bob (1919-)

Unquestionably the most successful manager in Football League history, Bob Paisley has won 13 major British and European honours; his nearest rivals Matt Busby and Bill Nicholson have each won eight.

Paisley has devoted nearly 50 years of his life

to Liverpool FC. He joined them as a player in 1939 shortly after winning an Amateur Cup winners' medal with Bishop Auckland. However, the Second World War intervened and he didn't make his League debut until 1946. A tough tackling wing-half, Paisley played for Liverpool 278 times. As a member of the championship winning team in 1946-47 he scored the goal against Everton that took the Reds to Wembley in 1950 but he was left out of the final team.

He retired in 1954 and joined the backroom staff and learned his managerial skills under men like Don Welsh, Phil Taylor and Bill Shankly, the man Paisley replaced in 1974.

In his nine seasons in charge at Anfield Paisley led the club to six championships; the Milk Cup on three occasions; three European Cup triumphs

and a UEFA Cup; win. Sadly, as in his playing days, he was not to enjoy FA Cup glory.

Since handing over to Joe Fagan in 1983 Paisley has continued to play a backroom role in the most successful English club and is still an adviser to current manager Kenny Dalglish.

Born: 23 January 1919, Hetton-le-Hole, Co. Durham
Football League debut: 7 Sept 1946 v Chelsea
Football League appearances: 253
Football League goals: 10
Honours
Player Division 1 1946-47
Manager Division 1 1975-76, 1976-77, 1978-79, 1979-80, 1981-82, 1982-83
European Cup 1977, 1978, 1981
UEFA Cup 1976
Milk Cup 1981, 1982, 1983
European Super Cup 1977
Awards
Manager of the Year 1976, 1977, 1979, 1980, 1982, 1983

Opposite: Kaz Deyna of Manchester City (right). An Olympic gold medallist with Poland in 1972, he went on to win 100 caps for his country

Left: Southampton's Chris Nicholl once scored two goals for each side in a 1st division game while he was at Aston Villa

The most successful manager in Football League history, Bob Paisley

Pele (1940-)

Brazilian-born Pele, Edson Arantes do Nascimento, was the greatest player ever to grace a football field. He was born into poverty in a small town 150 miles south of Sao Paulo but went on to become one of the world's best known sportsmen.

His first club was the tiny Noroste team and manager Di Breito was so impressed he took the youngster along to Santos for a trial. Until Pele popularised it, the name Santos was little known except as the port for Sao Paulo.

He was the regular wearer of the Santos No.10 shirt at 16 and made his debut for Brazil, scoring a goal in the 2-1 win over Argentina in July 1957. He was only 17 when he won his first World Cup winners' medal in Sweden the following year.

After more than 1,000 games for Santos, and over 1,000 first-class goals, Pele retired after playing his last game against Ponte Preta on 2 October 1974. Santos retired his No.10 shirt.

A year later he came out of retirement and joined the US football bandwagon in a $4 million dollar deal that took him to New York Cosmos. He played his last game for them in 1977, before a crowd of 75,000.

In 1989 the Pele Cup for international teams of over-35s was launched in Brazil.

Pele is still popular the world over and is often a guest at major footballing events as well as lending his valuable knowledge to broadcasting companies as a commentator and summariser.

Born: 23 October 1940, Tres Coracoes, Mina Gerais, Brazil
International caps: 111
Honours
World Cup 1958, 1962, 1970
World Club championship 1962-63 (Santos)
Sao Paulo League championship 1956, 1958-62, 1964-65, 1967-69 (all with Santos)
Brazilian Cup 1962-64, 1968 (all Santos)
Awards
South American Footballer of the Year 1973

Penalty

The penalty kick was adopted by the Football Association in 1891-92 (the Irish FA had introduced it the season before). The *first player to score from the penalty spot in the Football League* was John Heath of Wolverhampton Wanderers against Accrington on 14 September 1891. Alex McCall of Renton scored one against Leith Athletic on 22 August 1891, the first in Scotland.

The *most penalties converted by one player in a Football League season* is 13 by Francis Lee of Manchester City in 1971-72.

In 1988 Liverpool's John Aldridge became *the first player to miss a penalty in an FA Cup final at Wembley.* All other Wembley spot kicks were successfully converted, as follows:

George Mutch (Preston NE) v Huddersfield T, 1938
(Mutch converted his kick in the last minute of extra time to give Preston a 1-0 win)
Eddie Shimwell (Blackpool) v Manchester U, 1948

Pele scoring one of his 1280 first-class goals

Ronnie Allen (West Bromwich A) v Preston NE, 1954
Danny Blanchflower (Tottenham H) v Burnley, 1962
Kevin Reeves (Manchester C) v Tottenham H, 1981
Glenn Hoddle (Tottenham H) v Queen's Park R, 1982
Arnold Muhren (Manchester U) v Brighton & HA, 1983

1988 wasn't a good year for penalty takers at Wembley. In addition to Aldridge's miss in the FA Cup final, Nigel Winterburn of Arsenal missed a penalty in the Littlewood's Cup final against Luton town. He became the third player to miss a League Cup final spot-kick at Wembley. The others were:

Ray Graydon (Aston Villa) v Norwich C, 1975
Clive Walker (Sunderland) v Norwich C, 1985

● The most penalties saved in one game is three by Grimsby Town goalkeeper Walter Scott in the 2nd division game against Burnley on 13 February 1909. It didn't do him much good; Burnley won 2-0 . . . one of their goals came from another penalty, which Scott failed to save. Four is the most penalties awarded to one side in a Football League game.

● One of the costliest penalty misses was by Len Davies of Cardiff City against Birmingham in the final match of the 1923-24 season. The game ended 0-0: Had Davies scored Cardiff would have won the League Championship. They are still awaiting their first championship. Another costly miss was by Manchester city in the final match of the 1925-26 season against Newcastle United. City lost 3-2. A draw would have kept them in the 1st division.

● The longest penalty shoot-out in the world for a senior game was on 20 November 1988. Argentinos Juniors beat League leaders Racing Club 20-19 after 44 penalties in their Argentine League match.

Player of the year

See *Footballer of the Year*

Play-offs

As a result of the restructuring of the Football League in 1986-87 and 1987-88, end of season play-offs were arranged to arrive at the current format of 20 teams in the 1st division and 24 teams in the other three divisions.

Winners
1986-87
Div 1/2: Charlton A (retained 1st Division status)
Div 2/3: Swindon T (promoted from Division 3)
Div 3/4: Aldershot (promoted from Division 4)
1987-88
Div 1/2: Middlesbrough (promoted from Division 2)
Div 2/3: Wallsall (promoted from Division 3)
Div 3/4: Swansea C (promoted from Division 4)

– No team figured in the play-offs in both seasons.
– Chelsea was the only club to lose its 1st division status as a result of the play-offs.
– Aldershot and Swansea City both gained the best advantage from the new system, they were promoted after finishing 6th in the 4th division in 1986-87 and 1987-88 respectively.

The play-offs continued in 1988-89, but no longer had the relegation aspect as part of them. The current format is:

Division 1: Relegated: bottom three clubs (automatic)
Division 2: Promoted: top two clubs (automatic) plus
    winners of play-offs involving next four clubs
    Relegated: bottom three clubs (automatic)
Division 3: Promoted: top two clubs (automatic) plus
    winners of play-offs involving next four clubs
    Relegated: bottom four clubs (automatic)
Division 4: Promoted: top three clubs (automatic) plus
    winners of play-offs involving the next four clubs

(see also *Test matches*)

Points

From the formation of the Football League in 1888 to 1981 points allocation was 2 for a win and 1 for a draw. To encourage attacking football this was changed in 1981-82 to 3 points for a win, although the Scottish League retained the 2 points for a win system.

Most points in a season

Football League (2 pts for a win)

Pts.	(max)		Div	
74	(92)	Lincoln C	4	1975-76
72	(84)	Doncaster R	3N	1946-47
71	(92)	Watford	4	1977-78
70	(84)	Tottenham H	2	1919-20
70	(92)	Nottingham F	3S	1950-51
70	(92)	Bristol C	3S	1954-55
70	(92)	Aston Villa	3	1971-72
69	(92)	Lincoln C	3N	1951-52
69	(92)	Port Vale	3N	1953-54
69	(92)	Hull C	3	1965-66
69	(92)	Notts C	4	1970-71
68	(84)	Plymouth A	3S	1929-30
68	(84)	Liverpool	1	1978-79
68	(92)	Grimsby T	3N	1955-56
68	(92)	Bury	3	1960-61
68	(92)	Mansfield T	4	1974-75
68	(92)	Northampton T	4	1975-76
				(runners-up)

Football League (3 pts for a win)

Pts	(max)		Div	
102	(138)	Swindon T	4	1985-86
101	(138)	York C	4	1983-84
99	(138)	Northampton T	4	1986-87
98	(138)	Wimbledon	4	1982-83
97	(138)	Bournemouth	3	1986-87
96	(138)	Sheffield U	4	1981-82
95	(138)	Oxford U	3	1983-84

1st Division
90 (120) Liverpool, 1987-88
90 (126) Everton, 1984-85

Above: The world's greatest – Pele playing for New York Cosmos. Opposite: Pele playing for Brazil

2nd Division
88 (126) Luton T, 1981-82
88 (126) Chelsea, 1983-84
88 (126) Sheffield W, 1983-84 (runners-up)

Scottish League (2 pts for a win)

Pts	(max)		Div	
76	(84)	Rangers	1	1920-21
72	(88)	Celtic	P	1987-88

71	(84)	Rangers	1	1919-20
69	(72)	Morton	2	1966-67
69	(88)	Rangers	P	1986-87

Records for the other divisions
Div 1 (post 1975-76): 62 (78) St Mirren, 1976-77
Div 2 (post 1975-76): 63 (78) Forfar A, 1983-84
(Figures in brackets indicates max. points available)

Fewest points in a season

Football League (min 34 matches)

Because the early divisions of the Football League had only 12-16 teams comparisons with present days points totals are unfair.

Pts	(max)		Div	
8	(68)	Loughborough T	2	1899-1900
8	(68)	Doncaster R	2	1904-05
9	(68)	Darwen	2	1898-99
11	(80)	Rochdale	3N	1931-32
17	(84)	Tranmere R	2	1938-39
17	(84)	Stoke C	1	1984-85

Other divisions

Division 3:	21 (92) Rochdale, 1973-74	
	21 (92) Cambridge U, 1984-85	
Division 3(S):	21 (84) Merthyr T, 1924-25 and 1929-30	
	21 (84) Queen's Park R, 1925-26	
Division 4:	19 (92) Workington, 1976-77	

Portsmouth pulled off one of the biggest FA Cup final shocks in 1939 when they beat Wolves 4–1

Scottish League (min 30 games):

Premier Division:	11 (72) St Johnstone, 1975-76
Division 1 (pre 1975-76):	6 (60) Stirling A, 1954-55
Division 1 (post 1975-76):	10 (78) Queen of the South, 1988-89
Division 2 (pre 1975-76):	7 (68) Edinburgh C, 1936-37
Division 2 (post 1975-76):	16 (52) Meadowbank T, 1975-76
	16 (78) Berwick R, 1987-88*
	16 (78) Stranraer, 1987-88

*Did not finish bottom of the table
(In 1896-97 Abercorn completed their 18-game Scottish 1st division programme with just one win and one draw. Their 3 points is an all-time low for any British League club)

The following Football League clubs have had points deducted from them by the League:

	Div		Pts deducted
Sunderland	1	1890-91	2
Stockport C	3N	1926-27	2
Peterborough U	3	1967-68	19
Preston NE	2	1973-74	1
Newport C	4	1973-74	1
Aldershot	3	1974-75	1
Bristol R	3	1981-82	2
Mansfield T	4	1981-82	2
Tranmere R	4	1987-88	2
Halifax T	4	1987-88	1

All except Peterborough and Tranmere had their points deducted for fielding an ineligible player. Peterborough had their points deducted following financial irregularities and the deduction of the points assured them relegation from division 3 to division 4. Tranmere had their points deducted for failing to meet a fixture.

Portsmouth

Portsmouth rose to prominence in 1939 when they beat the mighty Wolves 4-1 at Wembley in one of the biggest shocks in FA Cup final history.

Founded in 1898 out of the old Portsmouth Town club, which was formed eight years earlier, 'Pompey' had the foresight to buy their Fratton Park ground in 1899 for a mere £4,950. After more than 20 years in the Western and Southern Leagues, Portsmouth became founder members of the 3rd division in 1920. They were promoted to the 2nd division in 1924 and three years later they began a 32-year spell in the top division.

The Second World War prevented any follow up to their 1939 cup success, but in the early post-war years they took the 1st division by storm, winning the title in 1949 and 1950. Guided by manager Bob Jackson, and including such notable players as Jimmy Scoular, Jimmy Dickinson and Jack Froggatt, 'Pompey' left the more fashionable teams in their wake.

In 1959 they lost their 1st division status when they finished bottom of the table with only 21 points. The slide continued and in 1978 they reached rock bottom, when they landed in the 4th division. Since then they have made a brief return to the top division, in 1987-88.

Ground: Fratton Park
Nickname: Pompey
Record attendance: 51,385 — v Derby County (FA Cup 6th round), 26 Feb 1949
First Football League season: 1920-21 Division 3 (12th)
Seasons in Football League: 62 (26 Division 1, 24 Division 2, 7 Division 3, 3 Division 3(S), 2 Division 4)

Honours

Division 1 champions 1948-49, 1949-50
Division 3 champions 1961-62, 1982-83
Division 3(S) champions 1923-24
FA Cup winners 1939

Postponements

The *most postponements of any first-class game* in Britain was during the winter of 1978-79 when the Scottish Cup second-round tie between Inverness Thistle and Falkirk was postponed 29 times because of weather. Falkirk eventually won when the game was played on 22 February 1979, 47 days after it was scheduled to have been played.

The *English record for a tie in the FA Cup* competition proper is 15 postponements of the Coventry City versus Lincoln city third-round tie in 1962-63.

Two winters have caused chaos to the Football League programme: 1946-47 and 1962-63. Twice in the later season only four games were played: 12 January 1963 and 2 February 1963. That season went on to 24 May and lasted 279 days. However, the 1946-47 season went on to 14 June and lasted a record 287 days. But 1962-63 was the worst on record for postponements, with over 400 games in England and Scotland called off during a six-week spell of bad weather.

Preston North End

'Proud' Preston may not enjoy the success their predecessors did, but they can claim the honour of being the first Football League champions 100 years ago. Furthermore their team of 'Invincibles' won the title without losing a game, and completed the League and Cup double without conceding a goal in the FA Cup.

The number of matches played in 1888-89 was considerably lower than today, as was the standard of opposition, but Preston's record will always stand. The record breaking does not stop there: in the 1887-88 FA Cup they beat Hyde United by a record 26-0, and when League soccer started their Jack Gordon had the distinction of scoring the first goal in the Football League.

Preston started life as the association football branch of the local cricket club, after it had abandoned its plans to play rugby. Their early successes were built around a Scotsman, William Sudell, who brought the 'art and science' of football to Deepdale. After their initial triumph in the new Football League, North End retained the title a year later but suddenly were no longer 'invincible' and dropped to the 2nd division.

It was not until George Mutch converted a last-minute penalty in extra time in the 1938 FA Cup final that a trophy returned to Preston. Despite the presence of the genius Tom Finney in the team in the 1950s, Preston often challenged for League and Cup honours but could not emulate their great 'Invincible' side, and North End, who have been runners-up 14 times in major competitions, have plummeted to the 4th division in recent years.

Ground: Deepdale
Nickname: Lilywhites, Invincibles, or North End
Record attendance: 42,684 — v Arsenal (Division 1), 23 April 1938
First Football League season: 1888-89 Football League (1st)
Seasons in Football League: 90 (46 Division 1, 31 Division 2, 11 Division 3, 2 Division 4)

Honours

Football League champions 1888-89, 1889-90
Division 2 champions 1903-04, 1912-13, 1950-51
Division 3 champions 1970-71
FA Cup winners 1889, 1938
Footballers of the Year
Tom Finney (FWA) 1954, 1957

Professional Footballers' Association (PFA)

There was an unsuccessful attempt to form a football players' union in 1893. A National Union of Association Players was, however, formed in 1898, but lasted only briefly.

The current body was formed in December 1907 as the Football Players' and Trainers' Union and affiliated to the TUC in 1908. The FA initially recognised the union but withdrew recognition when it joined the TUC, causing a rift between the two bodies which, happily, was healed at a meeting later that year.

Since then the Association, which changed its name to the PFA in 1958, has done much to improve standards for professional footballers, including negotiating better terms of contract between player and club.

The PFA also runs a benefit fund for players forced to quit the game early. The highlight of the PFA's calendar is its annual awards ceremony. (See *Footballer of the Year*).

Professionalism

Had it not been for professionalism creeping into soccer in the latter part of the 19th century, the game would never have grown to the proportions it has.

Between 1876 and 1885 northern clubs started paying players as the game became popular with working-class fans. The Football Association, which was run by middle- and upper-class officials, disapproved and so payments were made 'under-the-counter'. However, at a meeting on 20 July 1885 professionalism was legalised after many clubs, notably Preston North End, openly admitted to paying players.

Initially only northern and midland clubs followed Preston's move: southern clubs remained amateur until Luton Town in 1890, and Arsenal in 1891, turned professional.

The first professional is generally regarded as James Lang, who played for Clydesdale and Glasgow Eastern before joining Sheffield Wednesday in 1877. As he was not officially paid, the claim can never be fully substantiated, although Lang admitted in later life that he was the first Scot to move south in return for payment.

Following the adoption of professionalism, James Forrest of Blackburn Rovers was the first recognised professional to play for England. (see also *Amateur football*).

Promotion

Since 1898-99 automatic promotion and relegation has applied in the Football League; before then the 'ups and downs' were settled by a series of test matches.

This is how the promotion system has worked over the years:

From Division 2
1898-99 to 1972-73 Top two clubs promoted (in 1919-20 the 1st division was extended and Arsenal who finished fifth in the last 2nd division before the First World War were elected into the 1st division)
1973-1974 to 1985-86 Top three clubs promoted
1986-87 to present Top two automatically promoted, plus winners of play-offs

From Division 3
1920-21 Top club only promoted
1921-22 to 1957-58 Top club from each of the two 3rd division sections (north and south) automatically promoted
1958-59 to 1972-73 Top two clubs promoted
1973-74 to 1985-86 Top three clubs promoted
1986-87 to present Top two clubs promoted, plus winners of play-offs

From Division 4
1958-59 to 1985-86 Top four promoted automatically
1986-87 to present Top three clubs automatically promoted, plus winners of play-offs

● Five clubs have won the 1st division title the season after being promoted:

	Promoted	League Champions
Liverpool	1904-05	1905-06
Everton	1930-31	1931-32
Tottenham H	1949-50	1950-51
Ipswich T	1960-61	1961-62
Nottingham F	1976-77	1977-78

(all except Forest were promoted as 2nd division champions)

The following clubs have been promoted from the 3rd to the 1st division in consecutive seasons:
Charlton A 1935-37; Queen's Park R 1967-69

Since the reorganisation of the Scottish League in 1975-76 only two teams have gained promotion from the 2nd division to the Premier division in successive seasons:
Clydebank 1976-78; Dunfermline A 1986-88

Most
9 — Birmingham C, Grimsby T, Notts C
8 — Bolton W, Leicester C, Manchester C, Millwall, Preston NE, Sheffield W
7 — Bristol C, Cardiff C, Derby C, Doncaster R, Middlesbrough, Sheffield U

Ramsey, Sir Alf (1920-)

Dagenham-born Ramsey was a brilliant full-back in his playing days with Southampton and Tottenham Hotspur. He then became a shrewd and clever manager, turning the unfashionable

Ipswich Town into champions of the 2nd and 1st divisions in successive years, a feat he had achieved as a player with Spurs in 1950 and 1951. It was the way in which he developed players at Ipswich that made him the obvious successor to England manager Walter Winterbottom in 1963.

When he took the England job Ramsey vowed that he would guide his team to the World Cup final: three years later he did just that, and on home soil too.

The men who masterminded England's World Cup triumph: Alf Ramsey, the manager (left) and Harold Shepherdson, the physiotherapist

The man he appointed captain was to be the mainstay of his team. That man was of course Bobby Moore. Surrounded with other great players like Gordon Banks, Jackie Charlton, Bobby Charlton, Roger Hunt, Geoff Hurst and so on, England reached the 1966 World Cup final at Wembley and beat the West Germans 4-2 after a nerve-racking 90 minutes that went into extra time. For his services to football Ramsey was knighted in January 1967.

He took England to the quarter-finals four years later but in 1974 England failed to qualify for the final stages and the inevitable calling for his head resulted in his sacking early in the year.

Born: 22 January 1920, Dagenham, Essex
Football League debut: 26 Oct 1946 v Plymouth A
Football League appearances: 316
Football League goals: 32
International caps: 32
Honours
Player
Division 1 championship 1959-51 (Tottenham H)
Division 2 championship 1949-50 (Tottenham H)
Manager
World Cup 1966 (England)
Division 1 championship 1961-62 (Ipswich T)
Division 2 championship 1960-61 (Ipswich T)
Awards
PFA Merit Award 1986

Re-election

Before 1986-87 the bottom four clubs in the 4th division had to apply to the Football League for re-election at the League's AGM. The last four clubs to apply for re-election in 1986 were Exeter City, Cambridge United, Preston North End and Torquay United.

The following season re-election was scrapped and the bottom club in the 4th division automatically left the League and was replaced by the GM Vauxhall Conference League champions.

Since the early days of the League the bottom clubs have had to apply for re-election. Originally it was the bottom four clubs. When the 2nd division was formed in 1892, it was still the bottom four who had to apply for re-election, and then the bottom three and eventually the bottom two. When the two 3rd divisions came into being the bottom two clubs in each had to apply for re-election to the League each season, and this remained unaltered until the creation of the 3rd and 4th divisions in 1958 when it was the bottom four clubs in the 4th division who had to endure the nerve-racking experience of applying to retain their League status.

The following clubs have failed to be re-elected:

1889-90	Stoke C
1894-95	Walsall
1895-96	Port Vale
	Crewe A
1896-97	Burton W

1898-99	Blackpool
1899-1900	Loughborough T
1900-01	Walsall
1902-03	Doncaster R
1903-04	Stockport C
1904-05	Doncaster R
1906-07	Burton U
1907-08	Lincoln C
1908-09	Chesterfield
1909-10	Grimsby T
1910-11	Lincoln C
1911-12	Gainsborough T
1919-20	Lincoln C

Since the formation of the 3rd division in 1920, the comings-and-goings in the League has decreased. The following are the clubs unlucky with their application for their re-election in the period 1920-86, together with the clubs who replaced them.

		Replaced by:
1926-27	Aberdare A	Torquay U
1927-28	Durham C	Carlisle U
1928-29	Ashington	York C
1929-30	Merthyr T	Thames
1930-31	Newport C	Mansfield T
	Nelson	Chester
1937-38	Gillingham	Ipswich T
1950-51	New Brighton	Workington
1959-60	Gateshead	Peterborough U
1969-70	Bradford PA	Cambridge U
1971-72	Barrow	Hereford U
1976-77	Workington	Wimbledon
1977-78	Southport	Wigan A

Most applications for re-election:
(Since formation of 3rd division in 1920)
14 — Hartlepool(s) U
12 — Halifax T
11 — Barrow, Southport
10 — Crewe A, Rochdale, Newport C

Referee

The referee is the sole arbitrator in a game of soccer and his decision is final. He is aided by two linesmen whose task is to assist the referee, not to make decisions for him.

The first mention of a referee is in the rules of the game played at Cheltenham College in 1867. Most games at that time appointed umpires, normally two, to officiate at a match from a position outside the field of play.

The first official mention of a referee was in the FA Cup rules in 1871 when he was defined as being the person to make decisions should the two umpires not agree on any incident.

Umpires were first mentioned in the FA's laws in 1874 but it was not until 1880 that the referee first got a mention. In 1891 the umpires made way for linesmen and the referee took up a position from inside the playing area and became the sole arbitrator.

The Referees' Association was formed in 1893. From 1928 referees have been categorised (I, II and III) according to their ability. Class I referees officiate in games at senior level.

An argument that has raged over the years concerns the use of professional referees, but there is little proof that professional referees would serve the game any better than the dedicated amateur.

● The first time a whistle was used was in a game between Nottingham Forest and Sheffield Norfolk at Nottingham in 1878. Before that, referees called out.

● Once a referee reaches the age of 48 (qualifying date 1 August) he is taken off the Football League list unless granted an extension until his 50th birthday, which is the maximum age limit as laid down by FIFA.

Registration

Players must be 17 years of age before they can register with a Football League club on a full contract. Between the ages of 16 and 17 they can be signed on as apprentices.

A player must be registered with the Football League on one of their Registration Forms for 48 hours before playing in any match under their control.

There are five forms of contracts a player can be registered under with a Football League club: non-contract, full contract, monthly contract, apprentice and associated schoolboy.

Relegation

There has been automatic relegation in the Football League since 1898-99 (see also *Promotion*). Before then, promotion and relegation issues were settled by a series of test matches. This is how the automatic relegation system has worked since 1899:

Division 1 to Division 2
1898-99 to 1903-04 Bottom two clubs automatically relegated
1904-05 No clubs relegated (division extended from 18 to 20 clubs)
1905-06 to 1913-14 Bottom two clubs automatically relegated
1914-15 Bottom club only relegated (division extended from 20 to 22 clubs)
1919-20 to 1972-73 Bottom two clubs automatically relegated
1973-74 to present Bottom three clubs automatically relegated

Division 2 to Division 3
1920-21 Bottom club only relegated
1921-22 to 1972-73 Bottom two clubs automatically relegated
1973-74 to 1985-86 Bottom three clubs automatically relegated
1986-87 to 1987-88 Bottom two clubs automatically relegated
1988-89 to present Bottom three clubs automatically relegated

Division 3 to Division 4
1958-59 to 1985-86 Bottom four clubs automatically relegated
1986-87 to 1987-88 Bottom three clubs automatically relegated
1988-189 to present Bottom four clubs automatically relegated

In 1986-87 and 1987-88 a series of play-offs were played in which one other club from each division was eligible for relegation if they lost their play-off matches.

Only five British League clubs have never been relegated: Wigan Athletic, Scarborough, Rangers, Celtic and Aberdeen.

Sunderland went a record 68 years before being relegated from the 1st division in 1958. Arsenal are the only current 1st division team never to have been relegated since the First World War.

The following clubs have been relegated from the 1st to the 4th division in successive seasons:
Bristol C 1979-82
Wolverhampton W 1983-86

The following clubs have been relegated from the 1st to the 3rd division in successive seasons:
Bradford PA (Div. 3N) 1920-22
Northampton T 1965-67
Fulham 1967-69
Huddersfield T 1971-73
Crystal P 1972-74
Swansea C 1982-84
Notts C 1983-85

The clubs most often relegated have been:

10 — Bolton W, Bradford C, Notts C, Preston NE
9 — Birmingham C, Bristol C, Cardiff C, Doncaster R, Leicester C, Manchester C, Norwich C, Sheffield U, Sheffield W, Wolverhampton W

● In 1937-38 Manchester City were relegated from the 1st division. The season before they were 1st division champions . . . the only instance of such a reversal in fortunes in the Football League.

Replays

For most replays in FA Cup matches see *Longest matches*.

The most replays of a major British Cup final is two for the Football League Cup final between Aston Villa and Everton in 1977, and for the Scottish FA Cup finals in 1877, 1903, 1910 and 1979.

The FA Cup final has gone to a replay 12 times. The first replay of a Wembley final was in 1970 (the first replayed final since 1912). The following Wembley finals have needed replays:

1970 Chelsea 2 Leeds U 2 (Chelsea won the replay 2-1 at old Trafford)
1981 Tottenham H 1 Manchester C 1 (Spurs won the replay 3-2 at Wembley)
1982 Tottenham H 1 Queen's Park R 1 (Spurs won the replay 1-0 at Wembley)
1983 Manchester U 2 Brighton & HA 2 (Man. U won the replay 4-0 at Wembley)

● Wembley (as above) has been used for three replays. The Oval (1875, 1876) and Old Trafford

(1911, 1970) have each been used for two replayed finals.

● Many cup ties have been ordered to be replayed, often because of crowd invasions. But perhaps the most bizarre reason for a replayed match happened in the Scottish Cup in November 1884.

After losing 4-3 at Arbroath, Rangers protested that the pitch was not wide enough. It was measured and found to be 49 yards 1 inch wide instead of 50 yards. The game was replayed five weeks later and Rangers won 8-1.

Resignations

Two clubs have resigned from the Football League during the season: in 1931-32 Wigan Borough resigned after 12 games in the 3rd division (north). Their results were deleted from the records. The same happened when Accrington Stanley resigned towards the end of the 1961-62 season. They had fulfilled 33 of their 46 4th division fixtures at the time.

Rimet, Jules (Cup)

The first World Cup trophy was named after Jules Rimet, president of FIFA 1921-54 and one of the prime instigators of the World Cup tournament.

A solid gold trophy, it was designed by French sculptor Abel Lafleur. It stood only 12 inches (30.48 cm) high and weighed less than 9 lb (4.08 kg). In 1966 while on display before the World Cup in England it was stolen, to be recovered a few days later. It was stolen again in December 1983 after being presented permanently to Brazil after they had won it three times. This time it was not recovered because it had been melted down. The Brazilian FA had a replica made.

Robson, Bobby (1933-)

Bobby Robson had football in his blood from an early age. At the age of 17 he left his native Langley Park in the North-East for London, where he signed for Fulham. In a 16-year career with the Cottagers (two spells) and West Brom,

George Courtney booking Liverpool's Gary Ablett in the 1988 FA Cup semi-final against Nottingham Forest

wing-half Robson played in nearly 600 League games, and scored 133 goals. His only honours from the game as a player were 20 England caps.

At the end of his playing days he ventured into management, firstly with Vancouver Royals in the NASL, and then in 1968 with Fulham. Because of boardroom squabbles at the time, he lasted there less than a year and after a spell out of work was appointed Ipswich Town manager in succession to Bill McGarry.

Like Alf Ramsey before him, Robson worked wonders with the Suffolk club and in 1978 led them out at Wembley where they beat Arsenal 1-0 to win the FA Cup. He followed that with success in the UEFA Cup.

Despite offers from many top clubs like Barcelona over the years he stayed loyal to Ipswich. With his great record at Portman Road, he was the obvious successor to Ron Greenwood as England manager and in July 1982 took up his new duties.

To date his best performance as England boss was in the 1986 World Cup when he led England to the quarter-finals where they lost to Argentina.

Born: 18 February 1933, Langley Park, Co. Durham
Football League debut: 7 April 1951 v Sheffield W
Football League appearances: 584 (345 Fulham, 239 West Bromwich A)
Football League goals: 133 (77 Fulham, 56 West Bromwich A)
International caps: 20
Managerial honours
FA Cup 1978
UEFA Cup 1981

Above: England manager Bobby Robson in his days as manager of Ipswich Town

Left: The Jules Rimet trophy ... the first World Cup trophy which was subsequently presented to Brazil and later stolen and melted down

Robson, Bryan (1957-)

Captain of both club and country, Bryan Robson has been one of the successes of the England team under the reign of manager Bobby Robson.

Like his unrelated namesake Bryan hails from the north-east, which he left as a 15-year-old to join West Brom. He couldn't get into the Durham school's team as a youngster at just 5 feet 2 inches (1.57 metres) tall and weighing a mere 7 stone (44 kg) at the time. Albion built him up in both physique and stature, but he suffered a great setback in the 1976-77 season when he broke a leg three times. However, determination kept bringing him back and when his Albion boss Ron Atkinson took charge at Manchester United, he returned to the Hawthorns with a £1.5 million cheque and took Robson to Old Trafford.

A great partnership developed with Ray Wilkins, but it was as a skipper that Robson has been the biggest influence and he has twice led United up the Wembley steps as FA Cup winners.

Robson has now played well over 600 games at senior level and considering his career has been one constant battle against injury, notably to a suspect shoulder in recent years, it is a remarkable achievement.

Born: 11 January 1957, Chester-le-Street, Co. Durham
Football League debut: 12 April 1975 v York City
Football League appearances: 449 (197 West Bromwich A, 252 Manchester U)
Football League goals: 104 (39 West Bromwich A, 65 Manchester U)
International caps: 77
Honours
FA Cup 1983, 1985

Royalty

The first FA Cup final to be attended by a reigning monarch was the 1914 final between Burnley and Liverpool at the Crystal Palace in the presence of George V. George V was also the first monarch to attend a Football League game outside the capital, the Manchester City versus Liverpool game at City's old Hyde Road ground on 27 March 1920. He also attended the 1921 Cup final at Stamford Bridge between Spurs and Wolves and the first Wembley final in 1923.

The first queen to attend an FA Cup final was Queen Mary in 1928. Elizabeth II attended her first final as monarch in 1953 when she witnessed the marvellous Blackpool versus Bolton game and presented Stanley Matthews with his elusive winners' medal.

Not all kings and queens have been such patrons of the game. Edward II and III, Richard III, James II and IV of Scotland, and Mary Queen of Scots all put edicts on football (and indeed other sports). One of the reasons was that interest in the game prevented the men of England from taking part in archery practice, vital to the nation's defence.

However, Charles II patronised a game in 1681, and Edward VII was the first monarch to attend a modern-day game when, as the Prince of Wales, he attended a charity match at the Oval between the Gentlemen and Players in March 1886. He became patron of the FA in 1892. The Queen is the current patron of the FA.

Rules

See *Laws*

Accrington Stanley 1960–61. The following season they had to leave the League

Peter Swan (left) and Tony Kay were two former internationals banned following *The People* newspaper revelations in 1964

Rush, Ian (1961-)

During his seven years with Liverpool Ian Rush was the most prolific goalscorer in Britain with 200 goals for the Merseysiders in 300 games. A great opportunist, he was lethal in front of goal and it was his scoring ability which helped Liverpool to four League titles during the first of his two spells at Anfield.

He started his career in the 3rd division with Chester. After just 34 League appearances for the Cheshire club, which had yielded 14 goals, Bob Paisley paid £300,000 for the youngster. Many doubted the shrewdness of the acquisition, but in his first full season at Liverpool Rush scored 30 goals in 49 appearances.

Rush made his Welsh international debut in May 1980, the month after joining Liverpool, and went on to become one of the Kop's favourite sons. When he agreed to join Juventus in 1987 the Liverpool fans got up a petition to keep 'Rushie' at Anfield, even offering to raise money to pay him increased wages, but he still moved. After an unhappy year in Italy Rush returned to Liverpool in 1988 in a £2.8 million deal.

Born: 20 October 1961, St Asaph, North Wales
Football League debut: 28 April 1979 v Sheffield Wednesday
Football League appearances: 282 (34 Chester, 248 Liverpool)
Football League goals: 160 (14 Chester, 146 Liverpool)
International caps: 41

Honours

Football League 1981-82, 1982-83, 1983-84, 1985-86
European Cup 1984
FA Cup 1986, 1989
Milk Cup 1981, 1982, 1983, 1984
Awards
Footballer of the Year (FWA/PFA) 1984
Young Player of the Year (PFA) 1983
Adidas Golden Boot 1984

Scandals

The biggest scandal to hit British football was in 1964 when *The People* Sunday newspaper uncovered a series of Football League matches that had been rigged for betting purposes. Ten players, including England internationals Peter Swan and Tony Kay, were jailed on fraud charges and suspended from football for life.

In 1913 West Brom and England full-back Jesse Pennington was offered £55 to fix a match, but resisted temptation and reported the matter to the police. The culprit was jailed for five months. Two years later the FA suspended eight players for life after discovering that the Manchester United v Liverpool game on 2 April 1915 had been fixed. The players had their bans lifted in 1919 in recognition of their war service.

(see also *Betting*)

Scores, record

(for record scores in major Cup competitions see the entry under the appropriate competition)

Football League

		Div	
13-0	Stockport C v Halifax T	3N	6 Jan 1934
13-0	Newcastle U v Newport C	2	5 Oct 1946
13-4	Tranmere R v Oldham A	3N	26 Dec 1935
12-0	West Bromwich A v Darwen	1	4 April 1892
12-0	Small Heath v Walsall Town S	2	17 Dec 1892
12-0	Darwen v Walsall	2	26 Dec 1896
12-0	Woolwich A v Loughborough T	2	12 March 1900
12-0	Small Heath v Doncaster R	2	11 April 1903
12-0	Nottingham F v Leicester F	1	21 April 1909
12-0	Chester v York C	3N	1 Feb 1936
12-0	Luton T v Bristol R	3S	13 April 1936

The *record away win* is 10-0 by Sheffield United at Burslem Port Vale on 10 December 1892

Opposite: England and Manchester United captain Bryan Robson

Above: Ian Rush in Liverpool colours

Left: Rush playing for Juventus

Gordon Strachan, a
Scotland stalwart of
recent years

● The most goals scored in a 1st division game is
14 when Tottenham H beat Everton 10-4 on 11
October 1958. It was Bill Nicholson's first game
as Spurs' manager. The Aston Villa v Accrington
game (see above) also contained 14 goals.

Scottish League

Score	Match	Div	Date
15-1	Airdrieonians v Dundee W	2	1 Nov 1894
13-0	Aberdeen Res v Montrose	C	17 March 1951
13-2	East Fife v Edinburgh C	2	11 Dec 1937
12-1	Dundee U v East Stirling	2	13 April 1936
12-1	Motherwell v Dundee U	2	23 Jan 1954
12-2	King's Park v Forfar A	2	2 Jan 1930
8-0	Aberdeen v Motherwell	P	26 March 1979
8-0	Celtic v Hamilton A	P	5 Nov 1988
8-1	Rangers v Kilmarnock	P	20 Sept 1980

● On 8 March 1947 Dundee beat Alloa Athletic
10-0. Two weeks later they beat Dunfermline
also 10-0. Thirteen of their 20 goals were scored
by Albert Juliussen.

Scotland

It may have been the English who invented the
game of soccer but it was the Scots who turned it
into the skilful and professional game it is today.
In the early days of professionalism the northern clubs turned to Scottish clubs for their star
players.

Scotland's oldest club is the Queen's Park club
which was formed by members of the Glasgow
YMCA in July 1867, and Queen's Park were the
pioneers of the dribbling game. The club pro-

Zaire 2-0. They have never progressed beyond the first stage of the finals.

International competitions

World Cup

Qualified for final stages in 1954, 1958, 1974, 1978, 1982 and 1986 but have never progressed beyond the first stage.

European Championship

Have never reached quarter-final stage.

(See also *Scottish Football Association, Scottish FA Cup, Scottish Football League* and *Scottish League Cup*)

Scottish Football Association

The Scottish Football Association was formed after a meeting at the Dewar's Hotel, Glasgow, on 13 March 1873 between representatives from Clydesdale, Dumbreck, Eastern, Granville, Queen's Park, Third Lanark and Vale of Leven. Kilmarnock were not present but agreed to support any motions carried.

The meeting was called primarily to organise a knockout competition along the lines of the English Cup, but during the meeting the clubs decided to form their own Association!

The man behind the formation of the SFA was Archibald Rae, secretary of Queen's Park, and he was appointed the SFA's first secretary. Archibald Campbell of Clydesdale was the first president.

Scottish FA Cup

The Scottish Cup was born at the inaugural meeting of the Scottish Football Association in March 1873. The new association bought a cup and 12 medals for the winners at a cost of £56. Sixteen clubs took part in the inaugural competition which was won by Queen's Park.

Of the first 16 entrants, only Queen's Park, Kilmarnock and Dumbarton are still regular entrants.

Non-1st/Premier Division winners

East Fife are the only League team from outside the 1st division or Premier division to win the Cup. They were in the 2nd division when they beat Kilmarnock in 1938. Queen's Park were not in the League when they last won the Cup in 1893.

vided the majority of players for the annual encounter with England, and their players were superior to the English in most departments.

Although still in existence, the pioneering Queen's Park club have remained truly amateur after more than 120 years, and their early dominance of Scottish football waned considerably once professional clubs like Rangers, Celtic, Hearts and Hibernian were established.

The Scottish Football Association was founded in 1873, the year after they drew 0-0 with England in the first ever soccer international at Glasgow.

Scotland entered the World Cup for the first time in 1950. They first qualified for the final stages in 1954 but had to wait until the 1974 competition for their first win, when they beat

Most wins	Most finals appearances
29 — Celtic	45 — Celtic
24 — Rangers	40 — Rangers
10 — Queen's Park	12 — Aberdeen, Queen's Park

Biggest cup tie wins
36-0 Arbroath v Bon Accord (1st round), 12 Sept 1885
35-0 Dundee Harp v Aberdeen Rovers (1st round), 12 Sept 1885
20-0 Stirling A v Selkirk (1st round), 9 Dec 1984
16-0 Queen's Park v St Peters (1st round), 12 Sept 1885
6-0 Partick T v Royal Albert (1st round), 17 Jan 1931
(note that three of the above were all on the same day)
Most individual winners' medals
8 — Charles Campbell 1874-86 (all Queen's Park)
7 — James McMenemy 1904-21 (6 Celtic, 1 Partick T)
7 — Bob McPhail 1924-36 (1 Airdrie, 6 Rangers)
7 — Billy McNeill 1965-75 (all Celtic)

Scottish League

The Scottish League was formed in 1890 after the lesser known clubs found it increasingly difficult to arrange sufficient fixtures to satisfy their fans. It had 11 founder members: Abercorn, Celtic, Cowlairs, Cambuslang, Dumbarton, Hearts, Rangers, St Mirren, Renton, Third Lanark and Vale of Leven.

Renton were suspended from the League after playing five matches because they played a friendly against Edinburgh Saints, who the Scottish FA ruled was the old St Bernard's club under a different guise. St Bernard's had adopted professionalism, and clubs were therefore barred from playing them.

A second division was formed in 1893 but was suspended in 1915 and between 1915-21 there was just one division. The League was re-structured in 1921-22 into two divisions again, and with a total of 42 clubs. Automatic promotion and relegation was introduced for the first time.

After the Second World War the two divisions were known as Divisions A and B (instead of 1 and 2) until 1956. In the period 1946-47 to 1954-55 a third division, known as the C divisions, existed. It consisted largely of reserve teams from the A and B divisions. The C division champions automatically replaced the bottom club in the B division, provided they were not the reserve team of an A or B division team. Only four teams were promoted from the C division as champions: Stirling Albion (1946-47), East Stirling (1947-48), Forfar Athletic (1948-49) and Brechin City (1953-54). To confuse the issue even further, the C division was divided into two regionalised divisions in 1949, north-east and south-west sections. It was scrapped in 1955 and became the Reserve League with no automatic promotion to the Scottish League. A third division had previously existed for the three seasons between 1923-24 and 1925-26.

The next major re-organisation of the Scottish League was in 1975 when the League was re-formed into three divisions: Premier, 1st and 2nd. The top ten clubs from the 1st division in 1974-75 made up the Premier Division while the bottom eight clubs plus the top six in the 2nd

Scottish FA Cup
Finals

				Venue	Attendance
1874	Queen's Park	2	Clydesdale 0	Hampden Park	3,500
1875	Queen's Park	3	Renton 0	Hampden Park	7,000
1876	Queen's Park	1	Third Lanark 1	Hamilton Crescent	10,000
	Queen's Park	2	Third Lanark 0	Hamilton Crescent	6,000
1877	Vale of Leven	0	Rangers 0	Hamilton Crescent	10,000
	Vale of Leven	1	Rangers 1	Hamilton Crescent	15,000
	Vale of Leven	3	Rangers 2	Hampden Park	12,000
1878	Vale of Leven	1	Third Lanark 0	Hampden Park	5,000
1879	Vale of Leven	1	Rangers 1	Hampden Park	9,000
	(Vale of Leven awarded cup after Rangers did not appear for replay)				
1880	Queen's Park	3	Thornlebank 0	Cathkin Park	4,000
1881	Queen's Park	2	Dumbarton 1	Kinning Park	15,000
	Queen's Park	3	Dumbarton 1	Kinning Park	7,000
	(Replayed after Dumbarton protested after first game)				
1882	Queen's Park	2	Dumbarton 2	Cathkin Park	12,500
	Queen's Park	4	Dumbarton 1	Cathkin Park	14,000
1883	Dumbarton	2	Vale of Leven 2	Hampden Park	9,000
	Dumbarton	2	Vale of Leven 1	Hampden Park	12,000
1884	Queen's Park		Vale of Leven		
	(Queen's Park awarded game after Vale of Leven failed to appear)				
1885	Renton	0	Vale of Leven 0	Hampden Park	2,500
	Renton	3	Vale of Leven 1	Hampden Park	3,500
1886	Queen's Park	3	Renton 1	Cathkin Park	7,000
1887	Hibernian	2	Dumbarton 1	Hampden Park	12,000
1888	Renton	6	Cambuslang 1	Hampden Park	11,000
1889	Third Lanark	3	Celtic 1	Hampden Park	18,000
	Third Lanark	2	Celtic 1	Hampden Park	13,000
	(Replayed game on order of Scottish FA)				
1890	Queen's Park	1	Vale of Leven 1	Ibrox	11,000
	Queen's Park	2	Vale of Leven 1	Ibrox	14,000
1891	Hearts	1	Dumbarton 0	Hampden Park	10,836
1892	Celtic	1	Queen's Park 0	Ibrox	40,000
	Celtic	5	Queen's Park 1	Ibrox	26,000
	(Replayed after protested first game)				
1893	Queen's Park	0	Celtic 1	Ibrox	18,771
	Queen's Park	2	Celtic 1	Ibrox	13,239
	(Replayed due to frost)				
1894	Rangers	3	Celtic 1	Hampden Park	17,000
1895	St Bernard's	2	Renton 1	Ibrox	15,000
1896	Hearts	3	Hibernian 1	Logie Green	17,034
1897	Rangers	5	Dumbarton 1	Hampden Park	14,000
1898	Rangers	2	Kilmarnock 0	Hampden Park	,13,000
1899	Celtic	2	Rangers 0	Hampden Park	25,000
1900	Celtic	4	Queen's Park 3	Ibrox	15,000
1901	Hearts	4	Celtic 3	Ibrox	12,000
1902	Hibernian	1	Celtic 0	Celtic Park	16,000
1903	Rangers	1	Hearts 1	Celtic Park	40,000
	Rangers	0	Hearts 0	Celtic Park	35,000
	Rangers	2	Hearts 0	Celtic Park	32,000
1904	Celtic	3	Rangers 2	Hampden Park	65,000
1905	Third Lanark	0	Rangers 0	Hampden Park	54,000
	Third Lanark	3	Rangers 1	Hampden Park	55,000
1906	Hearts	1	Third Lanark 0	Ibrox	25,000
1907	Celtic	3	Hearts 0	Hampden Park	50,000
1908	Celtic	5	St Mirren 1	Hampden Park	55,000
1909	Celtic	2	Rangers 2	Hampden Park	70,000
	Celtic	1	Rangers 1	Hampden Park	61,000
	(Owing to riot the cup was withheld)				
1910	Dundee	2	Clyde 2	Ibrox	62,300
	Dundee	0	Clyde 0	Ibrox	24,500
	Dundee	2	Clyde 1	Ibrox	25,400
1911	Celtic	0	Hamilton A 0	Ibrox	45,000
	Celtic	2	Hamilton A 0	Ibrox	24,700
1912	Celtic	2	Clyde 0	Ibrox	46,000
1913	Falkirk	2	Raith R 0	Celtic Park	45,000
1914	Celtic	0	Hibernian 0	Ibrox	56,000
	Celtic	4	Hibernian 1	Ibrox	40,000
1920	Kilmarnock	3	Albion R 2	Hampden Park	95,000
1921	Partick T	1	Rangers 0	Celtic Park	28,300
1922	Morton	1	Rangers 0	Hampden Park	75,000
1923	Celtic	1	Hibernian 0	Hampden Park	80,100

Year			Venue	Attendance
1924	Airdrieonians 2	Hibernian 0	Ibrox	59,218
1925	Celtic 2	Dundee 1	Hampden Park	75,137
1926	St Mirren 2	Celtic 0	Hampden Park	98,620
1927	Celtic 3	East Fife 1	Hampden Park	80,070
1928	Rangers 4	Celtic 0	Hampden Park	118,115
1929	Kilmarnock 2	Rangers 0	Hampden Park	114,708
1930	Rangers 0	Partick T 0	Hampden Park	107,475
	Rangers 2	Partick T 1	Hampden Park	103,686
1931	Celtic 2	Motherwell 2	Hampden Park	105,000
	Celtic 4	Motherwell 2	Hampden Park	98,579
1932	Rangers 1	Kilmarnock 1	Hampden Park	111,982
	Rangers 3	Kilmarnock 0	Hampden Park	104,965
1933	Celtic 1	Motherwell 0	Hampden Park	102,339
1934	Rangers 5	St Mirren 0	Hampden Park	113,403
1935	Rangers 2	Hamilton A 1	Hampden Park	87,286
1936	Rangers 1	Third Lanark 0	Hampden Park	88,859
1937	Celtic 2	Aberdeen 1	Hampden Park	147,365
1938	East Fife 1	Kilmarnock 1	Hampden Park	80,091
	East Fife 4	Kilmarnock 2	Hampden Park	92,716
1939	Clyde 4	Motherwell 0	Hampden Park	94,799
1947	Aberdeen 2	Hibernian 1	Hampden Park	82,140
1948	Rangers 1	Morton 1	Hampden Park	129,176
	Rangers 1	Morton 0	Hampden Park	133,570
1949	Rangers 4	Clyde 1	Hampden Park	108,435
1950	Rangers 3	East Fife 0	Hampden Park	118,262
1951	Celtic 1	Motherwell 0	Hampden Park	131,943
1952	Motherwell 4	Dundee 0	Hampden Park	136,274
1953	Rangers 1	Aberdeen 1	Hampden Park	129,681
	Rangers 1	Aberdeen 0	Hampden Park	112,619
1954	Celtic 2	Aberdeen 1	Hampden Park	129,926
1955	Clyde 1	Celtic 1	Hampden Park	106,111
	Clyde 1	Celtic 0	Hampden Park	68,735
1956	Hearts 3	Celtic 1	Hampden Park	133,339
1957	Falkirk 1	Kilmarnock 1	Hampden Park	83,000
	Falkirk 2	Kilmarnock 1	Hampden Park	79,785
1958	Clyde 1	Hibernian 0	Hampden Park	95,124
1959	St Mirren 3	Aberdeen 1	Hampden Park	108,591
1960	Rangers 2	Kilmarnock 0	Hampden Park	108,017
1961	Dunfermline A 0	Celtic 0	Hampden Park	113,618
	Dunfermline A 2	Celtic 0	Hampden Park	87,866
1962	Rangers 2	St Mirren 0	Hampden Park	126,930
1963	Rangers 1	Celtic 1	Hampden Park	129,527
	Rangers 3	Celtic 0	Hampden Park	120,263
1964	Rangers 3	Dundee 1	Hampden Park	120,982
1965	Celtic 3	Dunfermline A 2	Hampden Park	108,800
1966	Rangers 0	Celtic 0	Hampden Park	126,552
	Rangers 1	Celtic 0	Hampden Park	98,202
1967	Celtic 2	Aberdeen 0	Hampden Park	127,117
1968	Dunfermline A 3	Hearts 1	Hampden Park	56,366
1969	Celtic 4	Rangers 0	Hampden Park	132,874
1970	Aberdeen 3	Celtic 1	Hampden Park	108,434
1971	Celtic 1	Rangers 1	Hampden Park	120,092
	Celtic 2	Rangers 1	Hampden Park	103,332
1972	Celtic 6	Hibernian 1	Hampden Park	106,102
1973	Rangers 3	Celtic 2	Hampden Park	122,714
1974	Celtic 3	Dundee U 0	Hampden Park	75,959
1975	Celtic 3	Airdrieonians 1	Hampden Park	75,457
1976	Rangers 3	Hearts 1	Hampden Park	85,354
1977	Celtic 1	Rangers 0	Hampden Park	54,252
1978	Rangers 2	Aberdeen 1	Hampden Park	61,563
1979	Rangers 0	Hibernian 0	Hampden Park	50,610
	Rangers 0	Hibernian 0	Hampden Park	33,506
	Rangers 3	Hibernian 2	Hampden Park	30,602
1980	Celtic 1	Rangers 0	Hampden Park	70,303
1981	Rangers 0	Dundee U 0	Hampden Park	55,000
	Rangers 4	Dundee U 1	Hampden Park	43,009
1982	Aberdeen 4	Rangers 1 aet	Hampden Park	53,788
1983	Aberdeen 1	Rangers 0 aet	Hampden Park	62,979
1984	Aberdeen 2	Celtic 1 aet	Hampden Park	58,900
1985	Celtic 2	Dundee U 1	Hampden Park	60,346
1986	Aberdeen 3	Hearts 0	Hampden Park	62,841
1987	St Mirren 1	Dundee U 0 aet	Hampden Park	51,782
1988	Celtic 2	Dundee U 1	Hampden Park	74,000
1989	Celtic 1	Rangers 0	Hampden Park	72,069

division became the new 1st division. The remainder formed the new 2nd division.

At the time of its change the League consisted of 38 teams, its current number. The Premier division was extended to 12 teams in 1986, and the 1st division was reduced from 14 to 12 teams. All Premier and 1st division clubs play each club within their division four times in a season, while 2nd division sides meet three times.

See Scottish League Championship table on pages 136-137.

● Because automatic promotion and relegation was not introduced until 1921 three clubs have won the 2nd division in successive years: Hibernian (1893-94/1894-95); Kilmarnock (1897-98/1898-99); Ayr U (1911-12/1912-13)

Scottish League Cup

The Scottish League Cup was a continuation of the Scottish Southern League Cup in 1946-47. Formerly played on a series of qualifying group matches and a knockout competition from the last-8 stage, it has been a knockout event since 1977-78.

The final is played in November or December, although it has been staged at the end of the season several times.

Finals (including the Southern League Cup) have been held at Hampden Park except the 1980 replay between Dundee United and Aberdeen, and the 1981 final between Dundee United and Dundee. Both matches were played at Dens Park, Dundee FC.

Since 1984 it has been known as the Skol Cup.

Finals

1940-41	Rangers 1	Hearts 1		
	Rangers 4	Hearts 2		
1941-42	Rangers 1	Morton 0		
1942-43	Rangers 1	Falkirk 1		
	(Rangers won on corners)			
1943-44	Hibernian 0	Rangers 0		
	(Hibernian won on corners)			
1944-45	Rangers 2	Motherwell 1		
1945-46	Aberdeen 3	Rangers 2		
1946-47	Rangers 4	Aberdeen 0		
1947-48	East Fife 1	Falkirk 1 aet		
	East Fife 4	Falkirk 1		
1948-49	Rangers 2	Raith R 0		
1949-50	East Fife 3	Dunfermline A 0		
1950-51	Motherwell 3	Hibernian 0		
1951-52	Dundee 3	Rangers 2		
1952-53	Dundee 2	Kilmarnock 0		
1953-54	East Fife 3	Partick T 2		
1954-55	Hearts 4	Motherwell 2		
1955-56	Aberdeen 2	St Mirren 1		
1956-57	Celtic 0	Partick T 0 aet		
	Celtic 3	Partick T 0		
1957-58	Celtic 7	Rangers 1		
1958-59	Hearts 5	Partick T 1		
1959-60	Hearts 2	Third Lanark 1		
1960-61	Rangers 2	Kilmarnock 0		

Scottish League

Champions

1890-91	Dumbarton/Rangers*	
1891-92	Dumbarton	
1892-93	Celtic	

	Division 1	Division 2
1893-94	Celtic	Hibernian
1894-95	Hearts	Hibernian
1895-96	Celtic	Abercorn
1896-97	Hearts	Partick T
1897-98	Celtic	Kilmarnock
1898-99	Rangers	Kilmarnock
1899-1900	Rangers	Partick T
1900-01	Rangers	St Bernard's
1901-02	Rangers	Port Glasgow
1902-03	Hibernian	Airdrieonians
1903-04	Third Lanark	Hamilton A
1904-05	Celtic	Clyde
1905-06	Celtic	Leith A
1906-07	Celtic	St Bernard's
1907-08	Celtic	Raith R
1908-09	Celtic	Abercorn
1909-10	Celtic	Leith A/Raith R†
1910-11	Rangers	Dumbarton
1911-12	Rangers	Ayr U
1912-13	Rangers	Ayr U
1913-14	Celtic	Cowdenbeath
1914-15	Celtic	Cowdenbeath
1915-16	Celtic	—
1916-17	Celtic	—
1917-18	Rangers	—
1918-19	Celtic	—

	Division 1	Division 2	
1919-20	Rangers	—	
1920-21	Rangers	—	
1921-22	Celtic	Alloa A	
1922-23	Rangers	Queen's Park	

	Division 1	Division 2	Division 3
1923-24	Rangers	St Johnstone	Arthurlie
1924-25	Rangers	Dundee U	Nithsdale W
1925-26	Celtic	Dunfermline A	Leith A

	Division 1	Division 2
1926-27	Rangers	Bo'ness
1927-28	Rangers	Ayr U
1928-29	Rangers	Dundee U
1929-30	Rangers	Leith A
1930-31	Rangers	Third Lanark
1931-32	Motherwell	East Stirling
1932-33	Rangers	Hibernian
1933-34	Rangers	Albion R
1934-35	Rangers	Third Lanark
1935-36	Celtic	Falkirk
1936-37	Rangers	Ayr U
1937-38	Celtic	Raith R
1938-39	Rangers	Cowdenbeath

	Division A	Division B	Division C
1946-47	Rangers	Dundee	Stirling A
1947-48	Hibernian	East Fife	East Stirling
1948-49	Rangers	Raith R	Forfar A
1949-50	Rangers	Morton	NE: Hibernian Res SW: Clyde Res
1950-51	Hibernian	Queen of the South	NE: Hearts Res SW: Clyde Res
1951-52	Hibernian	Clyde	NE: Dundee Res SW: Rangers Res
1952-53	Rangers	Stirling A	NE: Aberdeen Res SW: Rangers Res
1953-54	Celtic	Motherwell	NE: Brechin City SW:Rangers Res
1954-55	Aberdeen	Airdrieonians	NE: Aberdeen Res SW: Partick T Res
1955-56	Rangers	Queen's Park	

1961-62	Rangers	1	Hearts	1 aet
	Rangers	3	Hearts	1
1962-63	Hearts	1	Kilmarnock	0
1963-64	Rangers	5	Morton	0
1964-65	Rangers	2	Celtic	1
1965-66	Celtic	2	Rangers	1
1966-67	Celtic	1	Rangers	0
1967-68	Celtic	5	Dundee	3
1968-69	Celtic	6	Hibernian	2
1969-70	Celtic	1	St Johnstone	0
1970-71	Rangers	1	Celtic	0
1971-72	Partick T	4	Celtic	1
1972-73	Hibernian	2	Celtic	1
1973-74	Dundee	1	Celtic	0
1974-75	Celtic	6	Hibernian	3
1975-76	Rangers	1	Celtic	0
1976-77	Aberdeen	2	Celtic	1
1977-78	Rangers	2	Celtic	1
1978-79	Rangers	2	Aberdeen	1
1979-80	Dundee U	0	Aberdeen	0
	Dundee U	3	Aberdeen	0
1980-81	Dundee U	3	Dundee	0
1981-82	Rangers	2	Dundee U	1
1982-83	Celtic	2	Rangers	1
1983-84	Rangers	3	Celtic	2 aet
1984-85	Rangers	1	Dundee U	0
1985-86	Aberdeen	3	Hibernian	0
1986-87	Rangers	2	Celtic	1
1987-88	Rangers	3	Aberdeen	3 aet
	(Rangers won 5-3 on penalties)			
1988-89	Rangers	3	Aberdeen	2

Most wins
16 — Rangers		3 — Aberdeen, Dundee, East Fife
9 — Celtic		2 — Dundee U
4 — Hearts		

Most finals appearances
21 — Rangers
19 — Celtic
 8 — Aberdeen

East Fife, the only 2nd division winners of the Scottish FA Cup (1938), are also the only 2nd division winners of the League Cup when they beat Falkirk in 1948.

The following clubs have performed the double of Scottish League Cup and FA Cup in the same season:

Rangers 1948-49, 1961-62, 1963-64, 1975-76, 1977-78, 1978-79, 1981-82
Celtic 1966-67, 1968-69, 1974-75
Aberdeen 1985-86

Sendings off

The *red card system* for indicating a player is sent off was introduced by FIFA in 1968 and was first used at the Mexico Olympic Games. They were introduced into the Football League in 1976 and the first player to be shown one was David Wagstaffe of Blackburn Rovers, who was dismissed during the game with Orient on 2 October. The cards were scrapped in England in 1981, but reinstated in 1987.

Many players have been *sent off on their Football League debut*. The first was John Burns of Rochdale, against Stockport Co. 29 October 1921.

	Division 1	Division 2
1956-57	Rangers	Clyde
1957-58	Hearts	Stirling A
1958-59	Rangers	Ayr U
1959-60	Hearts	St Johnstone
1960-61	Rangers	Stirling A
1961-62	Dundee	Clyde
1962-63	Rangers	St Johnstone
1963-64	Rangers	Morton
1964-65	Kilmarnock	Stirling A
1965-66	Celtic	Ayr U
1966-67	Celtic	Morton
1967-68	Celtic	St Mirren
1968-69	Celtic	Motherwell
1969-70	Celtic	Falkirk
1970-71	Celtic	Partick T
1971-72	Celtic	Dumbarton
1972-73	Celtic	Clyde
1973-74	Celtic	Airdrieonians
1974-75	Rangers	Falkirk

	Premier Division	Division 1	Division 2
1975-76	Rangers	Partick T	Clydebank
1976-77	Celtic	St Mirren	Stirling A
1977-78	Rangers	Morton	Clyde
1978-79	Celtic	Dundee	Berwick R
1979-80	Aberdeen	Hearts	Falkirk
1980-81	Celtic	Hibernian	Queen's Park
1981-82	Celtic	Motherwell	Clyde
1982-83	Dundee U	St Johnstone	Brechin C
1983-84	Aberdeen	Morton	Forfar A
1984-85	Aberdeen	Motherwell	Montrose
1985-86	Celtic	Hamilton A	Dunfermline A
1986-87	Rangers	Morton	Meadowbank T
1987-88	Celtic	Hamilton A	Ayr U
1988-89	Rangers	Dunfermline	Albion R

* title shared after play-off game resulted in 2-2 draw
† joint champions

Most titles
38 — Rangers
35 — Celtic
8 — Hibernian
7 — Clyde, Ayr U

Since re-organisation in 1975 the following clubs have played in all three divisions:

Ayr U, Clydebank, Dumbarton, Dunfermline A, Falkirk, St Johnstone.
Arbroath, Stranraer and Stenhousemuir are the only current Scottish League clubs not to have won a League title.

(For details of most points, goals etc. see appropriate individual headings)

The *only player to be sent off in an FA Cup final* is Manchester United's Kevin Moran who was given his marching orders by Durham referee Peter Willis.

The *most players sent off in one Football League game* is 4. It has happened three times:

8 Jan 1985 Crewe A v Bradford PA (Division 3 (north))
13 Dec 1986 Sheffield U v Portsmouth (Division 2)
12 Dec 1987 Brentford v Mansfield T (Division 3)

● Four players were also sent off during the Littlewoods Cup tie (1st round, 1st leg) between Port Vale and Northampton T on 18 Aug 1987.

The *first players to be sent off for each of the four home countries in full internationals* were:

England: Alan Mullery, 5 June 1968 v Yugoslavia
Ireland: Billy Ferguson, 22 Oct 1966 v England
Scotland: Billy Steel, 27 May 1951 v Austria
Wales: Trevor Hockey, 26 Sept 1973 v Poland

The other England players to have been sent off are:

Alan Ball, 6 June 1973 v Poland
Trevor Cherry, 12 June 1977 v Argentina
Ray Wilkins, 6 June 1986 v Morocco (World Cup)

The following players have been sent off at Wembley:

Boris Stankovic (Yugoslavia) v Sweden, 13 Aug 1948 (Olympic Games)
Antonio Rattin (Argentina) v England, 23 July 1966 (World Cup)
Billy Bremner (Leeds U) v Liverpool, 10 Aug 1974 (Charity Shield)
Kevin Keegan (Liverpool) v Leeds U, 10 Aug 1974 (Charity Shield)
Gilbert Dresch (Luxembourg) v England, 30 March 1977 (World Cup qualifier)
Kevin Moran (Manchester U) v Everton, 18 May 1985 (FA Cup final)

The *fastest sending* off belongs to Ambrose Brown of Wrexham who was dismissed 20 seconds after the start of the 3rd division (north) match against Hull City on 25 December 1936. Not a very happy Christmas for Brown!

The *fastest 1st division dismissal* saw Liam O'Brien of Manchester United sent off after 85 seconds of the match against Southampton on 3 January 1987.

The *World Cup's fastest dismissal* is 55 seconds. That was all it took for Uruguay's Jose Battista to get his marching orders against Scotland on 13 June 1986.

The *most sendings off in an English season* is 242 in 1982-83. The figure was made up of: Football League 211, FA Cup 19, Milk Cup 12). The first time sendings off reached 100 was in 1975-76.

The *most players sent off in any one day in the Foobal League* is 13 on 14 December 1985 (four were also sent off in the Scottish League). A total of 15 players (12 FA Cup, 3 Football League) were sent off on 20 November 1982. This is the blackest day in British football for dismissals.

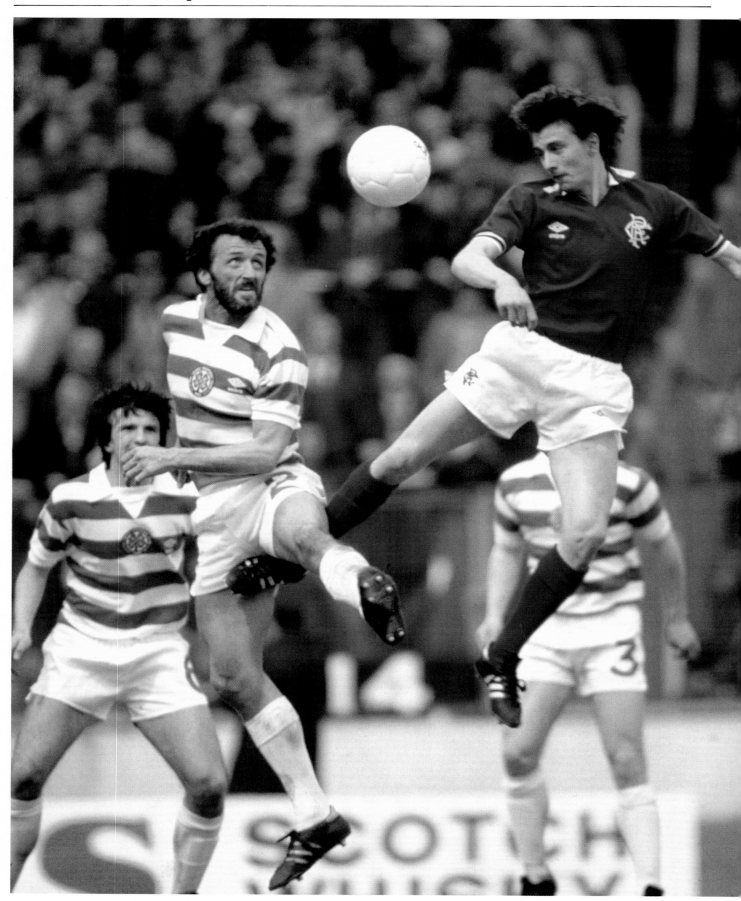

Opposite: There's nothing like a Rangers–Celtic match to get the adrenalin flowing in Glasgow

Above: Aberdeen have challenged the Rangers–Celtic monopoly in recent years

Left: Disgrace at Wembley in 1974. Kevin Keegan (Liverpool) and Billy Bremner (Leeds United) get their marching orders during the Charity Shield

Left: Bill Shankly, Emlyn Hughes, and the Charity Shield in 1974

● Nottingham Forest went from 1939 to 1971 without having a player sent off in the Football League.

● The first player to be sent off under the 'Professional Foul' rule was Lawrie Sanchez of Reading in the Football League Trophy match against Oxford on 14 August 1982. He had only been on the field eight minutes when he received his marching orders after finger-tipping a shot round the post.

● On 26 April 1978 Mark Halsey of Norwich City was sent off on his Football League debut, against Newcastle United. He was only 18 and 146 days old at the time, the youngest debutant to receive his marching orders.

Shankly, Bill (1913-1982)

Bill Shankly laid the foundations on which Bob Paisley and all subsequent Liverpool managers have built.

Born in Scotland, Shankly was a wing-half with Preston and won an FA Cup winners' medal in 1938. After handing over his number 4 shirt to Tommy Docherty, Shankly turned his attention to management, first with Carlisle, and then with Grimsby, Workington and Huddersfield Town, where he discovered Denis Law.

Shankly was recruited by Liverpool in December 1959 and immediately set about reforming the club. He dismissed many old faces, but retained the backroom staff. In came Scots Ian St John and Ron Yeats, who formed the backbone of the Liverpool team that won promotion to the 1st division in 1961-62. That was the start of the Liverpool success story that seems to open a new chapter as each season passes by.

Shankly led the club to its first League title since 1947 and in 1965 he led the team to its first ever FA Cup final success. Sadly Shankly never won the European Cup although he did win the UEFA Cup in 1973.

In 1974 Shankly surprised the Liverpool fans by announcing his retirement after the FA Cup final. Typical Shankly, he went out on a winning note.

Bill Shankly died of a heart attack in September 1982, and the Shankly Gates at Anfield are in memory of the great man.

Managerial honours
at Liverpool
Division 1 champions 1963-64, 1965-66, 1972-73
Division 2 champions 1961-62
FA Cup winners 1965, 1974
UEFA Cup winners 1973
Manager of the Year 1973
PFA Merit Award 1978

Sheffield United

Within ten years of joining the Football League Sheffield United had won the FA Cup twice and the Football League title once, maintaining the tradition the Sheffield, Nottingham and Derby area had for producing fine teams at the turn of the century.

Founded in 1889, they became founder members of the 2nd division in 1892, gaining promotion at the first attempt. For the next 43 years they remained a 1st division team. As the 19th century came to a close great men like giant goalkeeper 'Fatty' Foulke and Ernest Needham steered the club to the League title in 1898 and the FA Cup the following year. A second FA Cup win followed in 1902 and in 1915 they won the 'khaki' final at Old Trafford when they beat Chelsea 3-0.

The club's most recent major honour was in 1925 when they beat Cardiff in the Cup final in the first of two Wembley appearances. They lost the 1936 final to Arsenal. Since then, although they re-established themselves as a 1st division club in the 1960s, times have been hard for United who have lived in the shadow of neighbours Sheffield Wednesday. United last appeared in the 1st division in 1976 and within five years found themselves in the 4th division.

Ground: Bramall Lane
Nickname: Blades
Record attendance: 68,287 — v Leeds United (FA Cup 5th round), 15 Feb 1936
First Football League season: 1892-93 Division 2 (2nd)
Seasons in Football League: 86 (55 Division 1, 25 Division 2, 5 Division 3, 1 Division 4)

Honours

Division 1 champions 1897-98
Division 2 champions 1952-53
Division 4 champions 1981-82
FA Cup winners 1899, 1902, 1915, 1925

Sheffield Wednesday

Any team that wins four 1st division titles and the FA Cup three times has to be called successful, and Wednesday certainly have been: but they have to go back to 1935 for the last of those honours.

Founded by the Wednesday Cricket Club in 1867, they are the fifth oldest club in the Football League. They were known simply as the Wednesday until they adopted their current name in the 1929 close season.

They had a succession of home grounds in their early days, including Bramall Lane, now the home of Sheffield United, but in 1899 they moved to Owlerton which became Hillsborough.

Despite their lengthy history Wednesday were not founder members of the Football League. They joined in 1892 when they went straight into the newly extended 1st division. They have enjoyed considerable success over the years, but at the same time have gained a reputation as a 'yo-yo' team after making the journey from 1st to 2nd division, and vice versa, 14 times, including seven times in the 1950s.

In 1975 the club suffered the indignity of dropping into the 3rd division and were only saved from dropping to the lowest division in the League by a single point.

Ground: Hillsborough
Nickname: Owls
Record attendance: 72,841 — v Manchester C (FA Cup 5th round), 17 Feb 1934
First Football League season: 1892-93 Division 1 (12th)
Seasons in Football League: 86 (56 Division 1, 25 Division 2, 5 Division 3)

Honours

Division 1 champions 1902-03, 1903-04, 1928-29, 1929-30
Division 2 champions 1899-1900, 1925-26, 1951-52, 1955-56, 1958-59
FA Cup winners 1896, 1907, 1935

Sherpa Van Trophy

A descendant of the Anglo-Scottish Cup, the Sherpa Van Trophy has had five different names since its inauguration in 1981-82:
1981-82 Football League Group Cup;
1982-83 Football League Trophy;
1983-84 Associate Members' Cup;
1984-85/1986-87 Freight Rover Trophy and
1987-88 Sherpa Van Trophy.
The competition is open to associate members of the Football League.

Shilton, Peter (1949-)

Peter Shilton is not only England's most capped goalkeeper but also holds the record for the most Football League appearances stretching back to the day in May 1966 when he made his debut for Leicester City as a 16-year-old. An understudy to the great Gordon Banks at Filbert Street, it was under Banks' guidance, and that of coach George Dewis, that Shilton developed into one of the finest 'keepers in the world.

A schoolboy international, he was capped by the senior team for the first time against East Germany in November 1970. He had to share the No.1 jersey with Ray Clemence for a while, but since 1982 has virtually made it his own property.

At club level Shilton surprised a few people when he moved from Leicester to Stoke City in a £340,000 deal in 1974 and in 1977 he moved to Nottingham Forest for £270,000. At Forest he won two European Cup medals, a League championship, European Super Cup and Foot-

Sherpa Van Trophy

Finals

				Venue	Attendance
1982	Grimsby T 3	Wimbledon 2		Grimsby	3,423
1983	Millwall 3	Lincoln C 2		Lincoln	3,142
1984	Bournemouth 2	Hull C 1		Hull	6,544
1985	Wigan A 3	Brentford 1		Wembley	39,897
1986	Bristol C 3	Bolton W 0		Wembley	54,000
1987	Mansfield T 1	Bristol C 1		Wembley	58,586
	(Manchester won 5-4 on penalties)				
1988	Wolverhampton W 2	Burnley 0		Wembley	80,841

ball League Cup winners' medal. His next move took him to Southampton before moving nearer his Midland roots when he joined Derby County in 1987.

Shilton broke Terry Paine's record of 828 Football League appearances in the 1-1 draw with Watford at Vicarage Road on 30 April 1988.

Born: 18 September 1949, Leicester
Football League debut: 4 May 1966 v Everton
Football League appearances: 864 (286 Leicester C, 110 Stoke C, 202 Nottingham F, 188 Southampton, 78 Derby C)
International caps: 105
Honours
European Cup 1979, 1980 (both Nottm. F)
Division 1 championship 1977-78 (Nottm. F)
Division 2 championship 1970-71 (Leicester C)
Football League Cup 1979 (Nottm. F)
European Super Cup 1980 (Nottm. F)
Awards
Player of the Year (PFA) 1978

Shinpads

Shinpads were invented by Samuel Widdowson of Nottingham Forest. He is believed to have first worn them in 1874 but they were not mentioned in the rules until 1880 (Law 10), although the current laws of the game make no specific mention of pads.

Widdowson was a Nottingham lace-maker and Forest centre-forward from 1866 to the mid-1880s. He played for England once (in 1880 against Scotland) and later became chairman of Forest and a member of the FA committee.

Shortest players

The *shortest player to have appeared in the Football League* is Fred le May, an outside-right with Thames, Watford and Clapton Orient 1930-33. He was just 5 feet (1.52 m) tall.

Above: Tony Currie, a former favourite with the Sheffield United fans

Right: Glory days again for the Wolves ... seen celebrating after beating Burnley to win the 1988 Sherpa Van Trophy

Opposite: Peter Shilton of Derby County and England

The *shortest goalkeeper to appear in the Football League* is believed to be Jerry Best who kept goal for Coventry City between the two world wars. His height is quoted as 5 feet 6 inches (1.67 m).

The *shortest player to appear for England* is believed to be Fred Walden of Tottenham Hotspur who was just 5 feet 3 inches (1.60 m) tall.

The *shortest goalkeeper to play for England* is John Edward Davison of Sheffield Wednesday who was only 5 feet 7 inches (1.70 m) tall when he played his only game, against Wales in 1922.

Simod Cup

First played in 1985-86 as the Full Members' Cup, it is open to full members of the Football League. It became known as the Simod Cup in 1987-88.

Finals

				Venue	Attendance
1986	Chelsea 5		Manchester C 4	Wembley	68,000
1987	Blackburn 1		Charlton A 0	Wembley	40,000
1988	Reading 4		Luton T 1	Wembley	61,740
1989	Nottm F 4		Everton 3	Wembley	46,604

Skol Cup

See *Scottish League Cup*

Souness, Graeme (1953-)

Edinburgh-born Graeme Souness has enjoyed two successful careers, one as the skipper of Liverpool and the second as manager of Glasgow Rangers.

Souness was on Tottenham's books for three years but never played for them in a senior game, although he figured in the successful Youth Cup team of the early 1970s.

He moved to Middlesbrough in 1972 and under Jackie Charlton earned himself a regular place in the first team, helping them to the 2nd division title in 1973-74. But for Souness the move to Anfield for £352,000 in January 1978 was the start of a glorious era. In his first season he won a European Cup winners' medal, supplying the pass for Kenny Dalglish to score the winning goal against Bruges at Wembley.

The following season yielded the first of five League championship medals in six years and between 1981 and 1984 he appeared in Liverpool's four consecutive League Cup winning teams. He succeeded Phil Thompson as club skipper in 1982 and in his last season at Anfield led the club to the treble of League Championship, League Cup and European Cup.

He then joined Italian club Sampdoria in 1984 for £650,000 before becoming the Glasgow Rangers boss in 1986. At Ibrox he brought immediate success, reminiscent of his Anfield playing days. After the club was taken over in 1988 Souness was made a director.

Born: 6 May 1953, Edinburgh
Football League debut: 6 January 1973 v Fulham
Football League appearances: 423
Scottish League appearances: 49
Football League goals: 60
Scottish League goals: 3
International caps: 54

Honours
European Cup 1978, 1981, 1984 (all Liverpool)
Division 1 championship 1978-79, 1979-80, 1981-82, 1982-83, 1983-84 (all Liverpool)
Football League Cup 1981, 1982, 1983, 1984 (all Liverpool)
Scottish Premier Division 1986-87, 1988-89 (Rangers/player-manager)
Scottish League Cup 1986-87, 1987-88, 1988-89 (Rangers/manager)

South American Championship

The Copa Sudamericana was inaugurated in 1916, the year of the formation of the South American Football Confederation. Between 1916-20 only Argentina, Brazil, Uruguay and Chile competed. Paraguay first played in 1921, Bolivia made their debut in 1926, Peru in 1927, Ecuador in 1939, Colombia in 1945 and finally Venezuela in 1967.

Formerly an annual event, it has been contested every four years since the late 1940s.

The championship lost its popularity in the 1960s following the formation of the South American Cup for League clubs, but it was revived in 1975 after a gap of eight years.

Before 1975 the country with the most points after a round-robin competition were declared champions. Since reorganisation in 1975 the competing nations have been divided into three qualifying periods with the group winners, plus the defending champions, going through to a knockout competition. Between 1975 and 1983 all matches were played over two legs. Since 1987 they have been over single games with the final in a neutral country.

Winners

1916	Uruguay	1929	Argentina	1955	Argentina
1917	Uruguay	1935*	Uruguay	1956*	Uruguay
1919	Brazil	1937	Argentina	1957	Argentina
1920	Uruguay	1939	Peru	1959	Argentina
1921	Argentina	1941*	Argentina	1959*	Uruguay
1922	Brazil	1942	Uruguay	1963	Bolivia
1923	Uruguay	1945*	Argentina	1967	Uruguay
1924	Uruguay	1946*	Argentina	1975	Peru
1925	Argentina	1947	Argentina	1979	Paraguay
1926	Uruguay	1949	Brazil	1983	Uruguay
1927	Argentina	1953	Paraguay	1987	Uruguay

* extraordinary tournaments, cup not awarded.

Wins
13 — Uruguay
12 — Argentina
3 — Brazil
2 — Paraguay, Peru
1 — Bolivia

South American Cup

A forerunner was organised in 1948 on the suggestion of top Chilean side Colo Colo, and won by Vasco da Gama of Brazil.

The South American Champions' Club Cup was the first contested in 1960 and soon overtook the Copa Sudamericana as the leading South American tournament.

It is open to runners-up as well as the League champions of the South American countries. It became known as the Copa Libertadores (Liberators' Cup) in 1965. The winners of the cup play the European Cup winners for the World Club championship each year.

Winners
1960 Penarol (Uruguay)
1961 Penarol (Uruguay)
1962 Santos (Brazil)
1963 Santos (Brazil)
1964 Independiente (Argentina)
1965 Independiente (Argentina)
1966 Penarol (Uruguay)
1967 Racing Club (Argentina)
1968 Estudiantes (Argentina)
1969 Estudiantes (Argentina)
1970 Estudiantes (Argentina)
1971 Nacional (Uruguay)
1972 Independiente (Argentina)
1973 Independiente (Argentina)
1974 Independiente (Argentina)
1975 Independiente (Argentina)
1976 Cruzeiro (Brazil)
1977 Boca Juniors (Argentina)
1978 Boca Juniors (Argentina)
1979 Olimpia (Paraguay)
1980 Nacional (Uruguay)
1981 Flamengo (Brazil)
1982 Penarol (Uruguay)
1983 Gremio (Brazil)
1984 Independiente (Argentina)
1985 Argentinos Juniors (Argentina)
1986 River Plate (Argentina)
1987 Penarol (Uruguay)
1988 Nacional (Uruguay)

Most wins
7 — Independiente (Argentina)
5 — Penarol (Uruguay)
3 — Estudiantes (Argentina), Nacional (Uruguay)

Southern League

Formed in 1894, the Southern League was for many years the most prestigious league after the Football League. Arsenal suggested a League for southern-based clubs in 1892 but as they were a professional side other clubs refused to co-operate for fear of suspension or a ban from the local FA.

Once Arsenal joined the Football League Millwall resurrected the idea and this time a League for southern-based clubs was formed.

In 1920 all members of the Southern League 1st division applied to join the Football League and were duly accepted, and so was born the new 3rd division which the following year became known as the 3rd division (south) because of the formation of a northern section.

With the Southern League depleted it divided into two regional sections, English and Welsh. In 1923 the Welsh section was disbanded and eastern and western sections were created. In 1933 a third, central, section was created, but from 1936 all sections combined to make one division.

After the formation of the Alliance Premier League in 1979 the Southern League was reorganised once more, this time into Northern Premier and Midland Premier divisions. The two winners played off to decide the championship. In 1982-83 a single Premier Division was formed yet again, complemented by Southern and Midland divisions. The format has been unaltered since 1982, although the League became known as the Beazer Homes League in 1987.

The champions of the Premier division automatically gain entry into the GM Vauxhall Conference, the Football League feeder league.

Recent champions
1983 AP Leamington
1984 Dartford
1985 Cheltenham T
1986 Welling U
1987 Fisher A
1988 Aylesbury U
1989 Merthyr T

Most wins
7 — Southampton (incl. 1 Southampton Res.)
6 — Merthyr T
5 — Dartford, Merthyr T
4 — Chelmsford C

Spectacles

Players with poor eyesight are no longer restricted from playing soccer at the highest level because of contact lenses. Before their availability, the occasional player appeared in spectacles. The most famous was Belgian Josef Jurion (Anderlecht and La Gantoise) who was capped for his country 64 times between 1955-67. He wore spectacles on each occasion.

The Preston North End goalkeeper J F Mitchell wore glasses in the 1922 FA Cup final against Huddersfield Town, the only instance of a player wearing spectacles in an FA Cup final.

Sponsorship

Sponsorship in soccer, like all other sports, is crucial these days. To meet the spiralling costs of running a football club, whether it be a Football League or a non-league club, outside financial support is necessary, and the best way of obtaining this is from sponsorship.

All football grounds have advertising hoardings around them and most clubs, down to the local Sunday League team, have a sponsor of some sort, even if only to cover the cost of providing a team strip.

Liverpool skipper Graeme Souness with the Canon trophy

The top Football League clubs all have a main club sponsor who pays about £100,000 a year to have their name on the team's shirts, around the ground, and in the match-day programme. Naturally, big name sponsors only want to be associated with the top clubs so success inevitably yields more cash from sponsors.

Major tournament sponsors

Football League	**Scottish League**
Canon 1983-86	Fine Fare 1986-88
Today 1986-87	B&Q 1988-
Barclays Bank 1987-	**Scottish League Cup**
Football League Cup	Skol 1984-
Milk Marketing Board 1982-85	
Littlewoods Organisation 1986-	

The first major act of match sponsorship accepted by the Football League was the Watney Cup in 1970.

Substitutes

In the international between Wales and Scotland at Wrexham on 15 April 1889 A. Pugh of Rhostyllen replaced Wales' injured goalkeeper S. G. Gillam. At the same ground on 10 March 1908 Dai Davies of Bolton replaced Leigh Roose as Welsh goalkeeper when he was injured playing against England. Substitutes were not allowed at the time and while they were carried out with the blessing of both teams and the officials, they were ruled to be against the laws of the game.

It was not until 1932 that the International Board of FIFA agreed to allow substitutes in international matches with foreign countries, provided it was agreed beforehand.

In 1958 the board ruled that substitute goalkeepers could be brought on at any time during a match, and substitutes for other players at any time in the first half. But this ruling did not apply to competitive matches, only friendlies.

The Football League allowed one substitute a team, but only in case of injury, in 1965-66, and the following season the FA Cup and Football League Cup also allowed one substitute, again to replace an injured player only. The Scottish League followed suit the same season.

In June 1967 the International Board ruled that substitutes could be allowed during a match

Current Football
League sponsors
Barclays seen getting
plenty of exposure at
Goodison Park

for any reason, and increased the number to two. The Football League, however, stuck to its limit of one.

Two substitutes were allowed in major European matches (one other than a goalkeeper) from the 1968-69 season and in 1972 the international board permitted up to five substitutes for non-championship international matches.

The Scottish League allowed two substitutes a game from 1973 and in England this was permitted for FA Cup and League Cup games from 1986-87 and for Football League games from 1987-88.

The *first substitute to come on in a Football League game* was Keith Peacock of Charlton Athletic against Bolton Wanderers at Burnden Park on 21 August 1965. The *first official substitute in a Scottish game* was Archie Gemmell for St Mirren against Clyde in a Scottish League Cup tie on 13 August 1966.

The *first substitute to score in a Football League game* was Bobby Knox (Barrow) against Wrexham on 21 August 1965. The *first to score in a Scottish game* was Gus Moffatt of Motherwell in the League Cup against Dunfermline on 13 August 1966. Knox was also the first substitute to come on to the field, go in goal, and save a penalty, which he did for Barrow against Doncaster Rovers in December 1965.

The *first substitute to come on in an FA Cup final* was Derek Clarke for West Brom against Everton on 18 May 1968.

The *first goal scored by a substitute in an FA Cup final* was by Eddie Kelly of Arsenal against Liverpool on 8 May 1971. No other substitute has scored in an FA Cup final.

The *first substitute to score in a Football League Cup final* was Ralph Coates for Spurs against Norwich City in 1973. Coates scored the only goal of the game. Only one other substitute has scored in a League Cup final, Martin Hayes of Arsenal against Luton Town in 1988.

The *first player to score a goal after coming on as substitute for England* was Dennis Wilshaw (Wolverhampton W) who replaced Jackie Milburn against Belgium in Brussels on 18 May 1950.

● England international Stanley Mortensen made his international debut *against* England. One of the England reserves against Wales in a war-time game on 25 September 1943, he was called in to help the Welsh side out when they lost Ivor Powell injured after two minutes.

● Of the 92 clubs in the Football League at the time substitutes were first allowed in 1965, the last to bring on a substitute was Notts County who did not use a sub for the first time until 5 February 1966. On that occasion Dennis Shiels came on for Brian Bates against Lincoln City.

Sunday Cup

See *FA Sunday Cup*

Sunday football

From their formation in 1863 the Football Association was against the playing of football on Sundays. Even after many local amateur Sunday Leagues sprang up it did not recognise them and it was not until 1955 that Sunday League teams were no longer considered 'outlaws' by the FA.

The question of permitting Sunday Football League games was raised numerous times over the years and the first real move came in 1964 when the FA launched its own FA Sunday Cup. On 19 March 1967 Wisbech played Dunstable Town in the Southern League. This was the *first professional competitive match in England* to be played on a Sunday.

The first *FA Cup tie to be played on a Sunday* was on 6 January 1974 when 8,479 (the club's biggest of the season) saw Cambridge United and Oldham Athletic draw 2-2. The first goal was scored by Paul Edwards of Oldham. Three other matches (Bolton W v Stoke C, Bradford C v Alvechurch, Nottingham F v Bristol R) all took place later that same day.

The *first Football League game on a Sunday* was on 20 January 1974 when Millwall played Fulham at the Den in front of 15,143 fans. The home team won 1-0 thanks to a Brian Clark goal.

Sunderland

Sunderland had the embarrassment of dropping into the 3rd division for the first time in their long history in 1987. For a club with the one-time record for the most consecutive seasons in the 1st division, that drop was a hard blow.

One of the great clubs of English football, they were founded in 1879 as the Sunderland & District Teachers FC, becoming plain Sunderland two years later. They were admitted into the Football League at the expense of Stoke in 1890 and then followed an amazing sequence of success: champions in 1892 and 1893, runners-up in 1894 and champions again in 1895. They stayed in the top division for 57 consecutive seasons and were champions three more times. In 1908 they enjoyed a great moment when they beat Newcastle 9-1 at St James's Park; Newcastle ended that season as 1st division champions though!

During the inter-world war years Sunderland only enjoyed one brief spell of glory: in 1936 they won the League championship and the following year won the Cup for the first time.

After losing their 1st division place in 1958 they lost their way a bit and it was not until they appointed Bob Stokoe as manager in 1972 that great days were to return to Roker Park when they beat favourites Leeds United to win the FA Cup in 1973, while still a 2nd division side.

They returned to the 1st division in 1976 and again in 1980, but sadly for the north-easterners, also dropped to the 3rd division. Happily the movement of Sunderland FC appears to be an upward one these days.

Ground: Roker Park
Nickname: Rokerites
Record attendance: 75,118 — v Derby C (FA Cup 6th round replay) 8 March 1933
First Football League season: 1890-91 Division 1 (7th)
Seasons in Football League: 88 (69 Division 1, 18 Division 2, 1 Division 3)

Honours

Division 1 champions 1891-92, 1892-93, 1894-95, 1901-02, 1912-13, 1935-36
Division 2 champions 1975-76
Division 3 champions 1987-88
FA Cup winners 1937, 1973

Supporters' clubs

The National Federation of Football Supporters' Clubs was formed in 1927 with six members: Bournemouth, Brentford, Brighton & Hove Albion, Charlton Athletic, Northampton Town and Plymouth Argyle. Membership is not restricted to League clubs only, and many non-league clubs' supporters are members. The first non-league supporters to join were those of Barking FC.

Suspensions

Apart from life suspensions imposed on players for allegedly fixing matches or gross infringement of rules, the longest bans on a player for on-field activities went to Frank Barson, formerly of Barnsley, Aston Villa, Manchester United, Watford, Hartlepool's United and Wigan Borough. After being sent off in his Barnsley days he was banned for one and two months. At Villa the club banned him for 14 and 7 days in 1919-20 for breach of club discipline. He is reputed to have pulled a gun on the Aston Villa manager once! He had a relatively trouble-free time at Old Trafford but when he moved to Watford he was banned for seven months after being sent off against Fulham in an incident involving the police. After his move to Wigan he was suspended for three months after being sent off against Accrington. He quit playing League soccer in 1930-31 and had a spell at Rhyl and Stourbridge where he was also given his marching orders a few times. Barson is believed to have been suspended more than a dozen times during his career.

William Cook of Oldham was banned for 12 months for failing to leave the field after being sent off against Middlesbrough on 3 April 1915.

Willie Woodburn of Glasgow Rangers was suspended *sine die* by the Scottish FA in 1955 after being sent off for the fourth time in his career in the opening match of the 1955-56 season. Nearly two years later, on appeal, he had the ban lifted.

Since the introduction of the penalty points system for on-field offences in 1973-74 the heaviest ban imposed on a player was the nine-match ban on Arsenal's Paul Davis (plus a £3,000 fine) in 1988 following an incident against Southampton in the 1988-89 season. The longest other bans imposed on players for incidents on the field since 1969 have been:

9 weeks — Brian O'Neil (Southampton) Dec 1981
9 weeks — Denis Hollywood (Southampton) Dec 1981
8 weeks — Derek Dougan (Wolverhampton W) Nov 1969
8 weeks — John Fitzpatrick (Manchester U) Nov 1969
8 weeks — Mark Dennis (Queen's Park R) Dec 1987

Tallest players

Records concerning tallest players can never be regarded as completely accurate. However, the following are believed to have been the tallest players in the Football League and Scottish League:

6'8¾" Bill Carr (Bournemouth) 1920s
6'6" Albert Ironmonger (Notts C, Lincoln C) 1904-27
6'5" George Ephgrave (Aston V, Swindon T, Southampton, Norwich C, Watford) 1938-53
6'5" I McWilliams (Queen's Park) 1975-77
6'5" Andy Morris (Rotherham U, Chesterfield) 1984-

Television

See *Broadcasting*

Test matches

Following the introduction of the 2nd division in 1892 end-of-season test matches involving the top teams in division 2 and the bottom teams in division 1 were organised. The format changed over the six years they were in force, as follows:

1893-95 Single game played on neutral ground involving top three and bottom three clubs. The winners either retained their 1st division place, or were promoted
1896-98 A round robin series. The top two in the 2nd division played the bottom two in the 1st division. At the end of the series the two highest placed clubs were either promoted or retained their first division status

The following clubs were involved in the play-offs each season. Those in bold played in the 1st division the following season.

Automatic promotion and relegation was introduced in 1898-99.

Division 1
1893 Notts C, Accrington, **Newton Heath**
1894 **Preston NE**, Darwen, Newton Heath
1895 **Stoke, Derby C**, Liverpool
1896 Small Heath, **West Bromwich A**
1897 **Sunderland**, Burnley
1898 Blackburn R, **Stoke C**

Division 2
Small Heath, **Sheffield U, Darwen**
Liverpool, Small Heath, Notts C
Bury, Notts C, Newton Heath
Liverpool, Manchester C
Notts C, Newton Heath
Burnley, Newcastle U

(see also *Play-offs*)

Testimonials and benefits

Players who have given loyal service to a club are often rewarded with a benefit season, when a series of money-raising functions are organised for the player's benefit. However, testimonial matches can be organised for a player only

Right: Chelsea's Micky Droy is 6 feet 4 ins tall, making him one of the tallest Football League players

Opposite: Second division Sunderland sprang a surprise by beating Leeds United 1–0 in the 1973 FA Cup final

after 10 years' service with one club, and all testimonials must be authorised by the Football League. The proceeds from the gate receipts go to the player.

The *record attendance for a testimonial game* is 56,000 at Anfield on 11 April 1972 for Roger Hunt's Testimonial for Liverpool against an England 1966 World Cup XI.

Texaco Cup

An invitation event for teams not involved in European Club competitions, this was the predecessor of the Anglo-Scottish Cup. Inaugurated in 1970-71, it was first won by Wolverhampton Wanderers. Unlike its successor, however, Irish teams competed as well as ones from the English and Scottish Leagues in the first two seasons.

Finals

			Att
1970-71	Hearts 1	Wolverhampton W 3	26,000
	Wolverhampton W 0	Hearts 1	25,000
	Wolves won 3-2 on aggregate		
1971-72	Airdrieonians 0	Derby C 0	16,000
	Derby C 2	Airdrieonians 1	25,102
	Derby won 2-1 on aggregate		
1972-73	Ipswich T 2	Norwich C 1	29,698
	Norwich C 1	Ipswich T 2	35,798
	Ipswich won 4-2 on aggregate		
1973-74	Newcastle U 2	Burnley 1 aet	34,540
	(one game only, played at St James's Park)		
1974-75	Southampton 1	Newcastle U 0	17,100
	Newcastle U 3	Southampton 0	19,288
	Newcastle won 3-1 on aggregate		

(The competition was replaced by the Anglo-Scottish Cup in 1975)

Throw-in

The throw-in must be taken from the point where the ball goes out of play and by a member of the team not playing the ball last. A goal cannot be scored direct from a throw-in and a player receiving the ball from a throw cannot be offside. A foul-throw results in the opposing side taking a throw-in from the same spot.

Although a throw-in had been mentioned in the Sheffield Rules in 1858, it was not until the Football Association clearly defined the throw-in in its rules of 1863 that its use became standard. Before that the ball was returned to play by a kick from the touch line.

The first throw-ins were one-handed affairs. The current two-handed throw was introduced in 1882. It was only in 1895 that the rules prevented a player taking a run-up before launching the throw. The new rules stated that a player had to stand on the touch-line when taking the throw-in.

Tickets

The *first all-ticket FA Cup final* was in 1924. The Football Association took the steps after the inaugural final at Wembley the previous year resulted in nearly 75,000 getting into the ground unofficially. Since then, all Wembley FA Cup finals have been all-ticket.

It is not only Wembley matches that are all-ticket: clubs often make League games all-ticket when they are expecting big crowds so they can control the number of spectators, and also control the limit of tickets supplied to visiting fans.

The *first all-ticket match* is believed to have been the Scotland versus England international at Hampden Park on 15 March 1884 when just over 10,000 tickets were sold.

Above: Leicester City goalkeeper Gordon Banks is powerless to stop Bobby Smith scoring Spurs' first goal in the 1961 FA Cup final

Opposite: The man who led Spurs to the double in 1961, Irishman Danny Blanchflower – one of a handful of people to refuse to appear on the *This Is Your Life* television programme

Tottenham Hotspur

In 1901, six years after turning professional, Tottenham were in the Southern League, but they created a shock by beating Sheffield United to win the FA Cup at Crystal Palace. To this day, Spurs remain the only team outside the Football League to win the Cup since the formation of the League.

Founded in 1882 as Hotspur FC by a group of ex-grammar school boys, their first ground was at Tottenham Marshes, hence the change of name. They turned professional in 1895, moved to White Hart Lane in 1898, and three years later had that great Cup win.

However, it was not until 1908 that Spurs were elected to the Football League. They won promotion at the first attempt and in 1921 won the FA Cup for the second time despite not being established as one of the top 1st division teams at the time. But in 1950 Arthur Rowe's 'push and run' team won the 2nd and 1st division titles in successive season. From then on, apart from a season back in the 2nd division in 1977-78, Spurs have been one of the leading 1st division sides.

Ten years after their first League success manager Bill Nicholson guided the team to the first 20th century League and Cup double, skippered by Danny Blanchflower. They retained the Cup in 1962 and the following year became the first British club to win in Europe when they beat Atletico Madrid to win the Cup-winners' Cup. They won the FA Cup for a fifth time in 1967, when they beat Chelsea in the first all-London final this century.

They made it six Cup wins in six appearances in 1981 and the following year it was win number seven. The glorious Cup sequence was ended by Coventry City in 1987 when Spurs lost a Cup final for the first time. Their seven wins is nevertheless a record jointly held with Aston Villa.

Ground: White Hart Lane
Nickname: Spurs
Record attendance: 75,038 — v Sunderland (FA Cup 6th round), 5 March 1938
First Football League season: 1908-09 Division 2 (2nd)
Seasons in Football League: 70 (54 Division 1, 16 Division 2)

Honours

Division 1 champions 1950-51, 1960-61
Division 2 champions 1919-20, 1949-50
FA Cup winners 1901, 1921, 1961, 1962, 1967, 1981, 1982
Football League Cup winners 1971, 1973
European Cup-winners' Cup winners 1963
UEFA Cup winners 1972, 1984
Footballers of the Year Danny Blanchflower (FWA) 1958, 1961 Pat Jennings (FWA) 1963, (PFA) 1976 Steve Perryman (FWA) 1982 Clive Allen (FWA/PFA) 1987

Tours

The *first tour of any description* was made by the Royal Engineers who ventured north to play games in Derby, Sheffield and Nottingham in December 1873.

The *first English team to make an overseas tour* was Oxford University who toured Germany in 1875.

The *first Scottish club to tour abroad* was Queen's Park who toured Copenhagen, Denmark in 1898.

The *first club to tour the Americas* was Sunderland who toured the United States in 1894.

Transfers

The *first £100 transfer fee* was paid by Aston Villa when they bought Willie Groves from West Bromwich Albion in 1892. In 1902 Sunderland paid Sheffield United £500 for Alf Common. In February 1905 Middlesbrough paid Sunderland £1,000 for Common, *the first £1,000 transfer.* In an effort to curb these spiralling transfer fees the League imposed a limit of £350 on all transfers but clubs got around the restriction by selling two players for £700, one the sought-after player and the other a make-weight in the deal.

Seven years after the first £1,000 deal Blackburn bought Danny Shea from West Ham in the *first £2,000 transfer.* Before the First World War, in 1914, Manchester City paid the *first £2,500 fee* when they bought Horace Barnes from Derby County.

The *first £5,000 fee* was paid by Falkirk in February 1922 when they bought Syd Puddefoot from West Ham.

The magical *£10,000 milestone* was broken in 1928 when Arsenal paid £10,890 for Bolton's David Jack.

Since then transfer fees world wide have rocketed up into the million-pound bracket . . . and beyond.

Football League

£11,000	Jimmy Allen	Portsmouth to Aston Villa	July 1934
£14,000	Bryn Jones	Wolverhampton to Arsenal	Aug 1938
£15,500	Billy Steel	Morton to Derby C	June 1947
£20,000	Tommy Lawton	Chelsea to Notts C	Nov 1947
£20,500	Len Shackleton	Newcastle U to Sunderland	Feb 1948
£25,000	John Morris	Manchester U to Derby C	March 1949
£26,000	Eddie Quigley	Sheffield W to Preston NE	Dec 1949
£29,500	Trevor Ford	Aston Villa to Sunderland	Oct 1950
£34,000	Jackie Sewell	Notts C to Sheffield W	March 1951
£35,000	Cliff Jones	Swansea T to Tottenham H	Feb 1958
£45,000	Albert Quixall	Sheffield W to Manchester U	Sept 1958
£55,000	Denis Law	Huddersfield T to Manchester C	March 1960
£99,999	Jimmy Greaves	AC Milan to Tottenham H	Nov 1961
£115,000	Denis Law	Torino to Manchester U	July 1962
£125,000	Martin Chivers	Southampton to Tottenham H	Jan 1968
£150,000	Alan Clarke	Fulham to Leicester C	June 1968
£165,000	Alan Clarke	Leicester C to Leeds U	July 1969
£200,000	Martin Peters	West Ham U to Tottenham H	March 1970
£220,000	Alan Ball	Everton to Arsenal	Dec 1971
£225,000	David Nish	Leicester C to Derby C	Aug 1972
£350,000	Bob Latchford	Birmingham C to Everton	Feb 1974
£352,000	Graeme Souness	Middlesbrough to Liverpool	Jan 1978
£495,000	Gordon McQueen	Leeds U to Manchester U	Feb 1978
£500,000	David Mills	Middlesbrough to West Bromwich A	Jan 1979
£1,000,000	Trevor Francis	Birmingham C to Nottingham F	Feb 1979
£1,450,277	Steve Daley	Wolverhampton W to Manchester C	Sept 1979
£1,469,000	Andy Gray	Aston Villa to Wolverhampton W	Sept 1979
£1,500,000	Bryan Robson	West Bromwich A to Manchester U	Oct 1981
£1,900,000	Peter Beardsley	Newcastle U to Liverpool	July 1987
£2,000,000	Paul Gasgoigne	Newcastle U to Tottenham H	July 1988
£2,500,000	Tony Cottee	West Ham U to Everton	Aug 1988
£2,800,000	Ian Rush	Juventus to Liverpool	Aug 1988

In recent years the fees have involved players in part-exchange, and have also been subject to VAT. As figures are never quoted by the Football League or the clubs themselves, the figures are widely regarded as accurate estimates. Where other players were involved in a deal, the figure is the value of the player at the centre of the move.

British players to and from foreign clubs

£3,200,000	Ian Rush	Liverpool to Juventus	June 1987
£2,800,000	Ian Rush	Juventus to Liverpool	July 1988
£2,750,000	Gary Lineker	Everton to Barcelona	June 1986
£2,300,000	Mark Hughes	Manchester U to Barcelona	May 1986
£1,800,000	Mark Hughes	Barcelona to Manchester U	June 1988
£1,500,000	Ray Wilkins	Manchester U to AC Milan	June 1984

Milestones involving British players
(other than those included above):

First player to be transferred for two £20,000 fees
Bob Brennan (Luton to Birmingham July 1949; Birmingham to Fulham June 1950)
First £100,000 transfer between two Football League clubs
Alan Ball, Blackpool to Everton, Aug 1966 (£110,000)
First £100,000 involving a British player
Denis Law, Manchester C to Torino, July 1961
First Irishman to be transferred for £100,000
Gerry Daly, Manchester U to Derby C, March 1977 (£160,000)
First player transferred between Scottish clubs for £100,000
Colin Stein, Hibernian to Rangers, Oct 1968
First player transferred between Scottish clubs for £1 million
Ian Ferguson, St Mirren to Rangers, Feb 1988
Record fee between English and Scottish clubs
£1,500,000 Richard Gough, Tottenham H to Rangers, Oct 1987

Treble

Left: Liverpool's 'super-sub' David Fairclough

No Football League Club has completed the treble of Football League, FA Cup and Football League Cup in one season. However, both Celtic and Rangers have achieved the feat in Scotland.

Rangers: 1948-49, 1963-64, 1975-76, 1977-78
Celtic: 1966-67*, 1968-69
* Celtic also won the European Cup and the Glasgow Cup

The only team to win two major English titles and a European title in the same season is Liverpool. In 1983-84 they won the League, Milk Cup and European Champions' Cup.

Only three clubs have won the European Champions' Cup and their own domestic League and Cup competitions in the same year.

Celtic (Scotland) 1967
Ajax (Netherlands) 1972
PSV Eindhoven (Netherlands) 1988

Below left: Trevor Francis (left) Britain's first £1 million player

Below: The first £1000 footballer, Alf Common

Undefeated

The *longest unbeaten run in the 1st division* is 42 matches by Nottingham Forest from 20 November 1977 to 9 December 1978 (won 21, drew 21). The run was ended by Liverpool.

The *longest unbeaten run in Scotland* is 62 matches (49 won, 13 drawn) by Celtic between 13 November 1915 and 21 April 1917 when the run was ended by Kilmarnock, who won 2-0.

The *longest unbeaten sequence in one season* is 30 matches by Burnley in the 1st division in 1920-21.

The *longest unbeaten run from the start of the season* is 29 matches held jointly by Leeds United (1973-74) and Liverpool (1987-88). Liverpool also remained unbeaten in 29 games in the 1893-94 season which consisted of all 28 League games plus one Test Match.

Liverpool have been *unbeaten at home* in a record eight Football League seasons (1893-94, 1895-96, 1904-05, 1970-71, 1976-77, 1978-79, 1979-80, 1987-88). After losing 3-2 at home to Birmingham City on 21 January 1978 they did not lose in a League game at Anfield until 31 January 1981 when Leicester City won 2-1 thus ending a run of 63 games without defeat on home soil.

The *most FA Cup ties without defeat* is 24 by Blackburn Rovers between December 1883 and December 1886.

● Between 3 February 1957 and 7 March 1965 Real Madrid went 122 League games at home without defeat.

(see also *Defeats (fewest)*)

Union of European Football Associations (UEFA)

Founded in 1954 with 30 members, UEFA is the European governing body for member nations under its control. It does not interfere with the day-to-day running of national associations, but has control over clubs that take part in UEFA-organised competitions: the European Championship, the three major club competitions (Champions' Cup, Cup-winners' Cup and UEFA Cup) and other junior and youth tournaments.

One of UEFA's first tasks was to launch the European Cup in 1955. It was won by Real Madrid, who have the best record in all three major UEFA club tournaments with eight wins; they are followed by Liverpool with six.

UEFA Cup

Originally known as the International Industries Fairs Inter-Cities Cup, it was launched in 1955 as a tournament for European cities who sponsored international industrial fairs. Called simply the Fairs Cup, the first competition took three years to complete. The second tournament involved club sides and since 1960-61 it has been an annual event. All matches including the final are played over two legs, with the exception of the 1964 and 1965 finals which were single games.

In 1966 the competition changed its name to the European Fairs Cup and in 1971 it became the UEFA Cup.

A special game between Barcelona and Leeds United (the first and last winners of the Fairs Cup) was organised in 1971 to see who retained permanent possession of the trophy. Barcelona won 2-1 in front of their home fans.

Most wins
3-Barcelona
2-Borussia Moenchengladbach, IFK Gothenburg, Leeds U, Liverpool, Real Madrid, Tottenham H, Valencia
Most final appearances
4-Barcelona, Borussia Moenchengladbach
3-Anderlecht, Juventus, Leeds U, Tottenham H, Valencia
Biggest win
Single game
13-0-Cologne v Union Luxembourg (1st round), 5 Oct 1965

● Newcastle United won the 1969 Fairs Cup despite the previous season finishing only tenth in the English 1st division. They were eligible for the competition because of the 'one club one city' rule in force at the time.

United States of America

The most memorable date in United States soccer history is 29 June 1950, when a little known player, Larry Gaetjens, a naturalised Haitian immigrant from New York, was carried off the field shoulder high after he scored the only goal of the game which inflicted a 1-0 defeat on the mighty England side in the final stages of the World Cup in Brazil. It was one of the biggest upsets in World Cup history.

British settlers took football to the American colonies in the 17th century but the first reference to football in the United States was at Harvard in 1827. The first intercollegiate game was between Princeton and Rutgers in 1869, but this was more a form of rugby than the association game. By 1871 the dribbling game was popular in many of the universities and colleges and on 28 November 1885 the United States played their first international match against Canada at Newark. Canada won 1-0.

The United States Football Association dates to 1913 but they have had to battle constantly against the popularity of American football to gain a foothold. It changed its name to the United States Soccer Football Association in 1945 and to its present name, the United States Soccer Federation, in 1974.

As members of FIFA they were threatened with expulsion in 1978 if they did not conform to the rules of the game. The US game incorporated penalty shoot-outs from the 35-yard line if a game ended in a draw: the Americans don't like drawn games in any sport.

While professional soccer in the United States is on the decline, it will surely rise again because the sport is very popular at grass-roots level, and the staging of the 1994 World Cup in the United States will only enhance its popularity.

International competitions
World Cup
(Best performance)
1930 Semi-final (lost 6-1 to Argentina)

(see also *North American Soccer League* and *Major Indoor Soccer League*)

Uruguay

Considering its relatively small population, Uruguay has been proportionately outstanding in the soccer world. The first winners of the World Cup in their own country in 1930, Uruguay won the competition when they next competed in 1950.

Soccer was introduced to Uruguay by the British in 1870 and at the University of Montevideo in 1882 the first club was formed, consisting mostly of British students. The Uruguayan Football Association was formed in 1900 and a national League inaugurated, with four clubs. Two of the founder members were Nacional and the all-British Central Uruguay Railway team, who later became Penarol. These two teams have been outstanding in South American club history since the inauguration of the Copa Libertadores in 1960.

The first Uruguay national team was assembled and played its first international on 15 August 1905 against arch-rivals Argentina.

Six times winners of the South American championship by 1930, Uruguay hosted the first World Cup and beat Argentina 4-2 in the final. They did not compete in Europe in 1934 and 1938 but when it was next held in Brazil in 1950 Uruguay pipped the host nation for the title. Despite being the most successful South American nation since then, Uruguay has never progressed beyond the semi-final stages.

International competitions
World Cup winners
1930 (beat Argentina 4-2)
1950 (beat Brazil 2-1 in final match)
South American champions
1916-17, 1920, 1923-24, 1926, 1935, 1942, 1956, 1959, 1967, 1983, 1987

UEFA Cup
Finals
(Home team first)

Year			
1958	London 2	Barcelona 2	45,466
	Barcelona 6	London 0	62,000
1960	Birmingham C 0	Barcelona 0	40,500
	Barcelona 4	Birmingham C 1	70,000
1961	Birmingham C 2	AS Roma 2	21,005
	AS Roma 2	Birmingham C 0	60,000
1962	Valencia 6	Barcelona 2	65,000
	Barcelona 1	Valencia 1	60,000
1963	Dynamo Zagreb 1	Valencia 2	40,000
	Valencia 2	Dynamo Zagreb 0	55,000
1964	Real Zaragoza 2	Valencia 1	50,000
	(played over one leg, at Barcelona)		
1965	Ferencvaros 1	Juventus 0	25,000
	(played over one leg, at Turin)		
1966	Barcelona 0	Real Zaragoza 1	70,000
	Real Zaragoza 2	Barcelona 4 aet	70,000
1967	Dynamo Zagreb 2	Leeds U 0	40,000
	Leeds U 0	Dynamo Zagreb 0	35,604
1968	Leeds U 1	Ferencvaros 0	25,368
	Ferencvaros 0	Leeds U 0	70,000
1969	Newcastle U 3	Ujpest Dozsa 0	60,000
	Ujpest Dozsa 2	Newcastle U 0	37,000
1970	Anderlecht 3	Arsenal 1	37,000
	Arsenal 3	Anderlecht 0	51,612
1971	Juventus 0	Leeds U 0	40,000
	(abandoned after 51 minutes, waterlogged pitch)		
	Juventus 2	Leeds U 2	42,000
	Leeds U 1	Juventus 1	42,483
	(Leeds won on away goals)		
1972	Wolverhamton W 1	Tottenham H 2	38,362
	Tottenham H 1	Wolverhampton W 1	54,303
1973	Liverpool 0	Borussia Moenchengladbach 0	44,967
	(abandoned after 27 minutes, waterlogged pitch)		
	Liverpool 3	Borussia Moenchengladbach 0	41,169
	Borussia Moenchengladbach 2	Liverpool 0	35,000
1974	Tottenham H 2	Feyenoord 2	46,281
	Feyenoord 2	Tottenham H 0	59,317
1975	Borussia Moenchengladbach 0	Twente Enschede 0	42,368
	Twente Enschede 1	Borussia Moenchengladbach 5	21,767
1976	Liverpool 3	FC Bruges 2	49,981
	FC Bruges 1	Liverpool 1	32,000
1977	Juventus 1	Atletico Bilbao 0	75,000
	Atletico Bilbao 2	Juventus 1	43,000
	(Juventus won on away goals)		
1978	Bastia 0	PSV Eindhoven 0	15,000
	PSV Eindhoven 3	Bastia 0	27,000
1979	Red Star Belgrade 1	Borussia Moenchengladbach 1	87,500
	Borussia Moenchengladbach 1	Red Star Belgrade 0	45,000
1980	Borussia Moenchengladbach 3	Eintracht Frankfurt 2	25,000
	Eintracht Frankfurt 1	Borussia Moenchengladbach 0	60,000
	(Eintracht won on away goals)		
1981	Ipswich T 3	AZ 67 Alkmaar 0	27,532
	AZ 67 Alkmaar 4	Ipswich T 2	28,500
1982	IFK Gothenburg 1	SV Hamburg 0	42,548
	SV Hamburg 0	IFK Gothenburg 3	60,000
1983	Anderlecht 1	Benfica 0	60,000
	Benfica 1	Anderlecht 1	80,000
1984	Anderlecht 1	Tottenham H 1	40,000
	Tottenham H 1	Anderlecht 1 aet	46,205
	(Tottenham Hotspur won 4-3 on penalties)		
1985	Videoton 0	Real Madrid 3	30,000
	Real Madrid 0	Videoton 1	90,000
1986	Real Madrid 5	Cologne 1	80,000
	Cologne 2	Real Madrid 0	15,000
1987	IFK Gothenburg 1	Dundee United 0	50,023
	Dundee United 1	IFK Gothenburg 1	20,911
1988	Espanol 3	Bayer Leverkusen 0	42,000
	Bayer Leverkusen 3	Espanol 0 aet	22,500
	(Bayer Leverkusen won 3-2 on penalties)		
1989	Napoli 2	VFB Stuttgart 1	83,000
	VFB Stuttgart 3	Napoli 3	60,800

Right: Jules Rimet (left) presenting the trophy bearing his name to the president of the Uruguay FA after his country beat Argentina to win the first World Cup final in 1930

Below: Liverpool's run of 29 matches without defeat in 1987–88 ended at neighbours Everton

Spurs' skipper Alan Mullery after they had beaten Wolves in 1972 to become the first winners of the UEFA Cup

Wages

In the days before professionalism was legalised clubs were paying players about *2s 6d* (12½ p) a match. In the early 1890s, after professionalism was legalised, Sunderland paid players at the rate of 30s (£1.50) a game, an enormous amount in those days. The Football League tried to fix maximum wage limits in 1893, but were unsuccessful. However, in 1901 they fixed a limit of £4 per week.

Since then the following limits have been fixed:
1910 £5 a week maximum with increases from £4-5 given in two 10s (50p) stages after 2 and 4 years' service
1920 £9 a week maximum (new players started on £5 and worked up to the £9 maximum).
1921 £10 a week maximum
1922 £8 a week in the playing season and £6 a week during the close-season

(During the war special rates applied and players were paid £1 10s (£1.50) (later £2) a match plus travelling expenses)
1945 The close-season wage was increased to £7
1947 A *minimum* wage level was set for the first time thanks to the efforts of the Players' Union. The minimum wages were £7 a week in the season and £5 off-season, for all players over the age of 20. The maximum limits were raised to £12 and £10, based on length of service.
1951 Maximum limit raised to £14
1953 Maximum limits raised to £15 during season, and £12 in close-season
1957 Maximum limits raised to £17 and £14 respectively
1958 Maximum limit in playing season reached £20 per week, and £17 per week for the off-season

In 1961 the Football League succumbed to pressure from the Players' Union to have maximum wage limits lifted, and in an effort to avert a national strike, they agreed to their demands. Johnny Haynes of Fulham immediately commanded a wage of £100 per week, Britain's first footballer to receive such a sum.

Wales

The Welsh Football Association was established after a meeting at the Wynnstay Arms, Wrexham, on 2 February 1876 by a group of enthusiasts who wanted to arrange an international fixture with Scotland. The match duly took place on 25 March 1876 and the Scots won 4-0. The team consisted of north Wales players, and the southern contingent maintained it was not a fully representative Welsh team.

The leading Welsh clubs at that time, however, came from the north. The first club to be formed was the famous Druids FC from Ruabon, near Wrexham. The Wrexham club was itself founded in 1873 and is the oldest senior Welsh club still in existence.

The man responsible for getting the Welsh FA off the ground was Llewellyn Kenrick, regarded as the father of Welsh football. The Welsh Cup was founded in 1877 and is the third oldest Cup competition in the world.

Three Welsh clubs take part in the English Football League: Wrexham, Cardiff City and Swansea City. Until 1988 Newport were members. Cardiff City won the FA Cup in 1927, the only non-English team to have done so.

Wales has produced some great individual international players over the years: Billy Meredith, John Charles, Ivor Allchurch, Trevor Ford and Ian Rush, but they have never fared well as a national team and were often one of the poor relations of the home international championship.

International competitions

World Cup

1958 Reached quarter-final (lost to Brazil 1-0)

European championship

Never reached last-eight stage.

(see also *Welsh Cup*)

War-time soccer

Football League and FA Cup competitions were cancelled during both world wars, but soccer was still played. During the First World War the Scottish League carried on but the Cup was abandoned.

First World War

During the First World War a Lancashire and Midland section of the Football League was contested, and in the south there was the London Combination. To keep the fixtures going a subsidiary tournament was run in all three cases at the end of the main season.

Champions

	Lancashire	Midlands	London Combination
1915-16	Manchester C	Nottingham F	Chelsea
1916-17	Liverpool	Leeds C	West Ham U
1917-18*	Stoke C	Leeds C	Chelsea
1918-19*	Everton	Nottingham F	Brentford

* In these two seasons the Lancashire and Midlands champions met in a two-legged play-off to decide the outright champions. Leeds City won in 1918 and Nottingham Forest in 1919.

Second World War

League fixtures in both England and Scotland were organised regionally and in England there was a national cup competition until 1942 when it was split into two regions, north and south.

Champions

South Division A:	1939-40	Arsenal
South Division B:	1939-40	Queen's Park R
South Division C:	1939-40	Tottenham H
South Division D:	1939-40	Crystal P
Western Division:	1939-40	Stoke C
South-Western Division:	1939-40	Plymouth A
Midland Division:	1939-40	Wolverhampton W
East-Midland Division:	1939-40	Chesterfield
North-West Division:	1939-40	Bury
North-East Division:	1939-40	Huddersfield T
Scottish West & South Division:	1939-40	Rangers
Scottish East & North Division:	1939-40	Falkirk
North Regional League:	1940-41	Preston NE
	1941-42	Blackpool
	1942-43	Blackpool
	1943-44	Blackpool
	1944-45	Huddersfield T
	1945-46	Sheffield U
South Regional League:	1940-41	Crystal P
	1941-42	Leicester C
	1942-43	Arsenal
	1943-44	Tottenham H
	1944-45	Tottenham H
	1945-46	Birmingham C
Scottish Southern League:	1940-41	Rangers
	1941-42	Rangers
	1942-43	Rangers
	1943-44	Rangers
	1944-45	Rangers
League War Cup:	1939-40	West Ham U
	1940-41	Preston NE
	1941-42	Wolverhampton W
	1942-43	(north) Blackpool
		(south) Arsenal
	1943-44	(north) Aston Villa
		(south) Charlton A
	1944-45	(north) Bolton W
		(south) Chelsea
Scottish Cup	1939-40	Rangers
(Known as (a) Emergency Cup	1940-41	Hibernian
(b) Summer Cup (c) Summer	1941-42	Rangers
League Cup)	1942-43	St Mirren
	1943-44	Motherwell
	1944-45	Partick T
	1945-46	Aberdeen

International matches
These were not regarded as 'full' internationals.
Most capped players
Stanley Matthews (Stoke C) 29
Joe Mercer (Everton) 27
Tommy Lawton (Everton) 23

Watney Cup

This was a pre-season competition for the top goalscoring teams of the previous season. Eight Football League teams played on a knockout system over a single match. The final was also a single match at the ground of one of the finalists. The eligible teams were the two top scoring teams in each of the four divisions provided they were not promoted or eligible for one of the major European competitions. The competition was discontinued after the 1973-74 season.

Welsh Cup

The Welsh Cup was launched on 30 October 1877 when Newtown entertained Druids in the first match. The first final was held the following March and won by Wrexham who beat Druids 1-0. Nineteen teams took part in the first competition.

The Welsh Cup is the third oldest Cup competition in the world. It is open to Welsh teams and the English teams close to the Welsh border. The Cup has been won by several English clubs, but the only final without a Welsh team was in 1934 when Bristol City beat Tranmere Rovers at Chester.

Since 1961 the Welsh Cup winners, provided they were not English, have automatically qualified for the European Cup-winners' Cup. Swansea Town were the first winners to qualify.

Watney Cup

Finals

			Attendance
1970-71	Derby C* 4	Manchester U 1	32,049
1971-72	Colchester U 4	West Bromwich A* 4	18,000
	Colchester won 4-3 on penalties		
1972-73	Bristol R* 0	Sheffield U 0	19,000
	Bristol R* won 7-6 on penalties		
1973-74	Stoke C 2	Hull C 0	18,159

*home team

● Cardiff City in 1927 completed the double of the English and FA Cup in the same season. The only other Welsh Cup winners to appear in the English FA Cup final are Bristol City.

Recent winners

1980	Newport C	1985	Shrewsbury T[3]
1981	Hereford U[1]	1986	Wrexham
1982	Swansea C	1987	Merthyr T
1983	Swansea C	1988	Cardiff C
1984	Shrewsbury T[2]	1989	Swansea C

[1] did not qualify for Europe, place taken by Swansea C
[2] did not qualify for Europe, place taken by Wrexham
[3] did not qualify for Europe, place taken by Bangor C

Most wins
22 — Wrexham
20 — Cardiff C
8 — Druids, Swansea T/Swansea C
6 — Shrewsbury T

One of Wales' finest players, the 'Gentle Giant' John Charles

Wembley Stadium

The idea of a national stadium was first mooted in 1920 when it was suggested a site be constructed for the British Empire Exhibition of 1924. Work did not get under way until January 1922, but in less than 15 months the famous stadium was built at a cost of £750,000.

The focal point of the stadium are twin towers 126 feet/38.5 metres high. After its completion Sir Charles Clegg of the FA signed a 21-year lease on it. Four days later, on 28 April 1923, the first FA Cup final was played at Wembley. Unfortunately the organisers did not realise how many people would want to get into the ground to see its first Cup final. The official attendance is given as 126,047 but something nearer 200,000 were estimated to be inside the ground on the day.

Every FA Cup final has been played at Wembley since that day, but they are now all-ticket affairs. England play their home matches at Wembley, and other major finals for League and non-league teams are played at England's most famous venue.

In addition to soccer, Wembley was the venue for the main events at the 1948 Olympic Games. It has also been used for greyhound racing, American football, show jumping, hockey, speedway, and many other sporting events, including the final of the Rugby League Challenge Cup every spring. The indoor Wembley arena and pool was opened in 1934 and swimming, tennis, boxing, basketball, ice hockey, badminton takes place there. The Wembley Conference Centre and hotel complex opened in 1977.

Floodlights were installed in 1955 at a cost of £22,000 and in a major facelift in 1963 the stands were re-roofed and the open ends covered for the first time, giving cover to all 100,000 spectators.

Moves towards making Wembley an all-seater stadium got under way during the summer of 1988 reducing its capacity to 87,000 (63,000 seated and 24,000 standing). It was further reduced in 1989.

Opposite: Football's first £100-a-week player, Johnny Haynes of Fulham

Below: After playing for Wales 44 times Mike England went on to manage the national side

● The only team to play Football League matches at Wembley is Clapton Orient who played two 3rd division (south) games there in 1930 when their own ground was out of commission. Their first game against Brentford on 22nd November drew a crowd of 10,300 but their second game, against Luton town on 4 December, was watched by a mere 2,500.

● Bobby Charlton has made a record 48 appearances at Wembley (all matches).

West Bromwich Albion

West Brom started life as the football section of the West Bromwich Strollers cricket team who found themselves with nothing to do in the winter months. They changed their name to Albion in 1880 and in 1884 adopted as their crest a thrush perched on a crossbar. The local name for a thrush was a throstle, the origin of the club's nickname.

Having gained a reputation in the Staffordshire area they entered the FA Cup and in 1885 reached the last eight. The following year they reached the final before losing to the mighty Blackburn Rovers. They lost to Aston Villa a year later but in 1888 it was a case of 'third time lucky' when they beat Preston 2-1 at the Oval.

One of the 12 founder members of the League the following season, they stayed in the top division until 1901. They won their first and only League title in 1920 and in 1931 as a 2nd division club beat neighbours Birmingham in the Cup final at Wembley. They came close to completing the double in 1954, but after beating Preston to win the Cup were handicapped by injuries towards the end of their League programme and had to be content with 2nd place to Wolves.

Albion have a reputation for grooming top goalscorers. Arthur Rowley started his League career at Albion and other prolific Albion scorers have been Ronnie Allen, Derek Kevan, Jeff Astle and Tony Brown.

They won the FA Cup for a fifth time in 1968 but sadly that was the last honour the Throstles won.

Ground: Hawthorns
Nickname: Throstles, Albion, Baggies
Record attendance: 64,815 — v Arsenal (FA Cup 6th round), 6 March 1937
First Football League season: 1888-89 Football League (6th)
Seasons in Football League: 90 (68 Division 1, 22 Division 2)

Honours

Division 1 champions 1919-20
Division 2 champions 1901-02, 1910-11
FA Cup winners 1888, 1892, 1931, 1954, 1968
Football League Cup winners 1966

West Germany

Since the late 1960s West Germany has been one of Europe's most successful nations at both club and international level. Although their rise to the top of world football started with a shock World Cup final win over Hungary in 1954, it is since their defeat by England at Wembley in 1966 that they have emerged as one of the most successful nations.

The Deutscher Fussball-Bund (German Football Association) was formed in 1900 and joined FIFA in 1904. They retained their membership until 1946, but rejoined in 1950.

Soccer was introduced to Germany by the British in 1870 via the northern sea ports. In 1875 an Oxford University team toured Ger-

many and the following year the rules were translated into German for the first time.

In the 1880s many sporting clubs sprang up, all with football sections, but the first soccer-only club, SC Germania Hamburg, later to be known as SV Hamburg, was founded in 1887.

The first leagues were started in the 1890s but these were only regional, with the local champions playing off for the German title. It was not until the formation of the Bundesliga in 1963 that a national league was created. The first Bundesliga matches got under way on 24 August 1963 and the honour of scoring the League's first goals went to Friedholm Konietzka of Borussia Dortmund against Werder Bremen.

Since the formation of the League West Ger-man soccer has advanced dramatically: they have reached the World Cup final four times, winning in 1974, reached the European Championship final twice and provided no fewer than ten winners of the major European Club tournaments.

West Germany have fielded a host of fine top-class players in the last 25 years: Uwe Seeler, Franz Beckenbauer, Gerd Muller and Karl-Heinz Rummenigge are just a few.

International competitions

World Cup winners 1954 beat Hungary 3-2, 1974 beat Netherlands 2-1
European champions 1972 (beat USSR 3-0), 1980 (beat Belgium 2-1)

Jeff Astle scores the winning goal for West Brom in extra time as Albion beat Everton to win the FA Cup in 1968

Wins

Highest numbers

Football League season

Wins	Matches		Div	
33	42	Doncaster R	3N	1946-47
32	42	Tottenham H	2	1919-20
32	46	Aston Villa	3	1971-72
32	46	Lincoln C	4	1975-76
32	46	Swindon T	4	1985-86
31	42	Tottenham H	1	1960-61
31	46	Rotherham U	3N	1950-51
31	46	Grimsby T	3N	1955-56
31	46	Hull C	3	1965-66
31	46	York C	4	1983-84

The record for division 3 (south) is 30 by Millwall (1927-28), Plymouth A (1929-30), Cardiff C (1946-47), Nottingham F (1950-51), Bristol C (1954-55)

Scottish League season

Wins	Matches		Div	
35	42	Rangers	*	1920-21
33	38	Morton	2	1966-67
32	36	Morton	2	1963-64
32	38	Celtic	*	1915-16
32	38	Celtic	1	1935-36
31	42	Rangers	*	1919-20

*Scottish League (only one division)
In 1898-99 Rangers won all 18 league games

Post 1975

Wins	Matches		Div	
31	44	Rangers	P	1986-87
31	44	Celtic	P	1987-88
27	36	Aberdeen	P	1984-85
27	39	Forfar A	2	1983-84
27	39	Ayr U	2	1987-88
27	44	Celtic	P	1986-87
26	36	Celtic	P	1980-81
26	39	Motherwell	1	1981-82
26	44	Rangers	P	1987-88
26	36	Rangers	P	1988-89

Fewest
Football League season

Wins	Matches		Div	
1	34	Loughborough T	2	1899-1900
2	46	Rochdale	3	1973-74
2	34	Darwen	2	1898-99
3	46	Southport	4	1976-77
3	42	Stoke C	1	1984-85
3	38	Woolwich A	1	1912-13
3	34	Doncaster R	2	1904-05
3	30	Crewe A	2	1894-95
3	28	Norwich V	2	1893-94
3	22	Stoke	*	1889-90

*Football League (before formation of 2nd division)

The records for the other divisions are:
Division 3 (south): 6 (42 matches) Queen's Park R, 1925-26
6 (42 matches) Merthyr T, 1929-30
Division 3 (north): 4 (42 matches) Rochdale, 1931-32

The lowest totals by division since 1945 have been:
Division 1: Stoke C (as above)
Division 2: 4 (42 matches) Cambridge U, 1983-84
Division 3: Rochdale (as above)
Division 4: Southport (as above)
Division 3 (south): 7 (46 matches) Walsall, 1952-53
Division 3 (north): 6 (46 matches) Crewe A, 1956-57

Scottish league

Wins	Matches		Div	
0	22	Vale of Leven	*	1891-92
1	38	Forfar A	2	1974-75
1	34	Ayr U	1	1966-67
1	22	East Stirling	2	1905-06
1	18	Renton	1	1893-94
1	18	Abercorn	1	1896-97
1	18	Clyde	1	1897-98
1	18	Dundee	1	1898-99
1	18	Morton	1	1901-02

*Scottish League (only one division)

Post 1975

Wins	Matches		Div	
3	44	Morton	P	1987-88
3	36	St Johnstone	P	1975-76
3	36	Kilmarnock	P	1982-83
4	39	East Fife	1	1977-78
4	39	Queen of the S	1	1981-82
4	39	Stanraer	2	1987-88
4	36	Kilmarnock	P	1976-77
4	36	Motherwell	P	1983-84

Opposite: West German Karl Heinz Rummenigge, winner of the European Footballer of the Year title in 1980 and 1981

Above: Franz Beckenbauer holds aloft the FIFA World Cup Trophy after beating the Netherlands in the 1974 final

● Cambridge United went a record 31 Football League games without a win between 1 October 1983 and 28 April 1984.

● Between September 1922 and September 1925 Merthyr Town went 61 away games in the Football League without a win.

● In 1963-64 Morton had 23 consecutive wins in the Scottish 2nd division from the start of the season.

● The most consecutive wins in a season is 14 by Manchester U (1904-5), Bristol C (1905-06) and Preston NE (1950-51). All were in the 2nd division. The 1st division record is 11 by Tottenham Hotspur in 1960-61.

● In 1929-30 Brentford won all 21 home games in division 3 (south) to create a Football League record.

● The best winning start to a Football League season was by Reading in division 3 in 1985-86 when they won their first 13 matches. A 2-2 draw at home to Wolverhampton Wanderers on 23 October ended the run.

● Sheffield Wednesday and Stoke City have each failed to win away from home in a record five seasons. Wednesday were winless in 1898-99, 1900-01, 1926-27, 1957-58 and 1975-76. Stoke failed to win away in 1891-92, 1893-94, 1897-88, 1968-69 and 1984-85.

Wolverhampton Wanderers

In the 1950s and 1960s Wolverhampton Wanderers were one of the top 1st division clubs, but a quarter of a century later they were on the verge of extinction.

Founded as St Luke's at Blakenhall in 1877 they merged with the local Wanderers team after a couple of seasons and in 1880 adopted the name Wolverhampton Wanderers. By 1887 Wolves were one of the leading Midlands sides and were regarded as being as good as the then great Aston Villa side.

By 1887 a Wolves players, Chas Mason, had gained international honours. The following year they were elected into the Football League as founder members and finished third behind champions Preston. They also reached the Cup final, but again it was Preston who prevented any further glory. That same year Wolves moved to their present Molineux home, a one-time professional cycling centre.

They beat Everton to win the FA Cup for the first time in 1893 and as a 2nd division side in 1908 won the trophy a second time. They left the top division in 1906 and did not return until 1932. But before the Second World War broke out they were emerging as a top team once more. A setback in the 1939 FA Cup final when they lost to Portsmouth was forgotten in 1949 when they won the Cup a third time and in 1954 they won the League for the first time.

With great players like England goalkeeper Bert Williams and captain Billy Wright, Wolves went on to be the outstanding team of the day and in three successive years from 1958 won two League championships and the FA Cup in consecutive years.

They had two League Cup wins in 1974 and 1980, when they were led to victory by Emlyn Hughes, but the club then suffered internal problems and dropped to the 4th division in 1986.

The drop to the 4th division was dramatic and the climb upwards a far from easy one. But happily Wolves are making their way back to where they belong.

In 1988 a near full-house at Wembley saw them beat Burnley to win the Sherpa Van Trophy.

Ground: Molineux
Nickname: Wolves
Record attendance: 61,315 — v Liverpool (FA Cup 5th round), 11 Feb 1939
First Football League season: 1888-89 Football League (3rd)
Seasons in Football League: 90 (59 Division 1, 26 Division 2, 2 Division 3, 1 Division 3(N), 2 Division 4)

Honours
Division 1 champions 1953-54, 1957-58, 1958-59
Division 2 champions 1931-32, 1976-77
Division 3 champions 1988-89
Division 3(N) champions 1923-24
Division 4 champions 1987-88
FA Cup winners 1893, 1908, 1949, 1960
Football League Cup winners 1974, 1980
Texaco Cup winners 1971
Sherpa Van Trophy winners 1988
Footballers of the Year
Billy Wright (FWA) 1952
Bill Slater (FWA) 1960

Women's football

Women are known to have played football in the 16th century and in the 18th century a well known match between the married women and unmarried women of Iveresk, near Edinburgh, was inaugurated.

In 1884 a Preston-based club, Dick Kerr's XI, was established and they played many charity matches. In 1892 a women's team from Preston toured the United States.

The Football Association ruled in 1902 that women's teams could not join its ranks.

Women's football started to take off across Europe in the early 1920s and in 1920 England and France played their first international in front of 10,000 fans.

Interest waned in the latter part of the 1920s but by 1957 its popularity had increased once more and in Germany the first unofficial European Women's Championship was held in West Berlin. England beat the host nation 4-0 in the final.

By 1970 organised tournaments were held in many countries, and before the end of the 1970s many national football associations and federations officially recognised women's soccer, including the FA, who in 1971 reversed their 1902 decision.

Italy is currently the stronghold of women's soccer: crowds of 5-10,000 watch League games, and many of their players are full-time professionals. A couple of England's top players currently play in the Italian women's League.

The *first unofficial women's World Cup* was held in Mexico City in 1971. Commercially sponsored, the final was watched by 100,000 in the Aztec Stadium. Denmark were the winners.

The *first official international match in Britain* was at Greenock on 18 November 1972 when England beat Scotland 3-2.

The *first woman to qualify for the FA's highest coaching award* was Michele Cockburn from Guiseley, Leeds, who qualified in August 1987.

The *most capped women's international* is Carol Thomas who played for England 56 times between 1974-86.

● Playing for Norwich Ladies against Milton Keynes Reserves on 25 September 1983 Linda Curl scored 22 goals in her team's 40-0 win.

World Club Championship

An annual competition between the winners of the European Champions' Cup and South American Cup (Copa Libertadores), it was launched in 1960. Officially called the Intercontinental Cup, it is better known as the World Club Championship.

Between 1960-68 it was played as a two-legged competition and if both sides each won a game, or both were drawn, a third match was played. Between 1969-79 goal difference was used (with the exception of 1973 which was played over one match). Since 1980 all matches have been over a single game for the Toyota Cup, played in Tokyo.

The annual match became a 'bruising' affair in the 1960s and 1970s and there was no match in 1975 and 1978. Because of the reputation of the South American clubs the European Cup winners Ajax (1971 and 1973), Bayern Munich (1974), Liverpool (1977), Nottingham Forest (1979) have declined to take part, and their places have been taken by the beaten European Cup finalists.

World Cup

The World Cup, officially called the World Championship, is soccer's premier international sporting event.

It was inaugurated in 1930 at the suggestion of Jules Rimet. It had previously been debated at FIFA meetings in 1904, 1920 and 1924. A congress meeting in Amsterdam in 1928 voted in

World Club Championship
Results

Year					
1960	Real Madrid (Spain) 0:5	Penarol (Uruguay) 0:1		[1]Play-off at Montevideo	
1961	Penarol (Uruguay) 0:5:2	Benfica (Portugal) 1:0:1[1]		[2]Play-off at Rio de Janeiro	
1962	Santos (Brazil) 3:5	Benfica (Portugal) 2:2		[3]Play-off at Madrid	
1963	Santos (Brazil) 2:4:1	AC Milan (Italy) 4:2:0[2]		[4]Play-off at Montevideo	
1964	Inter Milan (Italy) 0:2:1	Independiente (Argentina) 1:0:0[3]			
1965	Inter Milan (Italy) 3:0	Independiente (Argentina) 0:0		**Most wins**	
1966	Penarol (Uruguay) 2:2	Real Madrid (Spain) 0:0		3 — Penarol, Nacional	
1967	Racing Club (Argentina) 0:2:1	Celtic (Scotland) 1:1:0[4]		2 — Inter Milan, Santos	
1968	Estudiantes (Argentina) 1:1	Manchester U (England) 0:1			
1969	AC Milan (Italy) 3:1	Estudiantes (Argentina) 0:2			
1970	Feyenoord (Netherlands) 2:1	Estudiantes (Argentina) 2:0			
1971	Nacional (Uruguay) 1:2	Panathinaikos (Greece) 1:1			
1972	Ajax (Netherlands) 1:3	Independiente (Argentina) 1:0			
1973	Independiente (Argentina) 1	Juventus (Italy) 0			
1974	Atletico Madrid (Spain) 0:2	Independiente (Argentina) 1:0			
1976	Bayern Munich (W. Germany) 2:0	Cruzeiro (Brazil) 0:0			
1977	Boca Juniors (Argentina) 2:3	Borussia Moenchengladbach (W. Germany) 2:0			
1979	Olimpia (Paraguay) 1:2	Malmo (Sweden) 0:1			
1980	Nacional (Uruguay) 1	Nottingham F (England) 0			
1981	Flamengo (Brazil) 3	Liverpool (England) 0			
1982	Penarol (Uruguay) 2	Aston Villa (England) 0			
1983	Gremio (Brazil) 2	SV Hamburg (W Germany) 1			
1984	Independiente (Argentina) 1	Liverpool (England) 0			
1985	Juventus (Italy) 2	Argentinos Juniors (Argentina) 2 aet	Juventus won 4-2 on penalties		
1986	River Plate (Argentina) 1	Steau Bucharest (Romania) 0			
1987	FC Porto (Portugal) 2	Penarol (Uruguay) 1			
1988	Nacional (Uruguay) 2	PSV Eindhoven (Netherlands) 2 aet	Nacional won on penalties		

Above: Action from women's soccer. On the right is Fulham's Brenda Sempare

Opposite: Billy Wright (Wolverhampton Wanderers) captained England 90 times

favour of organising a world tournament. In recognition of its recent Olympic triumph, and to commemorate its centenary, the inaugural tournament was given to Uruguay.

The Jules Rimet Trophy, to be played for every four years, was commissioned.

There was no competition in the war years 1942 and 1946. When Brazil won the trophy for the third time in 1970 they became the permanent owners and FIFA issued a second trophy called simply the FIFA World Cup Trophy.

The format has changed over the years, as has the number of competing teams. The current format is as follows:

All eligible nations take part in pre-qualifying group matches which are organised geographically according to which FIFA-affiliated union a country belongs. The following unions will run qualifying matches for the 1990 competition. The figures in brackets are the number of teams that will qualify from that group for the final stages.

Oceania/Israel (0 or 1)*
Asia (2)
Concacaf (N & Central America/Caribbean) (2)
South America (2 or 3)*
Africa (2)
Europe (13)

*One play-off match to decide which country qualifies

The defending champions and host nation are automatically eligible for the finals.

Most wins
3 — Brazil, Italy
2 — Argentina, West Germany (incl.1 as Germany), Uruguay

Most final appearances
5 — West Germany (incl.1 as Germany)
4 — Brazil, Italy
3 — Argentina

● Brazil and West Germany have both finished 1st, 2nd, 3rd and 4th in the World Cup.
● Brazil is the only nation to have qualified for all 13 competitions.

Finals

Year	Winner		Runner-up		Venue	Att
1930	Uruguay	4	Argentina	2	Montevideo	90,000
1934	Italy	2	Czechoslovakia	1 aet	Rome	55,000
1938	Italy	4	Hungary	2	Paris	50,000
1950	Uruguay	2	Brazil	1*	Rio de Janeiro	199,854
1954	West Germany	3	Hungary	2	Berne	55,000
1958	Brazil	5	Sweden	2	Stockholm	49,737
1962	Brazil	3	Czechoslovakia	1	Santiago	69,068
1966	England	4	West Germany	2 aet	London	93,000
1970	Brazil	4	Italy	1	Mexico City	107,400
1974	West Germany	2	Netherlands	1	Munich	77,833
1978	Argentina	3	Netherlands	1 aet	Buenos Aires	77,000
1982	Italy	3	West Germany	1	Madrid	92,000
1986	Argentina	3	West Germany	2	Mexico City	114,580

*Last four teams engaged in a final pool.
Uruguay played Brazil in the deciding match

Biggest wins
Final competition
10-1 — Hungary v El Salvador, 15 June 1982
9-0 — Hungary v South Korea, 17 June 1954
9-0 — Yugoslavia v Zaire, 18 June 1974
The highest aggregate score in a final round match is 12 goals when Austria beat Switzerland 7-5 on 26 June 1954
Qualifying competition
13-0 — New Zealand v Fiji, 16 Aug 1981
12-0 — West Germany v Cyprus, 21 May 1969
11-1 — Trinidad v Antigua, 10 Nov 1972

For leading goalscorers and appearances see under appropriate section.

3rd place play-offs

1934	Germany 3	Austria 2
1938	Brazil 4	Sweden 2
1950	Sweden *	
1954	Austria 3	Uruguay 1
1958	France 6	West Germany 3
1962	Chile 1	Yugoslavia 0
1966	Portugal 2	USSR 1
1970	West Germany 1	Uruguay 0
1974	Poland 1	Brazil 0
1978	Brazil 2	Italy 1
1982	Poland 3	France 2
1986	France 4	Belgium 2

*no play-off match, Sweden finished 3rd in final pool

● The first player to score four goals in any World Cup match was Paddy Moore for Ireland in their 4-4 qualifying match against Belgium at Dublin on 25 February 1934. It was the Republic's first ever World Cup game.

● Vava (Brazil, 1958, 1962); Pele (Brazil 1958, 1970) and Paul Breitner (West Germany 1974, 1982) are the only men to score in *two* World Cup finals.

● The first World Cup match played on artificial turf was between Canada and the United States in Vancouver on 24 September 1976. The first World Cup match played indoors was the return match of the above played at the Seattle Kingdome on 20 October 1976.

World Player of the Year

Inaugurated in 1982, the winner is the player who comes top of a poll organised by *World Soccer* magazine.

Winners
1982 Paolo Rossi (Juventus)
1983 Zico (Udinese)
1984 Michel Platini (Juventus)
1985 Michel Platini (Juventus)
1986 Diego Maradona (Napoli)
1987 Ruud Gullit (AC Milan)

Wright, Billy (1924-)

William Ambrose Wright was a quality half-back, but moreover he was an astute captain, leading both his club and England to many great wins.

Born at Ironbridge, he joined his only League club Wolves as a 14-year-old and turned pro-

fessional in 1941. He made his international debut in the first post-war game against Northern Ireland and in 105 appearances was skipper no fewer than 90 times, a record. On 11 May 1959 at Wembley he led England out in his 100th match to become Britain's first international 'centurion'.

During his time at Wolves he appeared in their 1949 FA Cup final winning team and led them to three Championship wins.

He retired in 1959 and became manager of the England Youth team before taking over the manager's chair at Arsenal in 1962. He operated a youth programme at Highbury and signed players like Frank McLintock. His youngsters were to be the backbone of the great Arsenal team of the early 1970s. Wright was replaced by Bertie Mee in 1966.

Married to Joy, the oldest of the Beverley Sisters, Billy Wright went into television and later became Head of Sport at ATV (now Central Television). Wright was awarded the CBE for his services to football.

Born: 6 February 1924, Ironbridge, Shropshire
Football League debut: 31 Aug 1946 v Arsenal
Football League appearances: 490 (all Wolverhampton W)
Football League goals: 13
International caps: 105
Honours (player)
FA Cup 1949
Division 1 championship 1953-54, 1957-58, 1958-59
Awards
Footballer of the Year (FWA) 1952

Youngest players

The following were the youngest players in each of the major British tournaments.

Football League
15 years 158* days Albert Geldard (Bradford PA v Millwall), Div. 2, 16 Sept 1929
(*some sources give 156 days)
15 years 158 days Ken Roberts (Wrexham v Bradford PA), Div. 3N, 1 Sept 1951
Division 1
15 years 185 days Derek Forster (Sunderland v Leicester C), 22 Aug 1964
FA Cup
15 years 88 days Andy Awford (Worcester C v Borehamwood), 3rd qual. round, 10 Oct 1987
FA Cup (competition proper)
15 years 288 days Scott Endersby (Kettering T v Tilbury), 1st round, 28 Nov 1977
FA Cup final
17 years 256 days Paul Allen (West Ham U v Arsenal), 10 May 1980
Scottish League
15 years 98 days Sam McMillan (Ayr U v Queen's Park), Div. B, 14 March 1953

The *youngest scorer in the Football League* is Ronnie Dix of Bristol Rovers who was 15 and 180 days when he scored in the division 3 (south) match against Norwich City on 3 March 1928
The *youngest goal scorer in the 1st division* is Jason Dozzell who was 16 and 57 days when he scored for Ipswich Town against Coventry City on 4 February 1984
When Alan Shearer scored a hat-trick for Southampton against Arsenal on 9 April 1988, at the age of 17 and 240 days he became the *youngest scorer of a hat-trick in the first division*
The *youngest scorer* in an FA Cup final is Norman Whiteside of Manchester United. He was 18 and 19 days when he scored against Brighton & HA on 21 May 1983. Whiteside is also the youngest scorer in a League Cup final. He was 17 and 323 days when he scored for United against Liverpool on 26 March 1983.
David Nish of Leicester City is the *youngest captain of an FA Cup final team.* He was only 21 and 212 days when he led his side out against Manchester City on 26 April 1969.

The *youngest captain of a League Cup final team* is Barry Venison who was only 20 and 222 days when he skippered Sunderland in the 1985 final against Norwich City.

Youngest internationals for each of the British Isles teams
N. Ireland: 17 years 42 days Norman Whiteside (Manchester U) v Yugoslavia, 17 June 1982
Scotland: 17 years 92 days Johnny Lambie (Queen's Park) v Ireland, 20 March 1886
Ireland: 17 years 200 days Jimmy Holmes (Coventry C) v Austria, 30 May 1971
Wales: 18 years 71 days John Charles (Leeds U) v Ireland, 18 March 1950
England: 18 years 183 days Duncan Edwards (Manchester U) v Scotland, 2 April 1955
Norman Whiteside of Northern Ireland is the youngest person to play in the World Cup finals. When he played against Yugoslavia in Zaragoza on 17 June 1982 he was 17 years 41 days old.

Other notable youngsters:

● Campbell Buchanan played for Wolverhampton Wanderers against West Bromwich Albion on 26 September 1942 at the age of 14 and 57 days in a war-time League game. Ex-Celtic goalkeeper Ronnie Simpson made his war-time debut for Queen's Park during the war against Kilmarnock on 11 August 1945. He was 14 and 304 days at the time.

● Derek Johnstone of Rangers was only 16 and 330 days when he played in the Scottish League Cup Final against Celtic on 24 October 1970.

West Ham's Paul Allen on the ball in the 1980 FA Cup final when 2nd division Hammers beat Arsenal 1–0

Manchester United's Norman Whiteside, the youngest player to appear in the World Cup

● The youngest ever international is believed to be G. Dorval who made his debut for Brazil against Argentina in July 1957. He was only 15 at the time.

● Eamonn Collins of Blackpool was only 14 and 322 days old when he came on as a substitute in the Anglo-Scottish Cup against Kilmarnock on 9 September 1980. This makes him the youngest debutant in a senior peace-time game in Britain.

● When Jimmy Greaves (Chelsea) scored against Manchester City at Stamford Bridge on 19 November 1960 it was the 100th goal of his career. He was only 20 and 261 days old at the time and became the youngest player to score 100 Football League goals.

Youth football

Youths are regarded as players between the ages of 16-18. It was not until 1926 that organised youths' football gained recognition from the FA when it appointed a standing committee to look into the area of youth football.

The two main international tournaments for youths are the UEFA Youth Tournament, first played in London in 1948, and the World Youth Tournament, first played in Tunisia in 1977.

World Youth Tournament
Winners
1977 USSR
1979 Argentina
1981 West Germany
1983 Brazil
1985 Brazil
1987 Yugoslavia

UEFA Youth Tournament
Winners
1948 England
1949 France
1950 Austria
1951 Yugoslavia
1952 Spain
1953 Hungary
1954 Spain
1957 Austria
1958 Italy
1959 Bulgaria
1960 Hungary
1961 Portugal
1962 Romania
1963 England
1964 England
1965 East Germany
1966 Italy/USSR*
1967 USSR
1968 Czechoslovakia
1969 Bulgaria
1970 East Germany
1971 England
1972 England
1973 England
1974 Bulgaria
1975 England
1976 USSR
1977 Belgium
1978 USSR
1979 Yugoslavia
1980 England
1981 West Germany
1982 Scotland
1983 France
1984 Hungary
1986 East Germany
1988 USSR
*shared title

Most wins
8 — England
4 — USSR
3 — Bulgaria, East Germany, Hungary

(see also *FA County Youth Cup* and *FA Youth Challenge Cup*)

Zoff, Dino (1942-)

Italy's most capped footballer, Dino Zoff played for his country 112 times between 1968 and 1983. The highlight was undoubtedly in Madrid in 1982 when he skippered Italy to a 3-1 win over West Germany in the World Cup final.

Born just outside Venice, Zoff was turned down by Juventus as a youngster because he was not tall enough. However, he was given his chance with Udinese and on his Italian League debut in September 1961 he conceded five goals, including a hat-trick from Fiorentina's goalscoring ace Kurt Hamrin.

Zoff moved to Mantova in 1962 and to Napoli in 1967. The following year he made his inter-national debut against Bulgaria in the Nations Cup (European Championship) quarter-final.

In 1972 Juventus acknowledged their earlier mistake and signed Zoff. In 1974 he set a world record when he went 1,143 minutes without conceding a goal in international football. He went on to beat Giacinto Facchetti's record of 95 Italian caps and at the age of 40 became a World Cup winning captain. After retiring he became coach of the Italian Olympic squad and in 1988 took over at his former club Juventus.

Born: 28 February 1942, Mariano del Fruili, nr Venice, Italy
International caps: 112

Honours
World Cup 1982 (Italy)
European Championship 1968 (Italy)
Italian League 1973, 1975, 1977, 1978, 1981, 1982 (all Juventus)
Italian Cup 1979, 1983 (both Juventus)

The great Italian goalkeeper Dino Zoff who led his team to World Cup glory in 1982

Author's note

The starting point of the *Hamlyn Encyclopedia of Soccer* was easy: it was at the letter A. The finishing point was just as easy: it was 26 letters later at Z. But just what went in between A and Z was not one of life's easy tasks.

Association football is one of the most widely played and watched sports the world over. In more than 100 years it has witnessed many great players and teams. Records, both major and trivial, have been broken and the game has constantly changed. As a result, it left me with plenty of material to work on, but it also provided me with the problem of what to leave out.

In order to include as much fascinating reading and interesting facts as space would permit, I have had to be ruthless in my choice of entries. To have made it an *Encyclopedia of British Soccer* would have been one problem solved, but how could I omit the likes of Pele, Franz Beckenbauer and Diego Maradona? British fans recognise them as well as their own domestic players.

The British soccer fan is now more aware of European and world soccer. For that reason overseas football and records are included. The bias is towards the British game but, in an effort to add as much variety as possible, you can read about the overseas nations and players.

When it came down to deciding which British players and teams should be included the job was a thankless one. I would have been happier if I could have written an *Encyclopedia of British Football Clubs* followed by an *Encyclopedia of British Footballers,* and so on; life would have been a lot easier.

When it came down to making my final selection I thought it best to stick to a rigid guideline and so the histories of Football League clubs in this encyclopedia are restricted to winners of the Football League Championship, the world's toughest league, which means that clubs like Stoke City are not included. Neither are the likes of Scunthorpe United, Doncaster Rovers and Port Vale. To fans of those clubs and all other clubs not included I apologise but at the same time duly acknowledge their important role in this great game.

When it came to making my choice of biographical entries I was torn between restricting it to the out-and-out record breakers and the stars of today. In the end I plumped for a mixture of the two, but don't take my selection as the definitive list of all-time greats. However, every player included has played a significant role in the game of soccer. Nobody has managed to squeeze a quart into a pint pot, or for those of you who don't remember the old imperial days, a litre into a half-litre pot; I hope I have achieved the nearest thing to it with the *Hamlyn Encyclopedia of Soccer.*

Ian Morrison, 1989